THE LIMITS OF WESTERNIZATION

Columbia Studies in International and Global History

COLUMBIA STUDIES IN INTERNATIONAL AND GLOBAL HISTORY

The idea of "globalization" has become a commonplace, but we lack good histories that can explain the transnational and global processes that have shaped the contemporary world. Columbia Studies in International and Global History encourages serious scholarship on international and global history with an eye to explaining the origins of the contemporary era. Grounded in empirical research, the titles in the series transcend the usual area boundaries and address questions of how history can help us understand contemporary problems, including poverty, inequality, power, political violence, and accountability beyond the nation-state.

Cemil Aydin, *The Politics of Anti-Westernism in Asia: Visions of World Order in Pan-Islamic and Pan-Asian Thought*

Adam M. McKeown, *Melancholy Order: Asian Migration and the Globalization of Borders*

Patrick Manning, *The African Diaspora: A History Through Culture*

James Rodger Fleming, *Fixing the Sky: The Checkered History of Weather and Climate Control*

Steven Bryan, *The Gold Standard at the Turn of the Twentieth Century: Rising Powers, Global Money, and the Age of Empire*

Heonik Kwon, *The Other Cold War*

Samuel Moyn and Andrew Sartori, eds., *Global Intellectual History*

Alison Bashford, *Global Population: History, Geopolitics, and Life on Earth*

Adam Clulow, *The Shogun and the Company: The Dutch Encounter with Tokugawa Japan*

Richard W. Bulliet, *The Wheel: Inventions and Reinventions*

Simone V. Müller, *Wiring the World: The Social and Cultural Creation of Global Telegraph Networks*

Will Hanley, *Identifying with Nationality: Europeans, Ottomans, and Egyptians in Alexandria*

The Limits of Westernization

A Cultural History of America in Turkey

Perin E. Gürel

Columbia University Press   New York

Columbia University Press
Publishers Since 1893
New York   Chichester, West Sussex
cup.columbia.edu
Copyright © 2017 Columbia University Press
Paperback edition, 2020
All rights reserved

The publication of this book is made possible in part by support from the Institute for
Scholarship in the Liberal Arts, College of Arts and Letters, University of Notre Dame.

Library of Congress Cataloging-in-Publication Data
Names: Gürel, Perin, author.
Title: The limits of westernization : a cultural history of America in Turkey / Perin Gürel.
Other titles: Columbia studies in international and global history.
Description: New York : Columbia University Press, 2017. | Series: Columbia Studies in
    International and Global History | Includes bibliographical references and index.
Identifiers: LCCN 2016046840 | ISBN 978-0-231-18202-7 (cloth)
    ISBN 978-0-231-18203-4 (pbk.) | ISBN 978-0-231-54396-5 (e-book)
Subjects: LCSH: Turkey—Foreign relations—United States. | United States—Foreign
    relations—Turkey. | Turkey—Civilization—Western influences. | Orientalism—United
    States.
Classification: LCC DR479.U5 G87 2017 | DDC 327.561073—dc23
LC record available at https://lccn.loc.gov/2016046840

Cover design: Milenda Nan Ok Lee

Cover image: © 2014 Greg Harris www.FlashDashBulb.com

For Marjane Honey—
May you always keep your love of learning and sense of humor entangled.

Contents

Acknowledgments

Do you remember the first time you realized that a book you had read and loved had an "author" largely outside your relationship with it? That feeling still jars me now and again. Yet, now that I stand close to the other side of this feeling, as a first-time author whose book will form its own relationships, a different uncanniness has set in: what seems surreal is not just the disconnect between book and author, but that a book like this will end up with only one ostensible author. From where I stand, referring to this object as a "single-authored monograph" seems profoundly simplistic. Footnotes and acknowledgments will not do justice to all the authors of this book, but here I try, doubtless forgetting some who have helped already.

The Limits of Westernization began developing at Yale University under the outstanding guidance of Matthew Jacobson, Laura Wexler, Seth Fein, and Joanne Meyerowitz. In addition to my official mentors, I benefited from a vibrant intellectual community of scholars including David Agruss, Sumayya Ahmad, Elizabeth Alexander, La Marr Bruce, Hazel Carby, George Chauncey, Kamari Clarke, Michael Denning, Wai Chee Dimock, Ziv Eisenberg, Ron Gregg, Inderpal Grewal, Zareena Grewal, Matthew Gunterman, Ainsley Hawthorn, Rana Hogarth, Sara Hudson, Nihan Ketrez, Mary Lui, Ana Raquel Minian, Jennifer Nelson, Melek Okay, Stephen Pitti, Sally Promey, Naomi Rogers, Graeme Reid,

Sasha Santee, Alicia Schmidt-Camacho, John Szwed, Quan Tran, Charles Veric, and Kariann Yokota. Melissa Hussain was a crucial motivator and sounding board online. During research trips in Turkey, I got support from other illustrious scholars including Işıl Baş, Deniz Tarba Ceylan, Sibel Irzık, Louis Mazzari, Özlem Öğüt, Arzu Öztürkmen, Cevza Sevgen, Alpar Sevgen, and Aslı Tekinay. I am also grateful for my named and unnamed Turkish interlocutors who contributed to chapters 3 and 4 as intellectuals in their own right.

At Dickinson College, Cotten Seiler and Amy Farrell read and commented on parts of the manuscript. Other brilliant scholars, including Linda Brindeau, Maria Bruno, Megan Glick, Laura Grappo, Helene Lee, Erik Love, Gwen Moore, Sharon O'Brien, Emily Pawley, Jerry Philogene, Toby Reiner, Susan Rose, Vanessa Tyson, and Edward Webb, formed my broader intellectual community.

At the University of Notre Dame, faculty and staff associated with American Studies (with special thanks to my then chair Robert Schmuhl) and Gender Studies were immediately supportive and inspiring. Z'etoile Imma organized and Jesse Costantino and Sarah Wells joined in for an interdisciplinary writing group for junior faculty. A group of fierce feminist colleagues from Notre Dame and St. Mary's, including Z'etoile, Emily Beck, Nicole Woods-Beckton, Dionne Irving Bremyer, Mary Celeste Kearney, Ann Marie Alfonso Short, and Jamie Wagman, kept me motivated, thinking, and joyful. An Institute for Study of the Liberal Arts (ISLA) grant allowed me to meet and work with Melani McAlister, whose *Epic Encounters* had inspired *The Limits of Westernization* more profoundly than any other work. Melani kindly served as an outside mentor providing suggestions for the revision of the entire manuscript. I also held two book workshops at Notre Dame: the internal one allowed me to benefit from the wisdom of Thomas Tweed, Jason Ruiz, and Gail Bederman, and the external one, generously sponsored by ISLA, helped me organize another dream-team meeting around my work, featuring Afsaneh Najmabadi, Cemil Aydın, and Naoko Shibusawa. Outside these structured occasions, who knows how many times Thomas Tweed and Erika Doss have patiently and generously commented on partial drafts of this book? I knew I was close to a final draft when Tom used the word "better" and Doss the word "fine" a couple of times. But we all know nothing can be truly fine in our department without the support of

Katie Schlotfeldt, and I owe a lot to her assistance, understanding, and patience. Speaking of patience, let's not forget that Annie Coleman's sweet, brilliant daughter Lou babysat Marjane while I wrote, revised, and then revised again, pretending my toddler was actually good at hiding during endless sessions of hide-and-seek.

Since *The Limits of Westernization* impetuously pushes the limits of inter/multidisciplinarity, I also sought advice from experts in various disciplines outside my own institutional homes. Alastair Bonnett, one of the world's leading social geographers, was kind enough to read an earlier version of the introduction, helping me think about the idea of "the West" with more nuance. A version of chapter 1 was published in *American Quarterly* in 2015 and benefited greatly from the feedback I received in the process. Michael McGaha and Sibel Irzık helped with chapter 2 on the Turkish novel. Chapter 3 on folklore became stronger with feedback from Roger Abrahams, Regina Bendix, Simon Bronner, Hasan El-Shamy, John Szwed, and Rosemary Lévy Zumwalt. Chapter 4 on sexual identities and politics benefited from the intellectual generosity of Mija Sanders, Evren Savcı, and Irvin Cemil Schick. Timothy Marr read and commented on parts of a draft. Ebony Coletu and Ira Dworkin helped me think more clearly about the latest developments in American Studies of the Middle East and North Africa. I am also very grateful to the anonymous reviewers for Columbia University Press (CUP) for their wise feedback on the entire manuscript. The CUP editorial team was exceptional from start to finish. Special thanks are due to Anne Routon, Miriam Grossman, and Debbie Masi—I doubt that they could have been any more astute and understanding.

I am grateful for the financial support I received from Yale University, Dickinson College, the Institute for Turkish Studies, and the University of Notre Dame while writing this book. I would like to thank the staff at the Yale University Library Manuscripts and Archives, the U.S. National Archives and Records Administration (NARA) in Maryland, and Dickinson College and the University of Notre Dame libraries, with special thanks to Denise Massa at the UND Visual Resources Center. In Turkey, I received significant research support at the archives of the Kadın Eserleri Kütüphanesi ve Bilgi Merkezi Vakfı (The Women's Library and Information Centre Foundation) and the Istanbul University Libraries, as well as from volunteers and staff associated with Lambdaistanbul,

Istanbul LGBTT, Sosyalist EBT, Social Policies, Gender Identity and Sexual Orientation Studies Association (SPoD), and Komik Büro.

My family and friends have supported this project since long before the writing stage. My mother Dilek Özçer often directed my attention to key developments in Turkish culture and used her sharp analytical mind to brainstorm with me about them. Chapter 3 on bilingual humor had two fathers: the late Alan Dundes, who inspired me to combine transnational American Studies with folkloristics, setting the course of my life's work, and my own late father Ercan Gürel, who knew how to tell a joke (bilingual or otherwise) better than any single person on earth. I miss him every day. I passed ideas by the Arsan family and Leyla Ata and collected jokes from them, too. Marjorie Searl and Alan Scott read and commented on entire versions of the manuscript. Even when Microsoft Word complained it could no longer do the job and abandoned me to my bilingual typos, they came through, doing far more than catching typos.

My husband James Searl has heard, read, retold, and helped transform the matrix that became this book for almost a decade. Of all the intellectual debts I owe, his may be the most unquantifiable. His music inspires me to write with a matching commitment to beauty and justice. He woke up early and stayed up late with baby Marjane so my brain cells could recover enough to type, not to mention clearing the time for me to type. Without him, there might not have been this "single-authored" book.

I will let you in on a final secret I discovered on this side of uncanny. The more and more distant this work of scholarly nonfiction got from the singular me who lives and breathes, and as more and more people helped me write it, the more it has become my autobiography. So thank you for being a part of that.

THE LIMITS OF WESTERNIZATION

Good West, Bad West, Wild West

About halfway through the 2010 Turkish blockbuster *Yahşi Batı* (*The Mild West*), a mock-Western, two Ottomans dressed in stereotypical cowboy outfits are riding through late nineteenth-century America. Their sultan has sent them on a mission: to present a priceless diamond to the U.S. president as a token of international friendship. However, at the beginning of the movie, bandits attacked their carriage and stole the diamond and their clothes. Since then, they have been searching for ways to make money and retrieve the diamond. One of the pair, a refined and educated agent of the Treasury, confesses with exasperation, "I need to reevaluate my infatuation with the West." His companion, a coarse secret service agent, replies that it does not make sense to think so highly of the West anyway. "A hundred years ago," he scoffs, "the Palace of Versailles did not have any toilets. The king went directly on the palace floor. They invented the waltz to avoid stepping in all the shit." They ride on, commenting on the decline of the Ottoman Empire using schoolbook clichés, until they hear a gunshot ring out. As they take cover, they see that the sound came from a female sharpshooter holding target practice. The secret agent's jaw drops. Clearly impressed with her skills, he cannot take his eyes off her beauty. "I see a sudden infatuation with the West developing in you," observes his companion sarcastically. "Well," replies the agent, "you have got to take the things that are good from the West."[1]

With that screen exchange, *The Mild West* reveals what the discerning viewer has already discovered: this movie is not really about the Wild West and the Ottoman Empire, but about contemporary Turkey and "the West," specifically the United States. The scene comments on what appears to be a love-hate relationship, connecting these troubled affects to the complexities of Turkey's westernization (*batılılaşma*). On the one hand, "the West" is disgusting; its supposedly civilized rituals of courtship (i.e., the waltz) are a mere cover for scatological realities. This is a West is to be avoided, somewhat like scattered excrement on the dance floor. On the other hand, the West is stunning and skilled; it must be observed and courted. Thus westernization becomes a double-edged sword, beneficial and malevolent, desirable and damaging. The United States may provide good elements for incorporation into the Turkish body politic; yet, if Turkey takes in too much or takes the "bad" things, it risks degeneration. Complicating these depictions is the fact that the viewer encounters them in a movie that mobilizes Turkish nationalist sentiments through the audiovisual grammar of Hollywood. The characters debating the merits of westernization are dressed like cowboys from a Clint Eastwood movie. This film, which comments on the complexities of westernization, in other words, would not have been possible without a type of westernization. But which type of westernization is that? The good, the bad, or the ugly?

The Republic of Turkey is a Muslim-majority progeny of the Ottoman Empire, the decline of which paralleled the rise of the United States in the late nineteenth and twentieth centuries.[2] In the early twenty-first century, U.S.–Turkish relations are marked by ambivalence. Officially, the two countries are NATO allies and strategic partners. Yet one does not need to search long to find condescending attitudes toward Turkey in U.S. newspapers and policy journals as well as in popular culture. Similarly, Turks demonstrated high levels of both "anti-Americanism" and pro-American sentiments in the first decade of the twenty-first century. In a 2001 Turkish poll, the United States ranked highest in response to the question, "Which country is Turkey's best friend in international relations?" Yet the United States also scored high, coming in second, when the question was reversed to "Which country is Turkey's number one enemy in international relations?"[3] Even more surprisingly, in a 2007 Pew Global Attitudes survey, Turkey gave the United States the lowest approval rating (9 percent) among all surveyed countries.[4] Such data have long made Turkish–U.S. relations a puzzler for international relations scholars. How can Turkey, a longtime ally, give the United States its lowest approval rating on record? How can "the West" be the best, and the worst? As the proxy wars in Syria and Iraq persist and Turkey reels after a violent, failed coup attempt with alleged ties to the U.S.-based Muslim cleric Fethullah Gülen, Turkish popular sentiments toward the United States continue to be complicated and in flux.

⟶ Focusing on the twentieth century as the crucible of contemporary U.S.–Turkish relations, *The Limits of Westernization* unpacks this love-hate relationship. In particular, it demonstrates how Turkish perceptions of the United States have formed in relation to local debates over *batılılaşma* (westernization). The "American century" saw Turkey transition from contiguous empire to nation-state, figuring its place in a world order increasingly influenced by a new kind of postterritorial empire that sought to remake that world in its own image.[5] Using Turkish and English sources, examining official, elite, and vernacular texts, I demonstrate how Turks responded to the rise of the United States as a world-ordering power through a preexisting lens that deemed westernization both necessary and potentially corrupting. Turkish stock figures and figures of speech, changing through time, contrasted America to Europe, representing it alternately as a good model for selective westernization or as the most dangerous source of degeneration. As U.S. policy makers cast Turkey in various figurative roles within their own prescriptive civilizational templates, Turks anticipated, manipulated, and contested these attempts through the local logics of westernization. Ultimately, the United States was not able to contain Turkey within its world-ordering blueprints, nor was the Turkish elite able to police cultural change through civilizational figures of "the West." Instead, alternate conceptions of modernity, and folk culture hybridized with American cultural exports, operated as resources for both popular anti-Americanisms and resistance to state-led westernization. The story of the twentieth century transitioning to the era of the War on Terror is, in part, a story of how local and U.S. elites attempted to figure peoples into civilizational templates that clash with the complexity of culture.

For over a century, Ottoman and, later, republican Turkish policy makers developed a mode of governmentality focused on Europe and, increasingly, the United States.[6] Led by its intelligentsia, the Turkish state repeatedly attempted what some scholars have called "modernization without colonization," and what I call authoritarian or selective westernization: selectively adopting Western institutions and technologies while trying to forestall unwanted changes in sociocultural norms.[7] As a type of governmentality, Turkey's selective westernization has operated both as general theory about governing through strategic, Western-inspired reforms, and a method of social engineering, creating a certain type of citizen-subject. Some of the most lasting selective westernization reforms, all implemented in the early twentieth century under Mustafa Kemal Atatürk, were sociocultural. These included the introduction of French-style secularism (*laïcité*), the adoption of the Latin alphabet, Western forms of dress, and the Gregorian calendar. Such reforms sought to create properly "modern" Turkish citizens—citizens who would strategically embody Western modes of self-presentation but remain loyal subjects of the Kemalist state.[8] Atatürk, after all, was the very same leader who fought for and achieved Turkish independence from Europe during and after World War I. The opening dialogue's quip about taking the "good things" from the West echoes key questions regarding such elite borrowings and their nationalist limits: Can we draw the boundaries of westernization? If so, where? What are the "good things" to take? What should we exclude?

These are impossible questions, since no power elite can fully direct the trajectory of sociocultural change in even the smallest and most homogenous nation. As a project of nationalist "development," authoritarian westernization aims to destabilize traditional structures with the intention of establishing and reifying new ones.[9] However, as Bernard Lewis noted in his canonical history of modern Turkey, "it is almost a truism that there can be no limited and insulated borrowing by one civilization of the practices of another, but that each element introduced from outside brings a train of consequences."[10] Despite official westernizers' commitment to order and mistrust of anomie (normlessness), cultural changes unleashed by increasing transnational contact often prove volatile.[11] Selective westernization carries within it the seeds of transculturation, that "extremely complex transmutation of cultures" interacting in asymmetrical relations of power.[12] Even the most resolute nationalist rulers can have no say over how (or even whether) their reforms will take root and hybridize with local cultural formations. More-over, since no cultural formation is ever entirely foreign or fully local, we can only speak of "cycles of hybridization" and indigenization.[13] Yet, since at least the nineteenth century, this has not stopped Turkey's leaders from attempting to determine the proper limits of westernization.

Throughout the twentieth century, the Turkish elite developed a distinct set of discursive practices to describe and police the "wild" as-pects of transculturation with the West. These include both figures of speech (e.g., metaphors, metonyms, symbols, and other rhetorical de-vices) and stock figures, representing the dangers of "over-" and "under-westernization." As in the opening dialogue, Turks have historically figured the boundaries of westernization using tropes of gender and sexuality. In the process, they have developed a local discourse regard-ing the dangers of excessive westernization, or "westoxication," which casts certain types of Western cultural influence as degenerative.[14] The limits go both ways. Turkey's ruling elite have deemed it aberrant to absorb the West too voraciously, but were also concerned with policing citizens they considered too closed off from Western-style modernity. Thus stock figures like the over-westernized, effete Istanbul dandy found their counterparts in the stereotype of the coarse, under-westernized, hypermasculine Easterner.[15] Turkey's political elite regularly mobilized the two technologies policing the limits of westernization (authoritarian westernization as a mode of governmentality and over- and under-westernization as discursive aggregates) against wild westernization as a type of transculturation.

I use the qualifier "wild" to signify the unpredictable aspects of vernacular transculturation. "Wild" as a biological and sexual metaphor implies hybridization with colloquial, even vulgar, methods of commu-nication deemed inappropriate for civic use. The concept goes beyond acknowledging how authoritarian westernization has failed to convert all subjects to a properly modern Turkish identity; it also underlines that there is no culturally pure resistance to elite-led westernization, even at the level of folklore. As Chen reminds us, the Middle East is "a half-Western Orient."[16] This is abundantly clear in the case of Asia Minor, which has both served as the borderlands for fluctuating understandings of "the West" and "the East" and been a rich site of transculturation since antiquity.[17]

The term also purposefully evokes the "Wild West," an American "myth" connoting hybridity, chaos, and violence.[18] Before World War II, France was the primary Western exporter of cultural materials to Turkey; after World War II, the balance slowly shifted along with the rise of English language education in the country. Consumers of foreign media also diversified, expanding from the truly elite readers of French novels in the nineteenth century to a more mixed group of moviegoers, pop music fans, and Internet users. Certainly folklore and popular culture showed marks of vernacular hybridity long before the mid-twentieth century. Wide-scale wild westernization—that is, the wide-scale transculturation of Western cultural exports with the local vernacular—however, coincided with the rise of the United States as the world's leading exporter of mass culture materials in the mid-twentieth century.[19] These foreign exports, many transporting the myth of "the Wild West," merged with local folklore, with unpredictable results. As in the film vignette opening this introduction, the Wild West (sometimes figured as "Texas") works as a metonym for the United States in Turkish representations. In contemporary Turkish popular and folk cultures, this imported trope operates hybridized with local perceptions of U.S. imperialism.

Even as they were "figuring" the limits of westernization, Turks have had to "figure out" the United States—the new West that rose to prominence in the twentieth century—and the role it could play in national projects of westernization. Most cultural histories of Turkish westernization to date have focused on the Europe-inspired reforms of the early twentieth century, which included the adoption of "the Swiss civil code, the Italian Criminal Code, the German Commercial Code," and the French system of laïcité.[20] Indeed, Turkey's rulers originally conceived of selective westernization in relation to various European polities directly encroaching upon their sovereignty. However, they developed it in response to a new American empire, which mobilized a wide array of tools (economic, political, military, and cultural) to shape the world's peoples as figures in various prescriptive civilizational schemas. Local commentators on "westernization" do not always differentiate between the United States and Europe; the moments of conflation and differentiation, as explored in this book, can both be politically significant.

In the late nineteenth century, U.S. intellectuals and policy makers began figuring America as the world's model, guide, and arbiter of modernity. Merging anthropology with eugenics, they mapped the world's peoples on a racialized scale of civilization, which cast the Ottoman Empire as the representative of Islamic barbarism through the stock figure of "the terrible Turk."[21] During and immediately after World War I, Wilsonianism touted the promise of liberal developmentalism alongside this racial logic, tacitly promising modernization and self-determination to all, while restricting access for nonwhite and non-Christian races. After World War II, during the Cold War with the Soviet Union, the U.S. power elite began to figure a new world order that deemphasized racial and religious differences. Policy-oriented intellectuals developed an anticommunist "modernization theory" inspired in part by Kemalism and its attempts to counter the figure of "the terrible Turk" through selective westernization.[22] These theorists imagined modernization as a series of steps modeled on America's own developmental experience, open to all, with U.S. guidance. In this new rubric, the Republic of Turkey would play a key role as an intermediary example of successful, pro-American modernization. Thus by the mid-century, the figure of the terrible Turk had receded in memory to be taken over by images of Turkey as apt pupil, contrasted to the "bad Arab" embodied by the likes of Gamal Abdel Nasser of Egypt. Yet the late twentieth century saw cracks in this logic, which expanded as American Islamophobia resurged after the Cold War. The events of September 11, 2001, made Muslim-majority Turkey a critical "front state" for the United States once again, recalling its role during the Cold War.[23] During the early years of the War on Terror, America's new figurative bogeyman, the "Islamic terrorist," allowed Turkey to be occasionally cast in the newly invented role of "moderate Muslim"—yet again a touted model for the rest of the Middle East. The recurring emphasis on racially and religiously inflected civilizational divides, however, showed the limits of U.S. internationalism in a supposedly postimperial and postracial world. Foregrounding shifting figures about and from Turkey—a country that continues to be a key player in U.S. plans to "modernize" the Middle East—helps demonstrate the transnational development of a powerful Orientalist trope, from "the Terrible Turk" to "the Islamic Terrorist."

Scholars of American empire have inherited, and built upon, Edward Said's *Orientalism* as a model for examining how cultural production may intersect with international relations. According to Said, Orientalism is the discursive aggregate through which European authors, artists, scholars, and colonial administrators have constructed an East that is timeless, mystical, and irrational (thus utterly different and inferior). This figurative East comprises the West's "deepest and most recurrent images of the Other" and has justified imperial ventures in the Middle East.[24] Though Said underplays the United States in this account, the theory of Orientalism has deeply impacted American studies of the Middle East.[25] Melani McAlister, for example, has demonstrated how U.S. policy makers' projection of the United States as a "benevolent" foil to colonialist Europe complicates the gendered oppressor/oppressed and East/West binaries that are central to Said's formulation of Orientalism.[26] Americanists building on Said's work have both identified Orientalist biases in U.S. constructions of the Middle East and observed multiple, even counterintuitive, American uses for Orientalist constructs.[27] They have explored responses to Orientalist and post-Orientalist cultural productions and policies outside the United States and within diasporic communities.[28] Such scholarship challenges reductionist "cultural" explanations for international relations by emphasizing transculturation, heterogeneity, and historical context. It refines and expands Said's model by making visible the myriad discursive challenges to Orientalism operating within the so-called West and across transnational connections.

Unfortunately, unlike Orientalism, the growing literature on Occidentalism, which, in part, analyzes Asian uses of "the West," has yet to make its mark on cultural studies of the United States and Middle East.[29] This is partially due to the persistence of "the vernacular tradition" of (monolingual) American studies, despite the field's transnational turn.[30] However, the Eurocentric contours of scholarship in other fields has reinforced this narrow course as well: not only have studies of Occidentalism from other disciplines (including Turkish studies) tended to focus on representations of Europe, bilingual Americanist research on foreign reactions to U.S. hegemony has also been dominated by European texts and archives.[31] Transnational Americanist scholarship conversant with Orientalism can deconstruct hegemonic representations of the civilizational other. However, without a dialectical analysis that also considers local Occidentalisms, it is difficult to truly decenter U.S.-based figures and "provincialize" the field.[32] Moving toward this goal, *The Limits of Westernization* models an interdisciplinary methodology that combines transnational American studies, with its focus on the movement of people, products, and ideas across nation-state boundaries, with comparative cultural studies.[33] Brian T. Edwards's call to "seek to achieve a balance of attention between moments of transnationally inspired cultural encounter and that which remains local and difficult to translate" resonates with me.[34] Of course, as Edwards also notes, it is sometimes their profound transnational-ness—i.e., the absence of the stereotypical "exotic"—that hinders the translation and circulation of Middle Eastern texts in the United States.[35] As a fractured and fluctuating network of Occidentalisms, batılılaşma operates at the intersection of transnational contact and international relations. It is both ironic and telling that this transculturated cultural formation remains largely invisible to the West it seeks to define and manage.

Of course, debates over "westernization" are far from invisible to Turkish scholars. However, disciplinary divides often influence the specific kind of westernization scholars investigate. When social historians study batılılaşma, they are often referring to autocratic westernization, tracing specific reform movements through primary documents such as manifestos, official speeches, and laws.[36] Literary scholars often explore depictions of over-westernization in Turkish literature and its political implications.[37] Sociologists, anthropologists, and qualitative political scientists, on the other hand, have examined constructions of inadequate modernization and the cast of real-life figures associated with "the East": Islamists, *arabesk* music fans, *gecekondu* (shantytown) residents, belly dancers, rural migrants, *travesti* (cross-dressed male sex workers as well as trans female sex workers).[38] Wild westernization, the least studied, is the domain of cultural studies, literary texts, and the visual arts. Ethnography-oriented collections like *Fragments of Culture: The Everyday of Modern Turkey*, "cultural climate" studies like Nurdan Gürbilek's *Vitrinde Yaşamak*, and novels like Elif Shafak's *Flea Palace* offer glimpses into vernacular transculturation in the shadow of the American century.[39]

In this interdisciplinary book, I build upon these rich disciplinary engagements. I also conducted historiographic and literary research and interviews in Turkey and the United States between 2006 and 2013. Despite disciplinary divides, tropes, stock figures, and plot patterns associated with batılılaşma crisscross official and unofficial texts. This book, therefore, connects official narratives in state-approved histories (chapter 1), to the semiofficial narratives in novels published by public intellectuals (chapter 2), and to the unofficial discursive domain of the vernacular—the everyday cultural terrain in which jokes (chapter 3) and beds (chapter 4) are shared. I closely read these texts with attention to figures of speech and stock figures, situate them in their context of circulation, and relate them to debates over U.S.–Turkish relations. Following this trajectory from the institutional toward the folkloric, I demonstrate how ideas about westernization and America not only operate in the high register of national history writing and policymaking, but also influence everyday affects and identities. The figures of westernization gain traction at the level of the vernacular, yet they are also transformed through transculturation in ways that challenge the authority of the Turkish state (and the United States) to determine the parameters of sociocultural change. As such, the book offers a glimpse of "multiple meanings [and uses] of America and American culture in all their complexity," demonstrating how "America" may influence local identities and cultural politics, sometimes even in the absence of direct U.S. government intervention.[40]

Chapter 1, "Narrating the Mandate: Selective Westernization and Official History," explores rhetorical maneuvers of forgetting and remembering employed in official and popular nationalist histories. At its center are varying representations of a critical moment, between 1918 and 1923, from the end of World War I to the end of the Turkish Independence War, when the United States became seriously engaged with the fate of the Middle East due to calls for a U.S. mandate over Turkey. The history and historiography of a short-lived Turkish Wilsonian Principles League, founded by women's activist Halide Edib, allow an insight into how intersectional tropes of gender, ethnicity, and class have infused debates about foreign relations in Turkey. The chapter shows how early twentieth-century Kemalists came to institutionalize selective westernization by utilizing the discourse of over-westernization to marginalize their former allies, including Edib. Using history as a tool of the state,

Mustafa Kemal Atatürk and his followers were able to justify their own authoritarian westernization reforms, which included banning the fez and mandating the Western-style hat, to counter the Western figure of "the terrible Turk." These discursive moves echo in later historical references to the League and Edib, making "the mandate" a key rhetorical figure in U.S.–Turkish relations.

Chapter 2, "Allegorizing America: Over-Westernization in the Turkish Novel," provides a selective cultural history of the Turkish novel, with a focus on allegories of mobility and love, which have haunted the genre since its strategic adoption into Turkish. The nationalist novel, defined in relation to both nonfiction history (chapter 1) and folklore (chapter 3), operates as the primary crucible for figures associated with over-westernization. Through an examination of these thesis-driven, allegorical novels, I analyze the gendered and sexualized depictions of the United States and of Americans, starting with the early twentieth century. Comparing these to stereotypes of Europeans, I demonstrate how representations of Americans hardened during the Cold War in response to U.S. attempts to figure Turkey as a model laboratory for capitalist modernization theory. The historical trajectory shows how the United States came to dominate discussions of over-westernization, while also demonstrating how the Turkish novel began to critique the allegorical push of both Kemalist selective westernization projects and the U.S. State Department as the century progressed.

Chapters 1 and 2 explore debates around Turkey's upper classes and their suspect loyalties. The last two chapters remind us that the discourse of over-westernization has a counterpart in representations of inadequate westernization. Turkey's political elite has mobilized the gendered and sexualized discourse of over-westernization against the upper classes, who are supposedly too eager to absorb Western norms (section one). Yet they have also condemned the working classes for being too backward, too Eastern, too premodern on gendered and sexualized terms (section two). In chapter 3, this type of inadequate modernization becomes a resource for bawdy political humor. In chapter 4, it manifests in panic narratives about inappropriate or illegible sexual identities and connected criminal tendencies.

Chapter 3, "Humoring English: Wild Westernization and Anti-American Folklore," examines humor about language and language humor, along with attendant rhetorical figures, particularly bilingual puns and homophonic substitutions, and comic stock figures. Bilingual Turkish humor, or "Turklish" humor, consists of several folkloric and vernacular subgenres, including riddles, jokes, and lengthy mock romances, all of which require some level of familiarity with the English and Turkish languages, as well as with Turkish and American popular culture. As such, these texts provide an excellent archive for studying vernacular transculturation with the United States. This chapter explores the historical trajectory and political uses of Turklish humor, which has become increasingly popular since the 1960s and 1970s. I argue that such bilingual texts formulate a vernacular, wild-westernized nationalism, which challenges the government's ability to determine the limits of sociocultural change. Bilingual humor also regularly revises figures imported from the United States, particularly that of the Wild West, to talk back to empire. One recent example has been the mobilization of humor to counter the post-9/11 figuration of Turks as compliant "moderate Muslims" in the War on Terror. However, in the process, such humor can bolster divides between Turkey's citizens based on foreign-language competency and properly "modern" behavior.

If the first three chapters explore the clash of westernization in various discursive registers, from the official to the literary to the folkloric, the fourth chapter foregrounds the question that has been in the background so far: How exactly do these discourses influence identities, performances, and politics on the ground? How do individuals from different backgrounds maneuver within these discursive constructs to embody, challenge, or transform the figures of westernization? Chapter 4, "Figuring Sexualities: Inadequate Westernization and Rights Activism," demonstrates how, just as the limits of westernization are often figured in the language of gender and sexuality, gendered and sexualized figures are read through the limits of westernization. The chapter focuses on the contested construction of sexualized masculinities and sexual politics through discourses engaging the symbolic East/West binary. It traces how *gey* (gay) identity became increasingly normalized in the late 1990s and early 2000s, as the Turkish state began granting some begrudging public legitimacy to gey and *lesbiyen* (lesbian) identities, in line with its selective westernization projects. This official "acceptance," however, has not prevented a rise in the murders of gey-identified men. Moreover, the normalization of a figuratively modern/Western gey identity coincided with the increasing marginalization of cross-dressed male sex workers and trans female sex workers (collectively known as travesti). Travesti and working-class sexual partners of gey men who do not identify as gey often bear the brunt of criminalizing discourses around the lower limits of westernization. They, in turn, have developed their own rhetorical tactics, manipulating the gendered, classed East/West connotations of sexual acts and identities. The chapter shows how the United States, as the symbolic home of gay identity and LGBT politics, remains connected to debates around transculturated figures of gender and sexuality. Grants and discursive imports from European and American institutions influence local queer praxes, as does backlash against an ascendant neoliberalism structurally and figuratively connected to the United States.

Chapter 1 emphasizes the American figure of the Terrible Turk, chapter 2 brings in depictions of Turkey as a good pupil for U.S.-led modernization, and chapter 3 introduces attempts to recruit Turkey as a moderate Muslim ally in the War on Terror. The same chronology marks a transition in Turkish perceptions of the United States from a central guide for selective westernization (immediately after World War I and during the early Cold War) toward America as the most dangerous source of westoxication (late twentieth century) and as a complexly degenerative force countering Turkey's proper modernization (in the first decade of the War on Terror). Each chapter in *The Limits of Westernization*, however, straddles the divide between the late nineteenth and early twenty-first centuries. The book demonstrates how important historical events, such as Turkey's formation as a nation-state, the Cold War alliance between Turkey and the United States, the 1980s switch to a free market economy, and the intensification of folk anti-Americanism in the early twenty-first century, have impacted different discursive fields. This approach allows the reader to see how each epoch has utilized the figures of the past, as issues and events that do not overlap temporally— the American mandate, contentions over Turkey's NATO membership, the 2003 Iraq war—coalesce symbolically. Thus some important figures such as Halide Edib, motifs like "the American mandate" and "mobility," and metonyms like "Texas," gain new valences from chapter to chapter.

With this strategy, I seek to draw attention to cultural history writing as a discursive act itself, employing narratives, characters, and figures of speech. The overlapping layers are here to encourage a "writerly" approach that does not reify the linear historical narrative.[41] In the postscript to the book, I discuss the ramifications of this approach for thinking about culture in U.S.–Middle East relations in general.

The Limits of Westernization argues that increasing connectivity to the United States in the twentieth century has led to unpredictable, vernacular cultural politics that clash with both the Turkish state's authoritarian projects of westernization and U.S. figurations of Turkey. My theoretical insights are indebted not just to multinational, multidisciplinary scholarship but also to Turkish folk and popular cultures, which have become increasingly adept at examining the dilemmas of Turkish westernization through humor. A 2008 cartoon published in a weekly humor magazine, for example, made fun of selective westernization by depicting an Ottoman father frowning at an Ottoman youngster, who has decorated his room with posters representing "The Industrial Revolution" and "Steam Power," as if they were pictures of famous American singers or actors. "Our youth have surely become infatuated with the West," thinks the father gloomily. The dry pictures underline the limited libidinal dynamics of selective westernization, contrasting this phenomenon with vernacular transculturation, which is much more likely to influence how contemporary Turkish teenagers decorate their rooms. The cartoon father's disdainful reaction to his son's "infatuation" with the West, of course, also constitutes a knowing stab at the sexualized discourse of westoxication.

The opening dialogue from *The Mild West* similarly refers to selective westernization ironically to make a salacious joke. The humor stems from the incongruity of applying an instrumentalist model of authoritarian westernization ("taking the good things from the West") to a passion-driven circumstance, that is, the Ottoman character's attraction to an American woman. Such popular texts mock twentieth-century metanarratives about the limits of westernization, challenging the idea that the Turkish or U.S. elites can control the politics of cultural change in the country. Often the challenge is launched in the bawdy vernacular. Of course, as a cartoon and a motion picture, these texts are themselves products of a long history of transculturation; therefore, their commentary on wild westernization inevitably functions on a meta level. Referencing the Ottoman Empire as the birthplace of Turkish dilemmas around batılılaşma, these products might be heralding (and constructing) alternative ways of figuring America in the twenty-first century. Past debates around the limits of westernization will provide resources for that future.

Over-Westernization

CHAPTER ONE

Narrating the Mandate

Selective Westernization and Official History

On December 5, 1918, a group of Istanbul intellectuals led by a Turkish woman named Halide Edib (Adıvar) sent a letter to Woodrow Wilson, urging the United States to take Ottoman Turkey under its imperial wing. Edib and her colleagues represented Wilson Prensipleri Cemiyeti, the Wilsonian Principles League (WPL), founded on December 4, 1918, approximately a month after the Mudros armistice announced the near-unconditional surrender of the Ottoman Empire in World War I. Expressing concern that "any system attempted by themselves is likely to degenerate into despotism," the signatories asked the United States to "lend its aid and experience" to Ottoman Turkey, appointing an American advisor-in-chief with all the necessary powers for between fifteen and twenty-five years.[1] Throughout the nineteenth century, the Ottoman Empire had lost "territory and military power at a corresponding rate to the expansion of the size and power of the United States"[2] (figure 1.1). The WPL's letter was an appeal for tutelage in the new methods of empire the United States had perfected (e.g., industrialization, professionalization, and "liberal developmentalism"), sent by an intelligentsia that still imagined an ethnically and religiously diverse Ottoman state.[3]

At the Paris Peace Conference, the Allies and the United States developed an international mandate system, resembling the type of protectorate rule familiar to Western imperial powers, including the

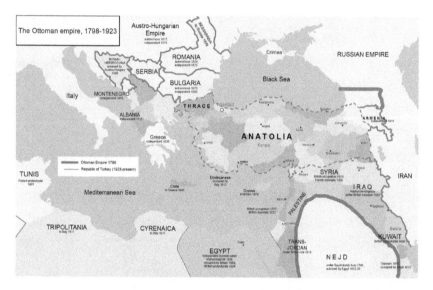

FIGURE 1.1 The loss of Ottoman territory during the nineteenth century and the boundaries of the Republic of Turkey. This work, "Ottoman Empire, 1798–1923," is a derivate of "Wikimedia Commons Map of Ottoman Empire in 1900 Latvian" by Juris Tiltins, used under public domain. "Ottoman Empire, 1798–1923" is licensed under public domain by Denise J. Massa, Visual Resources Center, University of Notre Dame.

United States, which had acquired its own overseas colonies at the turn of the century. The framework for mandates gave the victorious states power and responsibility over territories formerly belonging to the Ottoman and German empires and "inhabited by peoples not yet able to stand by themselves under the strenuous conditions of the modern world."[4] The mandate system appealed to WPL members with its promise of selective westernization and eventual independence, and they began to lobby specifically for a U.S. mandate over Turkey. Wilson, who "displayed a particular dislike of Turks," reinforced by Ottoman massacres of Armenians, never replied to Edib.[5] Yet he knew of the WPL's appeal. He related his thoughts on the matter to British Prime Minister Lloyd George at the Paris Peace Conference on May 6, 1919:

> [C]ertain authoritative Turks had expressed the view that the whole of Turkey ought to be under a single mandate. He himself thought that this was more than he could induce the United States to un-

dertake. The Turks were hated in the United States, and the only ground on which a mandate would be accepted in Turkey would be to protect subject races against the Turks.[6]

Unaware of the strength of Wilson's anti-Turkish feelings, Halide Edib also sent a letter to nationalist frontline commander Mustafa Kemal (Atatürk) on August 10, 1919, arguing that an American mandate over the remnants of the Ottoman Empire would be the "lesser of two evils," and the only way to avoid ethnic dissolution and division into European spheres of influence.[7] Ignored by Wilson and kept on the sidelines by Kemal, the WPL would have no direct impact on U.S., Allied, or even Turkish policy. On December 9, 1919, on the heels of the defeat of the Versailles Treaty and the League of Nations in the Senate, the United States withdrew from official participation in the Supreme War Council. By the time the Ottoman sultan consented to the devastating terms of the Treaty of Sèvres (August 10, 1920), which divided Turkey into multiple Allied territories and turned Istanbul and the Straits into demilitarized international zones, the Wilsonian Principles League had officially dissolved. In 1920, Edib and most other members joined the armed resistance led by Kemal. In 1923, following multiple military victories against Greece and the Allies, Kemal and his followers dethroned the sultan and founded a new, independent nation in Asia Minor and Thrace: the Republic of Turkey.

U.S. cultural historians have inherited from Edward Said's *Orientalism*, and productively complicated, the analysis of the discursive production of inferior otherness as fuel for imperial ventures.[8] Much has been written about how perceptions of racial superiority operated to justify economic, military, and territorial expansion within the logic of U.S. imperialism in the nineteenth and twentieth centuries. Ironically, however, the WPL incident can be registered as a double win for "race over empire," as racial ideas foreclosed avenues for imperial expansion.[9] First, Wilson's own racial prejudices and his approximation of American feelings against Turks prevented him from ever taking seriously the idea of incorporating Turkey into Pax Americana through the mandate system. Second, the final blow to the multiethnic, multireligious Ottoman ideal—a long time in the making as ethnic rebellions rocked the empire in the nineteenth century—led to the creation of a nation-state deeply committed to Turkish ethnic purity under Kemal.

While racial and religious prejudice on both sides limited the possibilities for the expansion of the U.S. empire into the Middle East at the time, the civilizational paradigm that drove the WPL to look to the United States as a guide toward a desired, Western-style modernization did not disappear. The dominance of Kemalist ethnic nationalism, and the military victories that backed it, allowed the government to vilify Edib and her colleagues as "over-westernized" traitors, even as the young republic implemented a radical cultural revolution modeled on a normative idea of Western civilization. The new state urged its citizens to become figures of nationalist modernity through reforms regarding dress and behavior. These early attempts to differentiate a "proper" nationalist mode of Western-inspired reform (i.e., "selective westernization"), which came to be embodied by Mustafa Kemal, from "over-westernization" or "westoxication," a gendered and sexualized discourse of corruption and degeneration, which tarred the memory of Halide Edib, have significantly shaped Turkish historical memories of the WPL and the United States. This institutionalization of selective westernization in the early twentieth century prepared the ground for Turkey's alliance with NATO and the United States at mid-century. Yet the peculiar rhetorical flourishes of contemporary Turkish anti-Americanism, which regularly employs the trope of "the American mandate," can be traced to this era as well.

As Homi Bhabha, building on the work of Benedict Anderson, has noted, nation-building depends on strategies of narration seeking to manage the ambivalences of constructing one people out of countless heterogeneities.[10] Narratives promulgated in nationalist histories thus employ a host of rhetorical maneuvers to police the contours of collective cultural memory, urging a nation's people to "disremember" some events and "overly remember" others.[11] Such collective disremembering and over-remembering constitute two sides of the same coin: figured as topics about which "everybody already knows," mythologized stories and connected stock figures foreclose questions and help consolidate the nation as an "imagined community."[12]

The construction of a state-oriented nationalist history was a key part of Kemalist authoritarian westernization. The alphabet reform (1928), the founding of the Turkish Historical Society (1931), the secularization and centralization of education operated together to make history a tool of the state. A hegemonic official "Turkish history thesis" formed and was institutionalized under Kemal's leadership in the 1930s.[13] Kemal himself modeled proper nationalist history writing with *Nutuk* (1927), his epic recounting of the Independence War and the founding of the Turkish republic.[14] Although challenged in academic works for decades, Kemalist history still holds sway in high school textbooks and, therefore, has become a part of Turkish popular memory. This official (and popular) history overly remembers the aftermath of the Great War as a time of Western invasion, elite "over-westernization," and redemption by Kemal's armies. Thus it narrates the birth of a modern republic out of the ashes of a failed, decrepit empire through the sheer will of one manly hero: Mustafa Kemal Atatürk, the "ancestor-father" of Turks.[15]

Moments of forgetting and remembering sustained by figurative language and stock figures also structure U.S. history taught in high schools, particularly in relation to racial violence and imperialism.[16] In fact, the interdisciplinary subfield of transnational American studies owes its birth to the impetus to examine the "absences" that have historically defined nationalist history-writing, particularly vis-à-vis the existence of an American "empire."[17] Yet, as in the Turkish case, the exceptional and abundant scholarship that followed these calls has not transformed the exceptionalist and triumphalist schoolbooks that relate American history through the theme of "unrelenting progress."[18] This hegemonic American history overly remembers Woodrow Wilson's fight for the League of Nations, while forgetting his racially and religiously motivated unwillingness to aid Anatolia's Muslims. The largely positive and tragic figure of Wilson as a liberal internationalist ahead of his time also obscures the president's legacy in instituting Jim Crow in the federal government and his rejection of a proposed racial equality clause for the covenant of the League of Nations. In both countries, official history (bearing the insignia of the Turkish Ministry of Education in one case and the approval of the local school board in the other) has become nationalist collective memory.

In this chapter, I tell both the transnational history of the WPL and the comparative story of its nationalist histories. Taking a cue from W. J. T. Mitchell, I consider memory as a complex narrative device, a rhetorical technique, and as a human faculty that simultaneously constructs and obscures knowledge.[19] Memory narrated is "intersubjective": one individual's account hails others.[20] It is also intertextual and trans-temporal; the constructions of the past always speak to the present. This chapter is organized around three specific narratives of forgetfulness in the early twentieth century, with attention to their continuing echoes: Halide Edib, who "forgot" to mention her leading role in the founding of the WPL in her memoirs; Mustafa Kemal, who "forgot" his strategic response to calls for a U.S. mandate over Turkey in *Nutuk*; and Woodrow Wilson, who forgot the wording of the only one of his Fourteen Points that mentioned Turkey. I argue that the interaction between memory as a narrative technology and emotionally charged, gendered stock figures, such as the westoxicated woman and the "terrible Turk," has shaped national histories and popular conceptions of the period after World War I. The controversial figure of Halide Edib, continuing debates over the proper limits of westernization, and Turkey's unequal relationship with the United States have made the WPL notorious in Turkish national history. The story, however, is invisible in the United States. This is partially because of gaps in the historiography of U.S. relations with the Middle East before the Cold War. Also influential have been the post–World War II redemption of Woodrow Wilson as a tragic, protoglobalist figure and the rise of the "bad Arab" to replace the "terrible Turk" as the trope for the dangerous Muslim as the twentieth century progressed.[21] The story of the unlikely mandate is, therefore, both the story of U.S.–Turkish relations at a critical time and the story of how rhetorical techniques of (over)remembering and forgetting, bolstered by stock figures, continue to shape national histories and imperial (im)possibilities.

FIGURING RACE AND BELONGING IN TWO EMPIRES

Turkey's most important bilateral relation since the end of World War II has been the unequal and volatile one with the United States.[22] Ottoman–American relations in the eighteenth century, however, consisted of the Ottoman Empire, then the richer and bigger state, blissfully ignoring the so-called New World.[23] Only in 1827, when the Ottoman navy experienced a devastating defeat at the hands of Britain, France, and Russia at Navarino, did Ottoman officials begin to eye the United States as a potential party to include in the "balance of power" game. In 1832, the United States came out of bilateral talks with an advantageous trade capitulation and secret (though stillborn) plans to help rebuild and modernize the Ottoman navy.[24] This was the first time the United States entered the Ottoman political lexicon as a possible resource for selective westernization. Yet this is also when it first became embroiled in the discourse of excessive westernization. As a concession in return for the navy deal, the Ottomans agreed to exempt Americans from the laws of the land through a one-sided extraterritoriality agreement. The United States, therefore, joined other Western nations who claimed this license, which stung for decades as a symbol of the colonization of Ottoman lands in everything but name.

The Ottoman state itself was of little concern to official U.S. policy, which focused on Latin America, Europe, and even East Asia more directly, and generally stayed within the ever-fluctuating boundaries of the Monroe Doctrine. Although the United States acquired its own overseas colonies after the Spanish-Cuban-American war of 1898, U.S. policy makers were focused on developing financial and cultural ways to control the world's resources without having to administer and provide services to nonwhite subjects.[25] Missionaries, tradesmen, and philanthropists ran the American expansion into the Ottoman Empire, in accordance with what Emily Rosenberg has called "the promotional state" of the nineteenth and early twentieth centuries.[26] When the United States got embroiled in Ottoman politics, its concerns were related either to trade or to civic mobilization on behalf of Ottoman Christians, particularly Greeks and Armenians. Missionaries, the main source of information about the Middle East for the American government and laypeople alike, would have by far the greatest influence on bilateral relations in the nineteenth century, giving the Turks "a terrible reputation" in the United States.[27] Figuring Armenians as proto-Americans in contrast to the barbarian Turks and Kurds, U.S. officials often referred to them as "the Yankees of the Orient," and naturalized more Armenians on Ottoman soil, thus exempting them from Ottoman laws, than had any European state done for any Near Eastern minority.[28] Thus, at the end of the nineteenth century, the United States was both inextricably involved in and politically uncommitted to the Middle East; the missions and their Armenian congregations both "belonged to" the United States and also were "not a part" of it.[29]

With the 1878 Treaty of Berlin, the nations of Europe claimed the right to act as guardians of Ottoman Christians, further straining the ties of belonging between the weakening Ottoman state and its restless Christian communities, many of whom had begun agitating for a right to form their own nation-states.[30] As the Ottoman Empire weakened and began to pursue centralization through selective westernization and political repression, the authorities blamed U.S. missions as breeding grounds for minority sectarianism.[31] Between 1894 and 1896, Sultan Abdulhamid II ordered the massacre of tens of thousands of Armenians in response to revolts in Harput and Maraş. Far from a simple Oriental reactionary, Abdulhamid II was an autocratic westernizer. He reformed Ottoman education and the judiciary along Western lines, even as he ferociously suppressed dissent of all kinds. Although part Armenian on his mother's side, he also employed the discourse of over-westernization to attack minority Christians as a fifth column by which the West could "get at our most vital places and tear out our very guts."[32] Outrage over the Hamidian massacres helped solidify the stereotype of the Terrible Turk in the United States, creating a fez-wearing, scimitar-wielding, hook-nosed, bearded monster who ruled over a harem of captured white maidens.[33]

The Committee for Union and Progress (CUP), popularly known as the Young Turks, forced Abdulhamid II's hand in setting up a constitutional monarchy in 1908—the second in Ottoman history. CUP, which ruled the empire until its defeat in World War I, built upon Abdulhamid's methods of control and consolidation, developing a "scientific" policy of ethnic engineering based on European models.[34] Their education in Western-style medical and military schools had given them a sense of European ideals of statecraft and nationhood. Many were also Turkish immigrants from the Balkans and had experienced the rise of violent ethnic nationalisms in Europe firsthand. They, in turn, signed the orders that led to the deaths of over a million Ottoman Armenians in forced deportations, labor camps, and massacres during World War I. Unlike Westerners, who read pure Islamic savagery into Ottoman actions, CUP leaders saw even their most atrocious ethnic engineering projects as compatible with selective westernization. The strategic moving around of populations, including Muslims, Jews, and Christians, across parts of the empire was their cold-blooded preparation for a future in which multinational empires were becoming untenable.[35]

The United States, a settler colony building a new type of empire predicated on open markets, appeared to be an exception to this rule of dying multiethnic empires. Therefore, toward the late nineteenth century, it drew the attention of the ruling Ottoman elite as a rising world power that appeared to effectively "manage" its own fractious ethnic groups on both the mainland and in its overseas possessions. Thus the moral repugnance Americans felt for "the terrible Turk" was increasingly met by a sense of the moral equivalency and structural similarity of the two empires on the Ottoman side. Ottoman leaders developed two connected rhetorical strategies to explain their violent suppression of minorities to American representatives, utilizing the good/bad West dialectic of selective and excessive westernization. The first involved blaming the United States and Europe for Christian separatism. The second was to suggest the Ottoman Empire was no different than the United States in the way it dealt with "treasonous" minorities. In 1903, Chekib Bey, the Ottoman ambassador in Washington, complained to Secretary of State Hay about the impact of American missionary schools: "Suppose I should establish . . . a school for [American] Negroes, and my teachers should tell the Negroes . . . that they ought not to submit to lynching and should rebel? Do you think I would remain in this country long or that my school would flourish?"[36] In 1914, CUP's ambassador to the United States, Rustem Bey, cast the Armenians as "political agitators" operating under instructions from European imperialists, and compared the massacres to "the lynchings which occur daily in the United States and the memory of the 'watercures' in the Philippines."[37] During the forced deportations of 1915, Talaat Pasha disgusted Ambassador Henry Morgenthau with his smug suggestion that the Ottomans were dealing with the Armenians as the Americans had dealt with the Indians.[38]

Such historical similes aimed to secularize and politicize the conflict between the Ottoman government and its minorities in opposition to Americans' insistence on religious interpretations. Yet they always backfired. The U.S. policy elite simply did not identify with the Ottoman rulers, despite America's own history of ethnic cleansing, land theft, and racial violence. In U.S. figurations, Turks, not Armenians, were the proper analogues for savage "Negroes" and "Indians." Not only did Wilson reportedly call Turks "the Mohammedan Apache," his ambassador to Germany would propose to move Turks in Anatolia to "park-like reservations such as were used for the American Indians" in 1919, even as the WPL continued to lobby for U.S. assistance.[39] The history of the failed American mandate over Turkey hinged on this "extreme Otherness" of the Turk in U.S. culture, in contrast with the parallels the Ottoman elite perceived between the Ottoman and American empires.[40]

THE WILSONIAN PRINCIPLES LEAGUE, HALIDE EDIB, AND THE UNLIKELY MANDATE

At the end of World War I, two empires, one bankrupt and moribund, the other enriched and energized, faced a chaotic postwar world. They had fought on opposing sides without declaring war on each other, mainly out of U.S. concern for American missionary lives and property. Woodrow Wilson, counting on global perceptions of America's high moral standing and powerful economy, was determined to be the architect of a new world. Ottoman Turks, on the other hand, were hoping to survive in it with a semblance of dignity. When President Wilson read a fourteen-point declaration on the peace process to the U.S. Congress on January 8, 1918, it seemed for a moment that both of these wishes might come true. Point 12, which addressed the destiny of the Ottoman Empire, suddenly made Wilson the most popular Western politician Asia Minor had ever known:

> The Turkish portions of the present Ottoman Empire should be assured a secure sovereignty, but the other nationalities which are now under Turkish rule should be assured an undoubted security of life and an absolutely unmolested opportunity of autonomous development, and the Dardanelles should be permanently opened as a free passage to the ships and commerce of all nations under international guarantees.[41]

Based on a December 22, 1917 memorandum by the president's group of experts, nicknamed The Inquiry, Wilson's Point 12 was ambiguous enough to please everyone.[42] Minorities within the Ottoman Empire read it as the promise of new nation-states; Turkish intellectuals saw in it the possible survival of their empire, as long as it granted equal rights and freedoms to all minorities. Point 12 was so popular among the Turkish intelligentsia that its invocation took on an apotropaic quality. The editors of major nationalist-leaning Turkish newspapers decided in the spring of 1918 to print it in full on the front page of their newspapers every day.[43] After the Allied-backed Greek invasion of Izmir on May 15th, 1919, protesters in Istanbul listened to feverish speeches made behind a banner which simply read "Wilson's Principle 12" (figure 1.2).[44] In the summer and fall of 1919, the United States sent two advisory teams to the region to produce policy recommendations—the King-Crane Commission to Syria and the Harbord Commission to Anatolia—and both were met with banners declaring the primacy of Wilson's principles.[45]

FIGURE 1.2 Turkish intellectual and women's activist Halide Edib was behind the most strident calls for a U.S. mandate over Turkey. In this photo, she is making a speech against the Greek invasion of 1919 while standing behind a banner that reads "Wilson's Principle 12" in Ottoman Turkish.

Halide Edib, the daughter of an elite Jewish convert with ties to the palace, the first Muslim woman to graduate from the American School for Girls in Istanbul (1901), and the founder of one of the Empire's most significant women's organizations, Teal-i Nisvan Cemiyeti (Society for the Elevation of Women, 1908), described how deeply the WPL's founders had been inspired by the Wilsonian principle of self-determination in her memoirs of 1928:

> Inspired and encouraged by the principles of Wilson, which had taken in the entire world of the defeated, a temporary association called the Wilsonian League was formed in Istamboul by a number of writers and publicists and lawyers. In the midst of blind hatred and the cry of "no quarter to the defeated," the only gleam of justice and common sense seemed to come from those principles.[46]

Edib's use of the passive voice clashes with her passionate words, signifying an author who wishes to distance herself from history but also to do justice to the strong emotions of the time. Interestingly, she refrains from naming names, including her own, thus protecting the identities of her colleagues. She does not mention her leadership in the WPL's founding or her role as the primary author and dominant signatory of the letter to Wilson.[47] In fact, she says little about the league in her memoir. Instead, she underplays the organization, arguing that it was meant to be temporary and that it dissolved quickly. She notes:

> The league started out in December, 1918, and died out completely in two months. But its value was very limited. Eastern Anatolia was against it from the very beginning. . . . America, whose sympathies seemed to be entirely on the side of the Armenians, having heard only of Armenian massacres and sufferings, appeared dangerous rather than helpful.[48]

By the time her memoir was published, Edib had come under attack by Kemal and his Republican People's Party for her appeal for an American mandate over Turkey, which partially explains her retroactive omissions. Yet in 1918 there was nothing unusual in the WPL's choice of the United

States as a potential protector. Although they fought on opposite sides during World War I, the United States and the Ottoman Empire had never declared war against each other, and the United States, in strong contrast to czarist Russia, England, France, Italy, and Greece, had never expressed any designs on Ottoman territory. As Edib notes, the American bias for minority Christians had alienated many Turks and Kurds in Eastern Anatolia. Still, in the WPL's opinion at least, the United States looked like the most reasonable power to court. The Fourteen Points had made Woodrow Wilson a messiah to many across the world.[49] WPL members, like the elite of several other nations, including Egypt, India, China, and Korea, saw the United States as both a potential ally against European imperialism and a potential guide to Western-style modernity.[50]

Certainly, many of the founders of the WPL were naïve about U.S. foreign policy, the mandate system, and the extent to which the United States could be "trusted to carry out a mission of peace and progress," in the words of one WPL member.[51] In her August 10, 1919 letter to Kemal, for example, Edib cited the Philippines as a positive model of benign U.S. rule, in which strategic westernization overcame atomization. As she wrote, America was "the only country that has succeeded in creating modern state machinery operating automatically in a country as wild as the Philippine Islands."[52] Edib and other WPL members felt the United States would make the perfect mandatory power for the Ottoman Empire, because its government was "without nationality or religion" and its population was heterogeneous, paralleling their own aspirations for a just and diverse state.[53] That Turkish intellectuals so idealized American racial and religious dynamics barely a decade after the atrocities of the Philippine-American War, in a heinous era marked by the Red Scare and race riots, as well as frequent military interventions in Latin America, is a surprising testament to the success with which Wilsonian rhetoric had differentiated America from Europe as it had Wilson from Theodore Roosevelt. Wilson himself, however, was no fan of the Ottoman elite, and no different in this in this regard than Roosevelt, who had once declared "Turkey," along with Spain, as the state he "would rather smash than any in the world."[54]

Woodrow Wilson's foreign policy was driven by strong religious convictions.[55] Like many Protestant Americans, the president's main interest in Turkey had been "missionary and theological."[56] Deeply influenced by missionary propaganda, he saw the Ottoman massacres of Armenians through apolitical, ahistorical, religious lenses. His perceptions of "the Turk" combined this religious antagonism with racial ideas about fitness for civilization and self-government. Wilson, therefore, was completely unwilling to embrace Turkey as a potential ward, although Turks were not the only ones making this request at the time. Looking for a buffer from Bolshevik Russia and a strong ally to protect England's oil-rich Arab mandates, Lloyd George aimed to draw Wilson into the Middle East, and proposed U.S. mandates in Anatolia, including the Straits and two regions designated as Turkish Asia Minor and Armenia, as early as January 30, 1919.[57] On March 20, Wilson told the Entente that, while he recognized the United States might need to accept responsibilities as a League member, he "did not want anything in Turkey," and would be "only too delighted" if Britain and France could take all responsibility for the region.[58] On May 21, 1919, two weeks after Wilson's insistence to the Allies that "[t]he Turks were hated in the United States," Lloyd George once again offered the United States mandatory rule over Armenia, Istanbul, and "a light mandate over the whole of Anatolia."[59] Wilson again rejected the need for any type of American mandate over Anatolia (overwhelmingly Turkish and Kurdish in population). "Wilson Warns U.S. May Refuse to Rule Turks," announced the *New York Times* on May 25, 1919.[60]

Wilson was not the only American unwilling to see "the Mohammedan Apache" as a victim, let alone imagine a situation in which it could be affiliated with the United States as a protégé. An editorial cartoon in the *Rocky Mountain News* in August 1919 depicted a gigantic, scimitar-wielding, fez-wearing Turkey, having just butchered a small, harmless, hat-wearing Armenian, smiling as piles of corpses lay behind him. The caption asked cynically, "Our Ward?" (figure 1.3). As Meltem Ahıska observes, the Ottoman Turks—Muslims ruling over Christian subjects—disrupted "the binary oppositions of East and West, colonizer and colonized that informs [Edward Said's] analysis."[61] Unlike the Arabs and Near Eastern Christians, who could be gendered feminine and sympathetic, the terrible Turk was depicted almost exclusively as male and belligerent, as a bloodthirsty tyrant without culture, refinement, or hope of rehabilitation. During World War I, "the Turk" functioned as a darker analogue to "the Hun," the German whose whiteness was revoked in

OUR WARD?

—(PEARCE) *Rocky Mountain News* (Denver), Aug., 1919

FIGURE 1.3 "Our Ward?" This is how many in the United States imagined calls for a U.S. mandate over Turkey in 1919. Depicted as a grotesquely powerful, irredeemable male monster, "the Turk" could not be seen a victim or potential protégé. Compare to figure 1.2, depicting Halide Edib, the Turkish woman leader who actually lobbied for the mandate.

popular American representations.[62] This racialized figure of the Turk clashed with elite Ottoman perceptions of America as a potential guide for proper westernization, a foil to predatory Europe, and a good model for rejuvenating their own multiethnic empire. Wilson and the U.S. public likely did not know that a diminutive American-educated women's activist was behind the most strident calls for U.S. assistance.[63] Although Edib wrote an open letter to the American public on August 7, 1919, and foregrounded her identity as a modern woman, claiming a hurt but proud identity Americans usually reserved for Armenians, her letter was not published.[64] Thus the brute figure of the Turk dominated talk of the mandate, instead of the Turkish woman intellectual who had lobbied for it.

After the defeat of the Versailles Treaty and the League of Nations, the United States continued as an observer in the Supreme War Council until January 11, 1921. In the San Remo conference of April 15, 1920, the council broke Anatolia into French, Italian, and Greek spheres of influence, roughly in accordance with secret treaties, and addressed a note to President Wilson proposing that the U.S. government accept the mandate for Armenia.[65] The San Remo plans ran counter not only to Point 12 but also to the recommendations of the King-Crane and Harbord Commissions sent to the Near East by the United States government. Yet they fit the president's own leanings. On May 24, 1920, Wilson asked a pro-Armenian but also increasingly isolationist Congress to support an American mandate over Armenia alone. In his speech asking for the executive power to accept a mandate, he suggested that the Great Powers' San Remo offer could only have been providential for the United States. He appealed to the American people's "genuine convictions and deep Christian sympathies" and their "earnest desire to see Christian people everywhere succored in their time of suffering."[66]

His detractors, on the other hand, chose to focus on the Harbord Commission's report, particularly as it concerned the financial and political burdens of an overseas mandate.[67] They also argued against overseas entanglements by citing the Monroe Doctrine and Lloyd George's dubious motives for drawing the United States into the oil-free and inhospitable region.[68] As Thomas Bailey put it, U.S. politicians had begun to suspect that "Uncle Sam was being played for a sucker" by the Allies, who claimed lucrative Arab mandates and left Armenia ("poor in natural resources but rich in the possibilities of trouble and expense") to the United States.[69] On June 1, 1920, the Senate rejected the Armenian mandate 52 to 32, and the United States exited the postwar settlement phase of the Great War without an official presence in the Middle East.

Of course, by that time, the resurgence of isolationism in the U.S. Congress and the warnings of the Harbord Report were only a few of the events complicating the resolution of the crisis. The Allied decision to postpone peace with the Ottoman Empire, the Greek invasion of 1919, and the harsh terms of the Treaty of Sèvres had led to a resurgence of Turkish nationalism across Asia Minor. The victories in the resulting Independence War, led by Mustafa Kemal and his comrades, and Western unwillingness to be drawn into another war, led the Allies to sign a new armistice (October 11, 1922). The ensuing Treaty of Lausanne (July 24, 1923) annulled plans for the dissolution of Turkey. However, it did not nullify anti-Turkish sentiment in the United States.[70] The Senate refused to ratify the Lausanne Treaty in January 1927, by a vote of 50 to 34, leaving the State Department scrambling to establish diplomatic relations and maintain trade agreements with the new nation. The rejection of Lausanne was based on widespread anti-Turkish sentiment in the country, as a *New York Herald Tribune* editorial argued:

> In rejecting the Lausanne Treaty with Turkey a minority in the Senate sacrificed common sense diplomacy to ancient prejudices and rancors. . . . Seldom has a decision in foreign affairs been taken with more irrelevant emotion and greater disregard for realities.[71]

However, emotion had never been "irrelevant" in Turkish–American relations. Nor did "irrelevant emotion" disappear from bilateral relations after 1927, although the Senate eventually agreed to most of the stipulations of Lausanne in a piecemeal fashion. The first sociological test for "nationality preferences" conducted in the United States in 1928 found "Turk" to be the most disliked group after "Negro" (figure 1.4).[72] The construction of official history out of emotionally charged cultural memories and stock figures also continued to determine the way Turkey and the United States remembered (or forgot) the fateful period after World War I, when a Turkish Wilsonian Principles League had courted an anti-Turkish Wilson with his own principles.

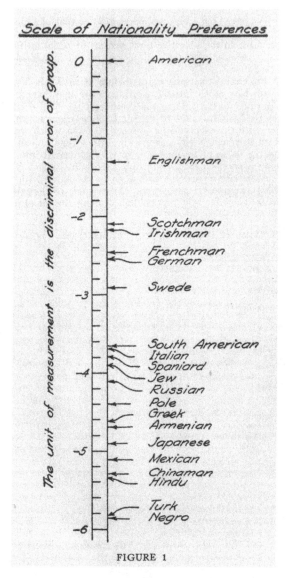

FIGURE 1

FIGURE 1.4 The first-ever sociological test of "nationality preference" conducted in the United States listed "Turk" and "Negro" at the bottom of the chart. Note the uneven mixture of races, regions, and nationalities (e.g., Chinaman, Jew, Spaniard, South American) mobilizing stock figures. "Turk" is the only Muslim signifier listed, operating as a racial and religious placeholder for a specific type of otherness.

KEMAL AND EDIB: TALLYING SELECTIVE AND EXCESSIVE WESTERNIZATIONS

Throughout the twentieth century and now into the twenty-first, the Wilsonian Principles League has been remembered in Turkish textbooks, popular nonfiction texts, novels, films, newspaper columns, and nationalist blogs, each time reflecting the concerns of the moment. The first history of the league, written by Mustafa Kemal, was no exception. Between October 15 and 20 in 1927, Kemal, the president of the young Turkish state, delivered a long-winded, meticulously detailed, and hyperbolic speech to the Turkish National Assembly, chronicling the role he played in the Independence War (1919–1923) and the founding of the republic (October 29, 1923). The Speech, or *Nutuk* as it is known in Turkey, is a testament to Kemal's love of epic history, his obsessive record keeping, and his willingness to harangue a captive audience for thirty-six hours and thirty-one minutes over five days. *Nutuk*, however, was not merely a history tome but also a project of political maneuvering: it glorified the author at the expense of ex-comrades, justifying Kemal's single-party regime and the Independence Tribunals of 1926, in which the Turkish revolution devoured its own children.[73] Kemal remembered and forgot historical events strategically, stigmatizing prominent figures of the nationalist movement and ironing out the ambiguities in his behavior during the chaotic Armistice years. America's rejection of the Treaty of Lausanne, amounting to a rejection of emerging Turkey, earlier that year must also be factored into Kemal's tone, particularly as it relates to the WPL and the United States.

Nutuk begins by passionately describing the dire straits in which Ottoman Turkey found itself on May 19, 1919, when Kemal landed in northeast Anatolia, ostensibly under orders to pacify and disarm the region but actually planning to unite and lead the scattered Ottoman armies into an armed resistance against the Allies. A common rhetorical convention in Turkish nationalist historiography, descriptions of the post–World War I, pre-Lausanne era make the resurrection of an independent Turkey in the next few years seem all the more miraculous. The Allies and the minorities, therefore, are not the only villains in *Nutuk*. The speech represents almost every locus of power in the country, from the sultan to the new minister of war to the Istanbul intellectuals, as working hand-in-glove with imperialists. According to Kemal, the post-Mudros era was one of utter chaos, hypocrisy, and treason—the results not only of ethno-religious atomization but also of an overactive civil society, selfish degeneracy, and lack of militarized will.

Inadequate centralization had been a significant Ottoman concern for centuries, ever since the empire began its painful decline in the eighteenth century. Blaming "over-westernization," late Ottoman intellectuals represented the decline of the state through metaphors of gender and maturity, as the lack of a strong father figure.[74] Ottoman nationalists decried the supposed degeneration of the westoxicated elite and called for all Turkish men to become soldiers and give up their lives and pleasures for the nation.[75] By the time he wrote *Nutuk*, Kemal had not yet taken the last name Atatürk, meaning the ancestor/father of Turks, but this was the position he claimed in the speech:

> Vahdettin, the degenerate occupant of the throne and the Caliphate, was seeking for some despicable way to save his person and his throne, the only objects of his anxiety. The Cabinet, of which Damat Ferit Paşa was the head, was weak and lacked dignity and courage.... Without being aware of it, the nation had no longer any one to lead it.

Kemal thus utilized Orientalist tropes about Eastern decadence, sloth, and cowardice to attack the old regime, casting himself as the masculine, determined, progressive leader. Such transculturated figures of inadequate modernity allowed Kemal and his followers to construct selective westernization as a necessity. Figures of over-westernization then set the limits around acceptable social change. The Armistice era did seem to Turkish nationalists as a veritable *Sodom and Gomorrah*—the name of a famous novel on Istanbul under Allied occupation—in which the greatest ethnic and gendered nightmares of Ottoman patriots seemed to be suddenly coming true: Christians ruling over Muslims, Turkish women publicly flirting with invading officers in Istanbul's dancehalls, and authorities handing parts of Anatolia to the imperialists on a silver platter.[76] The Wilsonian Principles League fit perfectly into this picture, and Kemal underlined a gendered as well as classed detail in describing it:

Certain prominent personalities—amongst them some women—in Istanbul were convinced that the real salvation of the country lay in securing an American protectorate over it. They stubbornly persisted in this idea and tried to prove that the acceptance of their point of view was the only thing possible.[77]

The WPL did indeed feature an elite cadre of Istanbulites, including professors, doctors, journalists, and lawyers. But the only woman active in the League was Halide Edib, its founder and leader. According to *Nutuk*, the WPL was perverse because of this unusual gendered arrangement—a woman at the helm—and the "stubbornness" it bred. Given that the league dissolved before the War of Independence, with most members, including Edib, joining the nationalists, Kemal's suggestion that these few intellectuals formed a formidable postwar force seems odd. Ironically, Kemal himself was a notoriously stubborn man, a quality that had led to his marginalization among nationalist circles prior to World War I.[78] Elsewhere in *Nutuk*, such persistence is featured as a positive, masculine quality, as when Kemal insists that his own uncompromising position had always been "Independence or Death!"[79] Later in his speech, Kemal devoted several pages to the question of an American mandate, reproducing letters and telegrams addressed to him in favor of the mandate. Among these was Edib's letter of August 10, 1919, read to the National Assembly and later reprinted in full, demonizing her in Turkish history as a woman in bed with the United States.

Halide Edib, however, cannot be so easily classified. "A teacher, journalist, author, statesman [*sic*], social worker, and soldier," as Professor Edward Mead Merle of Columbia University described her in his introduction to Edib's *Turkey Faces West* (1930), Edib wore many titles until her death in 1964, including that of political exile from the country she helped save.[80] For all her naïveté about the United States and Woodrow Wilson, Edib was considered nationalist enough to become a target for investigation after she gave a feverish speech against the Greek occupation of Izmir on May 23, 1919, in a big Istanbul protest meeting (figure 1.2). According to the *New York Times*, the British press soon labeled her as "a firebrand and a dangerous agitator."[81] The Allied high commissioner forbade further protests, and the sultan and the grand mufti sentenced Edib to death, making her the first Turkish woman sentenced to death by political decree. After lobbying for a U.S. mandate between 1918 and 1919, Edib joined the independence struggle alongside Mustafa Kemal in March 1920, serving as his aide-de-camp and earning the honorary rank of corporal. Her husband, Dr. Adnan Adıvar, also served as an advisor to Kemal and aided the formation of the National Assembly in 1920. A 1921 pamphlet describing the leaders of the nationalist movement spoke of Edib in glowing terms as "a venerable figure, who will go down in history as one of our greatest commanders."[82]

Edib served as a public relations officer for the nationalist resistance during the war and for the republic after its founding, translating articles from the foreign press and writing press releases for the government.[83] In this capacity, she represented the nationalist cause to foreign officials, countering Orientalist figures of the silenced and oppressed Muslim woman. In fact, in a 1925 letter to the U.S. secretary of state, U.S. High Commissioner Admiral Mark Lambert Bristol cited Halide Edib's influence on American representatives' initial sympathies toward the nationalist cause.[84] During this time, Edib also wrote two of the most famous novels of the nationalist movement, *Ateşten Gömlek* (The shirt of flame, 1922) and *Vurun Kahpeye* (Thrash the whore, 1923). Populated by brave and chaste nationalist heroines, both chronicle the struggles of the nationalist army against invaders and local collaborators, and they continue to be assigned in Turkish literature classes. Though clearly influenced by her American education and social milieu, Edib was certainly pro-independence. She had founded the WPL to lobby for guided modernization and a secure, independent country that gave equal rights to all citizens regardless of ethno-religious background. However, under the Kemalist single-party regime, there could only be one legitimate source of nationalism and selective westernization: the state.

The Adıvars' falling out with Mustafa Kemal took place after 1924, when Adnan Adıvar and several other important leaders of the liberation struggle founded an opposition party, the Progressive Republican Party (PRP). When an armed rebellion broke out in the Kurdish regions in 1925, Prime Minister İsmet İnönü quickly passed the Law on the Maintenance of Order, solidifying the government's grip over the country and banning any group it deemed a threat to national security. The law and the following tribunals silenced several opposition newspapers and clamped down on the PRP. When a plot to assassinate Kemal was foiled in 1926, the state ordered the arrest and trial of former PRP members, without regard to their lack of involvement in the plans. Several prominent leaders of the War of Independence were released under popular pressure; others, including some of Kemal's ex-comrades, were executed. Halide Edib and her husband escaped, having already left for self-imposed exile in 1925, before the trials began. Adnan Adıvar was cleared of all charges in 1926, but the couple lived in England and France, with sojourns in the United States and India, until Kemal's death in 1939.

In 1927, *Nutuk* symbolically sealed the end of Turkey's first experiment in democracy and consolidated the Kemalist single-party regime under the Republican People's Party. By vilifying Edib and the WPL as over-westernized, Kemal and his party were able to justify their own selective westernization reforms, which included the closing of Islamic shrines and convents, instituting a clothing reform banning the fez and replacing it with the European style hat, abandoning the Arabic script in favor of the Latin alphabet, and completely secularizing family law, thus abolishing polygamy and religious marriages. In addition to imposing Western styles of dress on men, the Kemalists encouraged women to unveil and take active positions in society. The new state also urged its citizens to embody the figures of proper modernity with their social behavior.[85] Edib followed the reforms from England and wrote opinion pieces in the Western press about the cultural revolution. In 1928, she visited the United States and gave well-publicized talks about "the new Turkey" at several colleges, intellectual clubs, and the Williamstown Institute.

Edib approved of most of Kemal's strategic westernization reforms. Her comments on the reform banning the fez constitute one of the notable exceptions. In an opinion piece published in the *Yale Review* in 1929, she noted that she found the new law misguided, because it "enriched European hat factories at the expense of the already impoverished Turks."[86] Recognizing, however, that Kemal's move was a strategic one against the Western figure of the Turk as a fez-wearing brute, she also mocked Westerners' knee-jerk reaction to Kemalist strategic westernization: "[T]he moment the Turks put hats on their heads, the general cry in the West was 'at last, the Turks are civilized; they wear hats!'"[87] Indeed, even at the height of anti-Turkish sentiment, the mainstream American press often congratulated the new nation and itself on what they saw as the Turkish adoption of Western, even specifically American, culture. "Turks Drop Arabic for *Our* Alphabet," the *New York Times* joyously reported in April 1928.[88] Many U.S. pundits saw Turkish authoritarian westernization as a bloodless conversion; Kemal's reforms confirmed and institutionalized American cultural superiority in their minds, all without the trouble of running an overseas mandate filled with "hated" peoples. When Edib spoke critically about the reforms to American audiences, on the other hand, she underlined their European-ness and cast Kemal as an undemocratic over-westernizer.[89]

American celebrations of the new Turkey were indeed dampened by a sense of competition with Europe regarding who represented the proper model for Turkey's development. The trope of the terrible Turk, which essentialized Turkish barbarism as an inherent racial attribute, compounded these doubts. Unlike some in the U.S. media who saw a willing pupil for the United States in Turkey's westernization, in their dispatches, official American representatives in Istanbul often matched Edib's criticism regarding excessive European influence, with added doses of anti-Turkish sentiment. G. Howland Shaw, the chargé d'affaires of the American embassy in Turkey between 1921 and 1936, for example, criticized the Kemalists for what he saw as their indiscriminate adoption of French political models. Like Edib, Shaw differentiated between European and American modes of governance, implying selective westernization reforms based on the former, such as anticlericalism and strict secularism, constituted "intemperate westernization."[90] Shaw, however, biologized this dependence on French institutions as stemming from the faulty grasping of the Orientals' "immature minds" after "ready made systems."[91] Such racialized language revealed the impossibility of modernity for nonwhite and non-Christian races in American eyes. Despite the liberal rhetoric of Wilsonianism and the promise of guided development inscribed in the mandate system, the very idea of civilization remained inherently white, American, and Protestant for U.S. policy makers in the early twentieth century.

Edib's speeches and publications in exile implicitly bolstered a Western prerogative in judging non-Western modernizations. However, she contested Euro-American racial logic with her scholarship and presence, suggesting it was possible for Turkey (and other non-Western countries) to modernize in ways that eluded Western preconceptions and control.[92]

She also critiqued the figures of westoxication animating Kemalist policy, seeing her own distorted image within them. After reading an article on *Nutuk*, Edib wrote an open letter to the British newspaper *The Times* objecting to Kemal's suggestions that WPL members were over-westernized traitors. Her letter called upon Kemal to talk about the Wilsonian League "simply as a past historical event" and frankly report "his own attitude of mind at the time."[93] Her objections also appeared in the *New York Times* in November 1927.[94] In Turkey, the Republican People's Party responded with an open letter calling Edib's memory "defective" and snidely suggested she rely on *Nutuk* as a memory aid.[95] Kemal's historiographic acumen, evident in his use of primary documents and archival data, only contributed to the text's place in the Turkish canon. Despite *Nutuk*'s exhaustiveness, however, Mustafa Kemal claimed that he could not remember a significant detail in his epic story: "his own attitude of mind at the time" regarding an American mandate over Turkish Asia Minor in 1919.

WHAT KEMAL FORGOT, AND WHY

Before the September 1919 meeting of the nationalist representatives in the Anatolian city of Sivas, Mustafa Kemal received several messages from Turkish opinion leaders and intellectuals, who called for the representatives to sign a unanimous statement requesting an American mandate.[96] They were apparently encouraged by Admiral Bristol, who had responded to their inquiries about an American mandate with the suggestion that the United States might consider it if it became clear that the majority of the Muslim population in Anatolia wanted it.[97] Woodrow Wilson chastised Bristol for encouraging the Turks on this issue, but Kemal himself humored pro-mandate appeals and wrote back demanding more information. While his confidants believed him to be for complete Turkish independence, most delegates in Sivas had no idea where he stood on September 8, 1919, at 2:30 p.m. when Kemal, in his role as chairman, opened the platform to discussions of the mandate question.[98]

The debate in Sivas was intense and extensive, hinging mainly on whether a U.S. mandate could be reconciled with nationalist aspirations. A pro-mandate motion was submitted and withdrawn, but confusion continued when another member made a fervent pro-mandate speech immediately following the withdrawal. Finally, as a compromise, the

Anatolian congress decided on September 9 to write to the American Senate and ask for a fact-finding mission.[99] Here is how Mustafa Kemal described this decision in *Nutuk*:

> I remember very well that a document to this effect was drawn up and signed by the Chairman of the Committee, but I cannot remember exactly whether it was sent off or not. In any case, I never attached any particular importance to it.[100]

The two subjects in this paragraph, the "I" and "the Chairman of the Committee" are, in fact, both Mustafa Kemal. This means that Kemal, the recounting historian, dissociated himself so much from the chairman who signed this letter asking for the sympathies of the United States that he can barely remember signing the document, much less sending it. The document was indeed signed by Kemal, given to *Chicago Daily News* journalist L. E. Browne, and eventually appended to the Harbord Commission Report, presented to the U.S. Senate in 1920, as Appendix F, "Resolution of National Congress of Sivas addressed to the Senate of the United States of America requesting that Senatorial committee visit and investigate conditions within the Ottoman Empire."[101]

This is a rare but significant lapse: *Nutuk* is not usually scant on details and has an overwhelmingly self-assured tone approaching that of an omniscient narrator. Kemal reproduces in full letters from intellectuals arguing for a U.S. mandate and criticizes them in detail, repeatedly stating that his own position had always been "independence or death." However, other documentation raises questions vivid enough to have led to some debate among Turkish historians.[102] Why did Kemal let the pro-mandate member speak and reignite the debate in Sivas, even after others had decided to withdraw their motion? Why didn't he make a clear speech against it? Why are his telegrams and letters to pro-mandate intellectuals filled with questions, not clear-cut rejections? Consider, for example, the following, from a telegram sent to pro-mandate Kara Vasıf Bey on August 19, 1919:

> It is of the utmost importance for you to study minutely the nature of the American mandate and the proposed American help, and find out whether these are in accord with our national aims.[103]

Most evidence suggests that Kemal wanted to leave the door open to U.S. aid without sacrificing Turkey's internal and external independence. Personal accounts of those who spent a great deal of time with the leader suggest he was averse to the notion of an American mandate, to the point of cynically mocking it.[104] However, U.S. government officials and visiting Americans, including Admiral Bristol and L. E. Browne, always conveniently ended up with the impression that Kemal wanted a U.S. mandate. For example, after meeting with Kemal on September 22, 1919, General Harbord wrote:

> The aim of the Nationalist, or National Defense Party, as its adherents style it, as stated by Mustapha Kemal Pasha, its head, is the preservation of the territorial integrity of the Empire under a mandatory of a single disinterested power, preferably America.[105]

Mustafa Kemal himself gave a note to the Associated Press on September 21, 1919, asking for U.S. help:

> The Nationalists recognize the necessity of the aid of an impartial and benevolent foreign country. It is our aim to secure the development of Turkey as she stood at the armistice. We have no expansionist plans. It is our conviction that Turkey can be made rich and prosperous if we can get a good government. Our government has been weakened through foreign interference and intrigues. After all our experience we are sure that America is the only country able to help us.[106]

Here Kemal utilized a "moral geography" of westernizations similar to the one utilized by the WPL, which cast Europe as the source of "over-westernization" (i.e., "foreign interference and intrigues") and the United States as an alternative source of selective westernization (i.e., "good government" and "development").[107] His statement was likely intended to please American policy makers, who compared their government's foreign policy to that of Europe's in similarly favorable ways. Yet it was hardly genuine. Two months later, Kemal met the French diplomat François Georges-Picot at Sivas, reportedly promising him a French "economic mandate" over Anatolia in return for Cilicia.[108] He also soon accepted the help of "an impartial foreign country" by signing a deal with Bolshevik Russia for aid and arms. Kemal thus played the different Western imperial states against each other rhetorically and politically, speaking to their specific civilizational templates and policy goals. The United States was no exception.

Most Turks are not aware of these tactics demonstrating Kemal's complex approach to the United States in the Armistice era, having internalized *Nutuk*'s version of the story as the eventual victory of manly resistance to the West over undignified groveling. Of course, unlike Kemal, WPL intellectuals were sincere in their appeals to the United States and their belief in the power of Point 12. Having placed their faith in Point 12 and America's anti-imperialist rhetoric, however, these pro-mandate intellectuals underestimated the strength of anti-Turkish sentiment among U.S. policy makers. In fact, by May 1919, Woodrow Wilson had not only acquiesced to the Greek invasion of Anatolia but had literally forgotten Point 12.

WHAT WILSON FORGOT, AND WHY

During the Paris Peace Conference on May 17, 1919, the Council of Four received a delegation of Indian Muslims, then under British rule, insisting that Turkey be dealt a fairer hand than currently planned. The delegation represented the Khilafat movement, which upheld the Ottoman sultan's role as the spiritual leader of all Muslims (*khalif*) and sought to influence Allied policy in Turkey's favor.[109] Appealing to Point 12, the delegates requested that Turkey be given the right to form a nation in Anatolia, Thrace, and Constantinople, lands that had been inhabited by Turkish-speaking peoples for centuries. They protested against the comparatively severe treatment of Turks: "Nobody has proposed to punish the Germans, who are the main offenders of the war, by taking Berlin from them. The Austrian Germans are to have Vienna. Why should Turks alone have their capital taken from them?"[110] Pointing out that the unjust dismemberment of Turkey would be perceived by the world's Muslims as "due to the fact that Turkey is a Mohammedan power," the delegation asked for the council's permission to read Wilson's Point 12 out loud to Wilson and the Allies.[111] This was more than a refresher. Strangely, as he admitted to the Allies two days later (May 19, 1919),

Wilson had forgotten his very own Point 12: "President Wilson said that what had impressed him in the evidence of the Mohammedan deputation was what they had said about Turkish sovereignty. He himself had forgotten that he had used the word in the 14 Points."[112]

Kemal forgetting his ambiguous role in discussions about the American mandate was a rhetorical decision as well as a political one. In terms of narrative continuity, his strategic ambiguity would have clashed with the central defiant thesis of *Nutuk*: "Independence or Death!" More importantly, it would have blurred the sharp black-and-white picture the speech draws between effete Istanbul intellectuals and the determined, militant father of the nation. These gendered figures, along with the figurative language he employed, made Kemal's case for him, justifying his strongman rule. His omission of the ambiguities of the past, therefore, epitomized the intersection between "characteristic amnesias" and strategic remembering, which Benedict Anderson has identified as central to nation-state consolidation.[113]

Unlike Mustafa Kemal, however, Woodrow Wilson was probably honest in his memory lapse. Approximately two months earlier, on March 20, 1919, he had told the very same council, "[F]or the purposes of peace all that was necessary to tell Turkey was that she would have nothing."[114] Deeply influenced by missionary propaganda, the president gladly partook in what Timothy Marr has called the American religio-political tradition of "fantasizing the symbolic termination of the Turkish empire."[115] As early as 1912, he had rejoiced, "There ain't going to be no Turkey" to Colonel House, when the latter proposed a new ambassador.[116] The sovereignty clause of Point 12 had actually been a political compromise: in 1917, the president had suggested Turkey be "effaced," that is, wiped out, eventually adopting the wording proposed by his advisors' memoranda.[117] Wilson could so easily forget the letter of Point 12 because, as far as the president was concerned, the point's spirit hinged on the protection of minority Christians from the Turk. While Kemal was manipulating figures in order to shape a nation's cultural memory, the American figure of the terrible Turk had already transformed Wilson's personal memories. Turks themselves were not able to challenge this stereotype, because the Allies had barred them from sending delegates to the Paris Peace Conference. Wilson had also clearly ignored multiple protest telegrams from Turkish demonstrators, not limited to the

WPL, as to the wording of Point 12.[118] Only when Indian Muslims gained a hearing through the British Empire did Wilson, an ardent Anglophile, have cause to listen and remember.

Thus, it is not surprising that Wilson regretted the letter of Point 12 soon after he remembered it. On August 16, following the withdrawal of British troops from the Caucasus, the president sent a telegram to Admiral Bristol, asking him to warn the Ottoman government that any attacks on Christians by state or nonstate actors would lead to the abolishment of the sovereignty clause of Point 12.[119] In classic Ottoman fashion, the grand vizier complained to the Entente powers, arguing that the United States, a country that had not been at war with Turkey and had even not signed the Armistice, was acting not only unfairly but also unilaterally. On August 25, French Premier Georges Clemenceau criticized the note at a meeting of the heads of delegations. Not knowing President Wilson had originated the memo, he told the council of his belief that Wilson would not have approved of this policy. He then "drew special attention to the twelfth Point to the Fourteen Points," reading it out loud for the council's benefit.[120] That Clemenceau, who had once mocked the religious ambitions of Wilson's Fourteen Points by noting that even God had been satisfied with *ten* commandments, would defend them against Woodrow Wilson, their ostensible author, is yet another sad irony of the Paris Peace Conference and another key node in this post–World War I thicket of history, memory, and political strategy.[121]

NATIONAL HISTORY AND THE GENDER OF THE AMERICAN MANDATE

These moments of forgetting continue to reverberate today in Turkish and American historiography. In the United States, the WPL is hardly the stuff of popular knowledge. Many American texts still cannot remember the letter of Point 12: summaries often omit the Turkish "sovereignty clause," and represent it as being about the "subject races." The tendency runs across a spectrum of texts from a 1920 issue of *World's Work* to a 1997 cultural literacy book addressed to a lay audience ("Autonomy for the subject peoples of the Ottoman Empire"), and to college textbooks in the early twenty-first century ("self-determination for national minorities in Europe").[122] The direct overlap between Woodrow Wilson's forgetting and widespread American disremembering in popular and educational histories should prompt questions about whether the ethno-religious biases of their Western primary sources continue to haunt contemporary histories. Yet some of this forgetting is determined by change as opposed to continuity. "The Arab" replaced "the Turk" as the synecdoche for troublesome Muslims as the two world wars transitioned into the Cold War.[123] Turkey, on the other hand, earned the condescending disinterest reserved in the American popular imaginary for relatively harmless developing nations, although a change might be afoot as the country gets refigured as a regional power player in the era of the War on Terror.

Two months, several unheeded letters, a few speeches, and a membership consisting of a handful of Istanbul intellectuals. . . . With no impact on U.S., Allied, or Turkish policy, perhaps the WPL deserves some of this forgetting. Unlike Americans, however, Turks "overly-remember" the American mandate, continuing to accuse contemporary politicians, activists, and intellectuals of being *mandacı* (pro-mandate) traitors. Discourse around the mandate intensifies in moments of crisis around U.S.–Turkish relations, and popular histories often reflect the current political climate. A 1955 article in a popular history journal, written at the high point in Turkish–American relations, for example, stated, "Not having faith in the nationalist cause at first cannot constitute a sin or national crime," and cited exemplary commanders (like İsmet İnönü) and civil intellectuals (like Halide Edib), who later joined Kemal as comrades.[124] In the 1960s and 1970s, as U.S.–Turkish relations worsened over the perceived inequalities of NATO membership, such popular history magazines published articles shaming former members of the WPL in an entirely different tone.[125]

Serious Turkish scholarship does transcend *Nutuk*'s history of the mandate.[126] These nuanced works, however, have not impacted official histories or popular memories. Here the WPL's slippage from sovereignty under Point 12 toward an American mandate and Kemal's savvy political flirtations with the United States both drop out of the picture. A 1997 high school history book even called the WPL "Amerikan Mandacılar Cemiyeti," or "the Organization of Those for the American Mandate," instead of using the group's registered name.[127] The discrepancy between U.S. and Turkish popular history is perhaps best reflected in Wikipedia, the online crowd-sourced encyclopedia: "The American Mandate over Turkey" is a central topic in the Turkish Wikipedia ("Vikipedi") under the entry for "Mandate (Diplomacy)." The English-language Wikipedia does not even mention it under the parallel entry.[128]

Official and popular histories in Turkey also omit the fact that neither U.S. public opinion nor Woodrow Wilson ever favored a mandate over Turkey. A 2008 dark comedy called *The Ottoman Republic*, for example, centered on the belief that had Mustafa Kemal died as a child, Turkey would have become an American mandate.[129] However, as this chapter has shown, the mandate question was hardly contingent on Turkey's call—not only because of the isolationist turn in the U.S. Congress, but also because of Wilson's own resistance to the idea. Despite increasing pressure from Lloyd George, Wilson, haunted by the figure of the terrible Turk, remained deeply unenthusiastic about the idea of U.S. custody over Turkish (and Kurdish) Anatolia.[130] This fact, embodied in the *New York Times* headline "Wilson Warns U.S. May Refuse to Rule Turks," clashes with popular and official Turkish history, which continues to propagate the flattering belief that the United States wanted to own Turkey and was only thwarted by Mustafa Kemal's armies. The false history of the mandate fuels conspiracy theories in the twenty-first century—the bread and butter of reactionary pundits and the theme of countless email chains, as well as of popular action films and books.[131]

The mandate trope remains a significant force in day-to-day politics. I give several examples later in this book, but one seems exceptionally worth reproducing here for how it echoes Kemal's words on the WPL. In January 2016, Turkey's Islamist-leaning President Recep Tayyip Erdoğan used language that could have been torn from the pages of *Nutuk* to vilify scholars who had signed a letter condemning the government's military campaign against Kurdish separatists in southeastern Turkey:

> [Despite the realities of terrorism], a group that calls itself "academics" releases a statement and accuses the state. Not only this, they invite foreigners to our country to follow the events. The name for this is colonial mentality and *mandacılık* (being mandacı).[132]

In contrast to his clear anti-Kemalist policies in other arenas, here Erdoğan mobilizes a popular memory of the WPL directly inherited from Kemal's oeuvre. His formulation accuses westoxicated intellectuals of inviting in "foreigners" (read: Westerners) to judge, control, and divide the country against the will of the nation, discursively collapsing the gap between the polarizing Justice and Development Party (AKP) government and "the people" through nationalist rhetoric.[133] This figurative lineage was largely lost in the English-language press, which translated "mandacılık" generically as "a fifth column," and made references to Erdoğan's authoritarianism (coded Islamic) to explain the AKP's crackdown on dissent.[134] Erdoğan's "father-like" authoritarianism and the official and unofficial witch-hunts that followed his statement, however, depended on specific local connotations and affects for their popular legitimation. Under his words lay an early twentieth-century story even his staunchest secularist opponents would have committed to heart.[135]

Gendered tropes of selective and excessive westernization have continued to color national(ist) histories, ever since Kemal's version of the story. Halide Edib's gender, in particular, has been inextricable from representations of the mandate. Works that are more forgiving of the pro-mandate intellectuals of the Armistice era emphasize the fact that she became a brave corporal alongside Mustafa Kemal after 1920, underplaying her gender and desexualizing her.[136] Halide Edib contributed to this vision, occasionally figuring herself as "Corporal Halide" in her memoirs, and describing herself as a genderless, ego-less soldier.[137] Most Turkish history writing on the WPL, however, takes the opposite route, employing the discourse of over-westernization with exuberance. A 1928 newspaper article, for example, called Edib a creature with the passions of the male and the female, unable to get satisfaction either way.[138] In his 1941 book on the Atatürk revolution, Kemalist statesman Mahmut Esat Bozkurt used a sexist proverbial expression to accuse Edib of "meddling in men's business with the cooking dough still fresh on her hands."[139] (Ironically, yet entirely in keeping with "state feminism" under authoritarian westernization, Bozkurt had overseen the abolishment of polygamy and men's rights to unilateral divorce as Minister of Justice in 1924.) Demonstrating how gender intersects with ethnicity and class in Turkish discourses around the limits of westernization, Bozkurt also underhandedly attacked Edib's family's Jewish roots in the same book, implying she was not truly Turkish: "The bothersome point is not that Rauf Bey or Halide Edib were mandacı. The problem is that there were also some Turks among this group."[140]

Even after her death in 1964, the figure of Halide Edib continued to be contested, often in gendered terms. On March 9, 1970, the Turkish Women's Association unveiled a bust of her in Sultanahmet, representing her work as a woman of the Independence War.[141] A group of leftist university students interrupted the opening ceremony, tearing up the ceremonial flowers and arguing that the statue belonged in the American embassy instead. On the night of March 13, 1970, unidentified individuals, assumed to be members of the same group, unhinged the bust with dynamite, in response to Edib's work for the American mandate.[142] The bust was quickly reinstalled the same year, yet it continues to shows signs of neglect and abuse (figure 1.5). Even scholarly articles insult WPL members as "spineless" and "weak-hearted," and praise Mustafa Kemal as having "a will of steel," in gendered terms.[143] Over a decade into the new century, several sexist nationalist manifestos about the mandate are sent to popular presses every year, outnumbering clear-headed studies about Edib's life and work.[144]

Gendered and sexualized histories of the WPL and Edib have also impacted Turkish fiction. The 1924 novel *Pervaneler* (The moths) by nationalist author Müfide Ferid Tek employs a Halide Edib–like character called Cemile, who is one of the first Turkish graduates of "Byzantine College," a reference to the American College for Girls in Istanbul. Depicted as an extremely ambitious and arrogant woman, Cemile lobbies for an American protectorate before becoming "vaguely" nationalist.[145] Tek further discusses the relations between the students and teachers at the Byzantine College as quasi-lesbianism.[146] The young girls are in awe of their American teachers, to the point of having jealous catfights over them, just as they are "in love" with America.[147] In the 2007 anti-American bestseller *Metal Fırtına* (Metal storm), on the other hand, the WPL makes an appearance in the figure of a westoxicated journalist/intellectual, famous for his love of wine, implying an effete, degenerate temperament given to pleasure and dissipation. This sexually ambiguous male figure welcomes a fictional U.S. invasion of Turkey in the hope that Turkey might finally become an American state.[148]

FIGURE 1.5 Bust of Halide Edib at Sultanahmet Square, where she gave an impassioned talk against the Greek invasion of 1919 (see figure 1.2). While the inscription celebrates her as "the symbolic woman of the Independence War," leftist protestors saw her as a symbol of the American mandate. The bust was erected, bombed with dynamite, and reerected within a few days in 1970, a time of intense street violence between the pro-American right and the pro-Soviet left in Turkey. Contested gendered figures like Edib have played a significant role in how twentieth-century U.S.–Turkish relations are remembered. Photo by Alan Scott.

As Hülya Adak has noted, a paradox saturates Edib's legacy: even as official history textbooks depict her as a mandacı traitor, high school literature courses approved by the same Ministry of Education assign her novels as required nationalist reading.[149] Yet some critics even tar Edib's literary output with the brush of over-westernization. Çetin Yetkin's flamboyantly sexist analysis of Edib's novels epitomizes this approach, and contains sections such as "The Turkish Woman Loves Foreign Men":

> Halide Edib, who made [the Turkish girl] Rabia fall in love with [the Italian] Peregrini, who made Seviye Talip leave her home to live with a Hungarian convert, who pushed the married Neriman into the arms of Dick and made Sevim marry an American in an ostentatious ceremony and move to the United States, must have really wanted to organize mass marriage ceremonies, taking advantage of the fact that Istanbul was filled with invading foreign soldiers—in other words, of the fact that the Ottoman capital was suddenly awash with foreign men! Since our author herself is a woman, and since every artist puts something of herself into her work, all this makes one wonder . . . . [150]

Of course, these are not just examples of "foreign" men, but Western men—Europeans and Americans. The preexisting discourse of over-westernization allows Yetkin to raise questions about Edib's supposed sexual degeneracy without having to articulate them. His ellipses nudge the readers to complete the image themselves.

Yetkin ends his insinuations by connecting Edib's romantic plots to her mandacı beliefs. He calls her "Corporal Haleede Aideeb" in a mock American accent, thus questioning the gender-neutral image of her as a nationalist soldier.[151] This sexist and ultranationalist reading of Edib's fiction as a sublimation of the author's westoxication directs us toward literary allegories of over-westernization in the Turkish novel, examined in the next chapter. His mixture of Turkish and English points to the complex uses of bilingual ("Turklish") humor, explored in chapter 3. Despite Edib's wishes and the objective tone she sought in *The Turkish Ordeal*, the WPL has not been remembered "simply as a past historical event." Nothing in U.S.–Turkish relations has.

As the first Turkish Muslim girl to graduate from the American College for Girls in Istanbul, "the first woman in Turkish history sentenced to death by political decree, and the first woman corporal in wartime," Edib lived in a time of rampant change for Turkey.[152] Her era coincided with the founding of the Turkish Republic and the solid footing of the United States as a global power, seen by some Turks as a potential source of selective westernization and, increasingly, of over-westernization. Throughout the twentieth century, nationalist history operated as the central discursive field for drawing the limits of westernization in gendered terms. Kemalist historical narratives employed forgetting and over-remembering to make complex historical figures into flat rhetorical figures: Kemal as "Atatürk," the resolute father of the nation, Edib as the westoxicated mandacı. In addition, through selective westernization reforms, including banning the fez and discouraging the veil, Kemalists sought to create citizens who embody a properly Turkish modernity. These figures were mobilized to counter stereotypes in the West, most significantly that of the terrible Turk. They also operated as mechanisms of internal social control. The next chapter explores the reverberations of this allegorical imperative in Turkish literature, specifically the novel.

CHAPTER TWO

Allegorizing America

Over-Westernization in the Turkish Novel

It is the summer of 1918. Istanbul is chafing under Allied occupation. A Turkish veteran, who has lost his legs in the Great War and now propels himself around on a wooden cart with wheels, using his bare hands, is riding the tram. The tram halts and an English lieutenant walks in with an elegantly dressed Turkish girl. The lieutenant motions with his whip and the Turks in the front row stand up and give their seats to the officer and his native accomplice. As she moves alongside the Englishman, nose in the air, the Turkish girl accidentally steps on the hands of the crippled veteran with her fashionable high heels. The veteran lets out a muffled yelp. "Shut up! Shut up, you dog!" yells the girl. "Why would anyone in this state even try to ride the tram?" A young Turkish man is watching the scene. Furious, he imagines getting up and strangling the girl, who reminds him of his own Europhile fiancée. At the next stop, he gets off the tram without uttering a word, feeling even more crippled than the veteran.[1]

Half a decade later, Istanbul has been liberated after the long war for independence. A young Turkish woman quickly jumps onto the Fatih-Harbiye tram, which connects the traditional Muslim neighborhoods to the fashionable westernized quarter, Beyoğlu, in Istanbul. She is thrilled to be the first passenger on board. Unbeknownst to her, her fiancé sees her and realizes she will not be meeting a female friend who lives in the

Muslim quarter of the city as she promised, but an "over-westernized" man who lives in Beyoğlu. Blood rises to his head; his ears are ringing. He wants to jump on board, but instead, he just stands there and watches the tram turn the corner.[2]

These two tram scenes are from famous novels of the early republican era: Yakup Kadri Karaosmanoğlu's 1928 *Sodom ve Gomore* and Peyami Safa's 1931 *Fatih-Harbiye*. Set in occupation-era Istanbul (1918–1923), *Sodom ve Gomore* depicts with suffocating disgust a class of bourgeois Istanbulites consorting and collaborating with the invading Western soldiers, even while in Anatolia a bloody war of independence rages. *Fatih-Harbiye*, named after the tram line that connects the conservative Muslim quarter of the city (Fatih) to the Europeanized district historically populated by Christian minorities, depicts how the tram remained a symbol of connection and disconnection, mobility and immobility in Turkish culture, long after the nationalist liberation of Istanbul. Both stories are love allegories, commenting on the conflict between multiple urban Turkish cultures through the torturous relationship between a westoxicated young ingénue and a traditionally inclined young man. They are also allegories of progress gone wrong, represented by the disconnect between the male and female characters, particularly the impotence of the former and the newfound mobility and autonomy of the latter.

Just as importantly, both *Fatih-Harbiye* and *Sodom ve Gomore* are novels—a Western literary form introduced to Turkish in the mid-nineteenth century, which has, since then, followed a unique course intertwined with what literary historian Jale Parla has called "that inexhaustible subject of Turkish writing": "the effects of Westernization."[3] This chapter offers an interpretive and thematic cultural history of the intertwining of westernizations, allegory, and the novel between the late nineteenth century, when the genre first became popularized in Ottoman lands, and the early twenty-first century, when controversial Turkish novelist Orhan Pamuk won the Nobel Prize in literature. The focus remains on several novels that employ allegorical methods and the double themes of mobility/progress and love: Recaizade Mahmud Ekrem's *Araba Sevdası* (The carriage affair, 1896), Karaosmanoğlu's *Sodom ve Gomore* (Sodom and Gomorrah, 1928), Fakir Baykurt's *Amerikan Sargısı* (The American bandage, 1967), and Pamuk's *Yeni Hayat* (The new life, 1994). "Love" and "mobility/progress," broadly conceived, are two central tropes through which westernization has been imagined in Turkish literature and culture.[4] Approximately three decades, roughly equal to a generation, separate each novel from the next.

Initially written by public intellectuals with ties to the state, the Turkish novel started out as a project of selective westernization and became the primary forging ground for figures of elite "over-westernization." The following survey reveals how the allegorical novel increasingly constructed over-westernization as a female vice by the early twentieth century and demonstrates how America replaced Europe as the primary agent of westoxication in the Turkish cultural imagination in the mid-twentieth century. Interpreted as a political, semiofficial form commenting on Turkish history, thus a close kin of the nationalist histories explored in the previous chapter, the Turkish novel could nevertheless break with the authoritarian mission of the state. By pushing allegory to its wild limits, the novel flourished within the cracks in the political elite's ability to determine the limits of westernization.

THE PERSISTENCE OF ALLEGORY

By focusing on the intersections of allegory and the novel in a non-Western literary tradition, this chapter intervenes in several literary debates and historical narratives, beginning with the discrediting of allegory and the simultaneous "rise of the novel" in modernity.[5] Allegory is a figurative mode of representation harboring a level of deeper "true" meaning beyond the manifest. An allegorical narrative operates as an extended metaphor.[6] In other words, allegorical characters and events always stand for something more abstract than themselves, coding for a wider truth. The novel, on the other hand, is closely aligned with formal and thematic realism, empiricism, and a focus on the distinct qualities of human experience.[7] The novel, according to conventional literary critical wisdom, seeks a particular, individual truth, not a timeless truth imbued with universal morals. While allegory as a literary strategy can be found in any genre, including the novel, the post-Enlightenment West has broadly experienced the rise of the realistic novel and a devaluing of allegory.[8] As Jorge Luis Borges put it in his mid-century essay "From Allegories to Novels," openly allegorical fiction became synonymous with "aesthetic error" in modernity: "I know that at one time the allegorical art was considered quite charming . . . and is now intolerable. We feel that besides being intolerable, it is stupid and frivolous."[9]

Recent transnational and transhistorical reconsiderations of the Enlightenment-narrative accounts of the rise of the novel, however, have challenged this understanding of allegory as a primitive and premodern precursor to the novel.[10] Several important critics have questioned the received wisdom on "the fall of allegory." Northrop Frye's work, for example, points to a continuum of allegorical literature in the West from naïve, one-dimensional texts to complex paradox literature.[11] More recently, Fredric Jameson has utilized Marxist literary theory to locate in allegory a particularly useful and complex tool for dialectical analysis.[12] Jameson argues that expectations of one-to-one correspondence between manifest and latent content do not do justice to the layered richness of allegory. Instead, he suggests the form can be used for a neo-Marxist critique of power relations and to "generate spaces where the connections between structural inequalities and personal feelings can be made clear though not simplistic."[13] As such, allegory-infused literature is particularly suited to flesh out the complex connections between base and superstructure, i.e., the dialectic between the relations of production and structures of meaning and affect. Allegory can help an author comment on socioeconomic problems without employing the openly didactic transparency of much socialist realist fiction. Allegory, according to Jameson, is also not simplistic or one-dimensional, but essentially "profoundly discontinuous, a matter of breaks and heterogeneities, of the multiple polysemia of the dream."[14]

The two tram scenes I described at the beginning of this chapter can help us clarify how even apparently simple allegories can mobilize several layers of meaning, from the personal/libidinal to the civic/cultural and economic/material. As Jale Parla has argued in her "Car Narratives: A Subgenre in Turkish Novel Writing," vehicles like tramcars regularly function as a metonym for the whole process of industrialization and westernization in Turkish literature because they became the first visible "machines" in daily life, preceding factories and industrial machines by several decades due to the underdevelopment of Ottoman manufacture.[15] Urban tramcars forced a public mixing of the sexes, ethnicities, and religions and gave newfound mobility to Muslim women. Building on sexualized anxieties surrounding over-westernization, these scenes juxtapose the male protagonists' immobility and impotence to the phallic tram, which gives its female occupants a threatening mobility. The same phallic effect marks the high heels, which pierce through the hands of the legless veteran, the castrating whip of the English officer, and the shocking agility with which the heroine of the second scene jumps onto the tram, becoming its first passenger/penetrator. Both men are watching their fiancées transgress, not their wives or casual lovers; the insecure tie of betrothal makes their situation even more precarious. The trope of a fickle and fleeting lover recalls both Ottoman courtly poems addressed to a cruel and doe-like mistress and what sociologist Meral Özbek has called "the unrequited Turkish love for 'The West.'"[16] The crippled veteran, in turn, represents the wounded empire and the threat of castration in general. As such, the tram appears at first as a dreamlike, psychosexual, Freudian symbol.

However, the tram also codes for a central structural and economic reality of Ottoman history: the lack of state control over the country's transportation networks. Long before European armies took control over Istanbul, European treasuries had captured important parts of the empire's economic base and infrastructure. The empire's material dependency, apparent in its 1875 declaration of bankruptcy and sealed with the founding of the Ottoman Public Debt Administration in 1881, through which the Istanbul regime ceded control over the bulk of its economy to Europe, was particularly visible in questions of mobility and commerce.[17] Ottoman railways were almost entirely built and governed by Western powers: by 1923, Germans owned 68 percent of the country's railways, the British controlled 11.5 percent, the French 15.4 percent, and other powers 5.1 percent.[18] Christian minorities, furthermore, ran approximately 90 percent of domestic commerce networks in association with Western traders in Ottoman Turkey.[19] For this reason, trains and trams are loaded symbols in early nationalist fiction and memoirs.

The westoxicated woman's haughty question to the crippled veteran—"Why would anyone in this state try to ride the tram?"—reminds the reader that not everyone had equal rights to transportation in Ottoman cities during the occupation. The post–World War I Mudros Armistice placed ports, railways, and other strategic points officially under Allied rule. Many of the struggles of the Independence War, therefore, hinged upon the problem of mobility. Women's activist and author Halide Edib, who herself was accused of being over-westernized, mentions the gendered and ethnic dangers of riding trams in occupation-era Istanbul in her novel *Ateşten Gömlek* (Shirt of flame).[20] The tram also makes an appearance in Edib's 1928 memoir, *The Turkish Ordeal*, as a space of danger for Muslim women and children.[21] Nationalists, including Edib, formed secret organizations to smuggle men and arms outside occupied Istanbul. Narratives of heroism from and about the period pay great attention to the movement of people, materials, and armies, imbuing the village women directing ox carts and captains steering ships with great symbolic importance.[22]

The two allegorical scenes, therefore, connect their protagonists' emasculation vis-à-vis their westoxicated fiancées to Turkey's economic impotency vis-à-vis the West, refer to historical and structural realities of Turkish mobility in the early twentieth century, connect heterosexual frustration to international power inequalities, and hint at greater troubles with industrialization. It is difficult to privilege one explanation over another, let alone construct "a one-to-one table of equivalences."[23] Instead, the reader must engage figures that cut across the political and the libidinal.

However, renewed respect for allegory as a complex signifying process, as opposed to an atavistic precursor to the novel, is not the only theoretical problem associated with the intertwining of the novel and allegory, particularly within the so-called "Third World." In 1986, Fredric Jameson sparked a critical controversy with the publication of his essay "Third-World Literature in the Era of Multinational Capitalism" in the influential cultural studies journal *Social Text*. In this essay, Jameson differentiated between First World and Third World literatures, the latter defined roughly as literatures produced by members of nations that have borne the brunt of Western imperialism, with a bold generalization: "all Third-world texts are necessarily . . . allegorical, and in a very specific way they are to be read as what I will call national allegories."[24] According to Jameson, Third World texts lacked the radical split between the public and the private, the libidinal and the political, that binds First World artistic production. This, in turn, allows them to function as multivalent mirrors into society:

Third-world texts, even those which are seemingly private and invested with a properly libidinal dynamic, necessarily project a political dimension in the form of national allegory: the story of the private individual destiny is always an allegory of the embattled situation of the public third-world culture and society.[25]

This essay immediately met criticism for its apparent reduction of all Third World texts to a formula and its proposal of a clear binary opposition between the so-called Third and First Worlds.[26] Since then, however, several scholars have reconsidered the argument's merits and weaknesses, both generally and within specific national and transnational contexts.[27]

In Turkey, distinguished literary critics Murat Belge and Sibel Irzık have been at the forefront of the movement to reconsider Jameson. In a 1997 article, Belge argued that it is as difficult to disagree with the critics of Jameson's totalizing tone as it is to ignore the way allegory has permeated the Turkish novel since its earliest beginnings.[28] Belge complicates Jameson's explanatory emphasis on multinational capitalism and colonialism by citing several other reasons for the persistence of allegory in the Turkish novel: the creation of a specific type of author/public intellectual through state-led westernization; the dominance and inadequacies of official histories as explanatory narratives; the demands of the international literary market; and non-Western intellectuals' felt need to transcend the empirical narrative strategies exhausted by Western novelists. The first two reasons, in particular, explain the special political status of the novel within Turkey. According to Belge, whether they agree with Kemalist selective westernization or not, Turkey's top novelists have been influenced by it and have felt the need to comment on it.[29] Their novels, in turn, are taken seriously, if not as official histories like *Nutuk*, then as thesis-driven tracts in conversation with official histories.[30] Reading a Turkish novel as national allegory, in other words, is not (necessarily) a reductionist Orientalist move, but one enabled by local conditions of production and interpretation.

Local political conditions also influence what the Turkish novel has done with and about allegory as a literary form. In her 2003 article "Allegorical Lives: The Public and the Private in the Modern Turkish Novel," Sibel Irzık concurs that the Turkish novel has played a public political role since its beginnings. She then takes the reconsideration of Jameson further via insightful close readings of postwar Turkish novels. Irzık delineates how characters in these novels seem to feel burdened by the allegorical impulse of the republic itself. As explored in chapter 1, selective westernization as a mode of governmentality sought to turn individuals into representative figures for the new, modern Turkish nation. According to Irzık, post–World War II Turkish novels, in particular, depict characters who seem aware of this figurative impulse and feel trapped by it. The clear combination of allegory and a clear unease about it in these novels suggests that "the notion of national allegory is not so much in need of confirmation as it is in need of complication, and even, in a certain sense, reversal and irony."[31]

It is also possible to modify Jameson's dictum by considering how the vibrant folk tradition of mystical allegory has haunted Turkish literature, from the very first clumsy Ottoman novels to Orhan Pamuk's labyrinthine masterpieces. Islamic mysticism, or Sufism, flourished in the centuries following the spread of Islam in the Middle East, Central Asia, South Asia, and Africa. Sufis propose that the universe itself is one big allegory, as everything in it harbors the "hidden reality" of God.[32] Allegorical interpretation (ta'wīl) of the sacred texts, and of devotional poetry and prose, therefore, has been vital to Islamic exegesis long before poststructuralist debates. The Sufi tradition is particularly important for this project, as love and progress, the two metaphorical tools for the representation of westernization, parallel the two guiding metaphors of Sufism: love (ishq) and the journey or path (tariqa).[33] In this tradition, the yearning of the soul for the divine transcendent, often expressed in an allegory of earthly love, and the travels and travails the soul must pass through before it can merge with God, expressed in allegorical adventure tales, represent the highest truths of universal human existence.[34] The persistence of allegory in Turkish literature, therefore, is not only structurally produced by the realities of selective westernization, but also by the less tangible heritage of folk Islam and Sufi mysticism. This rich tradition of Islamic letters itself is outside the scope of this chapter, except insofar as its allegorical narratives of starcrossed lovers and quest tales constituted a formidable influence, a tradition to be rejected, reclaimed, or reworked for various modern Turkish novelists.

Nineteenth-century Ottoman novelists like Ahmed Mithat and Recaizade Mahmud Ekrem defined their work against the supernatural and
allegorical masterpieces of mysticism, often listing them alongside "old
wives' tales" as detrimental to the maturation of a newly rational citizen
subject. However, the same novelists were rarely able to escape allegory
as a signifying strategy. Even when the allegories they wrote tended to
extol the virtues of industry and rationalism, they depended on the
mode's didactic possibilities. In the early twentieth century, Turkish novelists like Karaosmanoğlu, Safa, and Edib wrote nationalist allegories
approaching the mystical in their depiction of nationalist conversation
experiences. Following the chaotic switch to a multiparty system in the
1950s and throughout the Cold War era, novelists wrote allegories of both
small-scale and large-scale hierarchy, such as the "village novels" exploring the hard, bitter power of rural Anatolian landlords (Yaşar Kemal,
Mahmut Makal) and the softly suffocating bonds of the United States
(Fakir Baykurt). Although sympathetic to folk traditions, many of these
novelists still tended to see them as detriments to true enlightenment.
Authors active between the military coups of 1972 and 1980 (Adalet
Ağaoğlu and Bilge Karasu) wrote political allegories documenting a period of strife and uncertainty for Turkish democracy.[35] After the 1980
coup, which pushed Marxist politics further underground and reduced
state control over media through the installation of free-market reforms,
Turkish novelists wrote self-referential allegories and postmodern
novels reflecting the mystical aspects of Turkish folk religion (Latife
Tekin, Orhan Pamuk, and Elif Shafak). In each instance, the novelists operated as public intellectuals, and their works depended on the alchemy
of allegory to comment on and influence the political culture.

OTTOMAN WESTERNIZATION(S) AND
THE RISE OF THE NOVEL

In the late Ottoman Empire, the state's attempts to centralize through
selective westernization led to the rise of a new secular Turkish literature. With the 1839 Tanzimat reforms came the founding of secular
educational institutions alongside the already existing Islamic schools,
increased translation activity, proliferation of printing presses, and the
rise of a mass media in the form of privately owned newspapers.[36] While

the reforms and the policy of "Ottomanism," seeking to promote a state-based nationalism to counter rising ethnic nationalisms, could not prevent the eventual dissolution of the empire, the Tanzimat did lead to the creation of a new bureaucratic class, loyal to both the ideals of selective westernization and to the survival of the Ottoman state.[37] Members of this new intelligentsia had been trained in government service, publishing, and/or journalism and had been exposed to French literature as translators. They translated European novels into Turkish and wrote the first Ottoman Turkish novels.[38]

Ottoman intelligentsia saw the importation of the novel into Turkish itself as potentially revolutionary because of the genre's perceived commitment to a disenchanted worldview.[39] The realism, empiricism, and didactic potential of European prose forms such as plays and novels appealed to this generation of reformers. As "movement" and "progress" (*terakki*) became keywords of selective westernization, the plot-driven form of the novel seemed more and more a panacea for the empire's perceived ills.[40] Early Ottoman authors situated their fiction against traditional "Eastern" literature, which they criticized severely for its surreal elements, dependence on allegory, and rhetorical embellishments. With its homoerotic imagery, apparent lack of utilitarian value, and immoral aloofness, classical courtly (*Divan*) literature seemed to be yet another decadent backwardness to be corrected in the Tanzimat era.[41] The folk traditions with their moral tint were closer to these reformers' hearts, yet they were still riddled with the supernatural. The early Ottoman novelists took pains to anchor their fictions in secular time and place and prioritize realism over rhetorical flourish. Rebelling against the Neoplatonism of classical Ottoman allegory, they developed an obsession with clarity and a transparent style reminiscent of journalism.[42] Ahmed Mithat (1844–1912), the great popularizer of the novel form in Ottoman Turkey, once boasted of never having written anything "which may be called literary."[43]

Products of Tanzimat era westernization, public intellectuals like Mithat also appointed themselves critics of its unwelcome aftereffects: economic dependency, excessive bureaucratization, and over-westernization. In their fiction and nonfiction, they repeatedly asked the central question of the era: "Where shall we draw the boundary of Westernization?"[44] Interestingly, they found their answers in the form of allegory. In 1876,

Mithat sparked a sociocultural phenomenon with his widely popular [*Felatun Bey ve Rakım Efendi* (Mr. Felatun and Master Rakım). This carelessly written and utterly craftless novel personified selective and excessive westernization in two men, both with jobs in the post-Tanzimat bureaucracy, with French mistresses, and with an interest in European culture. While Felatun's education is haphazard and his French is comical, Rakım is an intellectual with full grasp of French as well as Arabic and Persian. Unlike the hard-working producer Rakım, who thrives in love as well as business, the over-westernized Felatun consumes everything without appreciating the value of anything. Felatun's French mistress does not care for him and pushes him to spend more and more money on spoiling her. Rakım's French mistress, on the other hand, even gives his wife-to-be free piano lessons. As the levelheaded Rakım prospers, Felatun wastes his fortune and barely makes it out of Istanbul with a government post in the provinces. Rakım is the obvious model for the reader and a mouthpiece for the writer. Yet Felatun steals the show as one of the most memorable characters in nineteenth-century Ottoman literature, being the first manifestation of its longest-lasting trope: the over-westernized dandy (*züppe*).[45]

The dandy is, of course, a cross-cultural figure.[46] However, he gained specific local resonances related to the clash of westernizations in the late Ottoman Empire. Fiction and nonfiction writers alike cast young men like Felatun, with cushy government jobs, superficial Western tastes, and a flair for consumption, as effeminate, ineffectual, westoxicated phonies. The dandy, the slave of the fashionable, always in love with the very idea of love, "just like a woman," epitomized the opposite of the warlike manly values the Ottoman Turkish nationalists sought to instill in the middle classes.[47] Authors contrasted his superficial "love" for the West, allegorized in his affairs with Western or minority Christian women, with his inability to comprehend the strategic value of Western reason and industry. The dandy was always in love, yet never able to form a stable, respectable union; he was in constant movement, rushing from balls to carriage rides to teas to shopping trips, but never actually *progressing*. In short, he became a symbol for all that had gone wrong in the empire after the Tanzimat.

The dandy appears over and over in the Turkish novel of the late nineteenth century, becoming reincarnated most successfully in Bihruz

Bey, the protagonist of the 1896 novel *Araba Sevdası* (The carriage affair) by Recaizade Mahmut Ekrem.[48] Bihruz Bey is an even livelier character than Felatun because the author focuses completely on him, instead of creating a selectively westernized foil for the reader to emulate. Bihruz's two favorite pastimes are dressing in the latest and most expensive European fashions (completely independent of the weather) and taking his fancy horse-drawn carriage on tours in the leisure district of town, where he and other pretenders turn round and round, looking at each other in their fancy Sunday outfits, celebrating their European-ness. Moreover, in true dandy style, Bihruz's carriage has been purchased through debt; like the Ottoman state, it keeps breaking down. The actual driver of the carriage, technically under Bihruz's pay but in reality an independent and mobile individual, is a Christian called Andon.

Bihruz Bey, like all allegorical dandies, is in love with an idea of love gleaned from French romances and classical Ottoman court literature.[49] In one of his famous wanderings, he glimpses a blonde woman in another expensive carriage and immediately falls in love with her, or more correctly with his idea of her, in Don Quixote fashion. Although Bihruz imagines the "*blond*" to be a young Western-educated girl in her family's carriage, the woman is a notorious courtesan in a rented carriage.[50] Toward the end of the novel, when a false friend fools Bihruz, saying the woman is dead, the dandy imagines she must have wasted away out of her love for him, and he spends his days trying to locate her hidden grave in the hopes of reading a French poem over it. The woman, on the other hand, is alive and well and barely aware of Bihruz's existence. When he finally encounters her, all he receives is a mocking. The novel ends in a jarring anticlimax with his deflated last word to her: "*pardon.*"[51]

Unlike nineteenth-century Latin American novelists who "hypostatize desire as truth," and unlike Sufi texts that posit love as the ultimate reality of the soul's yearning for union with God, *Araba Sevdası* exemplifies how late nineteenth-century Ottoman authors remained cautious of the loss of rationality associated with certain kinds of desire.[52] Falling in love with silly European fashions, falling in love with carriages that go nowhere, and with sirens who never return their feelings, dandies served as warnings to young Turkish men expected to take control of the crumbling empire.

The Carriage Affair, however, is not only a novel depicting and criticizing over-westernization. It is also a mirror for vernacular transculturation, allowing Ekrem to delve deeply into the identity crisis brought on by unpredictable dimensions of cultural contact. Bihruz's comical attempts to locate and woo the courtesan he imagines to be an upperclass maiden give us glimpses into the multilinguistic mixing of the era. According to Moran, in his attempt to fully represent the cultural and linguistic hybridity of elite late Ottoman culture, Ekrem might in fact have been the first novelist ever to use the narrative technique of stream of consciousness.[53] The passage Moran uses to make this point allows us direct access to Bihruz's psyche and depicts mental codeswitching, from Turkish to French and back again.[54] The use of bilingual stream of consciousness here, about a year before Édouard Dujardin's *Les Lauriers sont coupés* (1887), considered the first novel to use the technique in a single language, should warn us against aligning local westernizations with a lack of creativity and innovation.

Freed from the formal conventions binding traditional literature and committed to the everyday, the late Ottoman novel became not just a tool of selective westernization and a treatise on over-westernization, but also a window into wild westernization, representing a society undergoing rapid transculturation. All of these threads work together to create a canon that is often uninspiring and insipid but sometimes capable of great innovation and subtlety, exceeding the boundaries of the genre. As Turkish novelists lived through sociohistorical transformations in international relations and gender norms, they used allegory with varying degrees of complexity to make political statements. As the nineteenth century transitioned into the twentieth, those statements would focus more and more on Turkish women and the United States.

AMERICA AND THE GENDER OF OVER-WESTERNIZATION

Just as Orientalism helped Europeans and Americans represent the East (and themselves) in gendered terms, corresponding to various political goals, Middle Eastern artists and authors used rhetorical figures of gender and maturity in imagining the relations between the East and the West. Similarly, as gendered representations of the East and the West shifted according to time and context in the United States, so did Turkish westernizations. Tanzimat intellectuals had originally imagined selective westernization as a peaceful marriage between a masculine, established, older East and a thrilling, youthful West.[55] Later authors could not be so certain of Eastern control over westernization. The late nineteenth century saw the apex of racist science and imperialism, complicating the image of the West for Ottoman intellectuals.[56] As European policies toward the Ottoman Empire degenerated into the so-called "Eastern question," which was not so much a question as a determination to divide the lands of the moribund empire, Europe in Turkish literature became fully masculinized as an upstart invader.[57] Turkey's regeneration in this scenario depended on the rise of a new masculine force, i.e., Mustafa Kemal and his army, and the elimination of weak links: westoxicated women and the effeminate young men who fall for their charms.

The phallic penetration of Western armies into the forbidden bosom of the nation coincided with the feminization of over-westernization and its depiction as a tragedy as opposed to a farce. Felatun and Bihruz were perfect examples of the over-westernized dandy of late nineteenth-century Ottoman fiction because they were both fatherless young men, undereducated wastrels, aimless *flâneurs*, and comic figures. In the first decade of the twentieth century, over-westernization, and the excess of passion and spastic movement associated with it, came to have a different face. The trope of the misguided Ottoman Turkish dandy was slowly overshadowed by the trope of the over-sexualized, smart, literate, and treacherous young woman.[58] This shift coincided with the rising popularity of Western-style education for the daughters of upper- and middle-class Turks and the increasing presence and mobility of Muslim women in urban life.[59]

For many Turkish authors, unbridled education and active participation in civic life made such upper-class Turkish women unacceptable as wives and mothers. Ahmed Mithat, for example, constructed a memorable character called Ceylan (meaning Doe), who gets ideas about *marriage libre* from reading Western radical feminists, in his 1908 novel *Jön Türk*. Ceylan seduces the main protagonist, Nurullah, and becomes pregnant, in the hope that a marriage proposal will be imminent. Instead, Nurullah lets his family arrange his marriage to Ceylan's foil, a meek virgin with just the right amount of education and a perfectly controlled library. The allegorical novel ends with the suicides of both Ceylan and her dandyesque father, who is blamed for the haphazard over-westernized education his daughter has received.[60] Author Ömer Seyfettin, similarly, found in his own failed marriage to a chic Istanbul lady a lesson on feminine over-westernization. In a diary entry on December 7, 1917, he complained of "non-nationalist," "Europeanized" Turkish women, calling them "puppets, some of whom have been educated like the French, some like the English, others like the Germans."[61] He anticipated writing a novel about a man looking for a wife and running into these figures.

In the 1920s, some nationalist intellectuals complicated these depictions, mobilizing their own allegorical figures of selective westernization. The famous novelist Reşat Nuri Güntekin, for example, did not see any contradictions between his iconic protagonist Feride's education in the American College for Girls, her flighty mobility, and her transformation into a chaste, enlightened village teacher in his canonical novel *Çalıkuşu* (The wren, 1922). Similarly, Halide Edib believed that a Western-style education, when combined with Islamic morals and a sense of national identity, would create the ideal mothers for the new nation.[62] Her novels complicated the femme fatale/innocent wife dichotomy of male novelists by combining the strength, intelligence, and mobility of the former with the spiritual ethics of the latter.[63] Aliye, the heroine of *Vurun Kahpeye* (Thrash the whore, 1923), for example, is an idealistic, well-educated teacher from Istanbul who goes to Anatolia to serve her country during the War of Independence. She protects her chastity despite overtures from the leader of the invading Greek militia, remains true to the national cause, and battles the religious extremism of the village elders. Perhaps in a reflection of the stigmatization Edib herself was increasingly feeling, Aliye becomes the victim of slander and is lynched by a mob screaming "Thrash the whore."[64] Halide Edib's novels thus insisted that appearances could be deceiving and that a woman's mobility ("excess of physical prowess"), eclectic education, and quest for self-realization did not necessarily imply over-westernization.[65] Chastity and modesty, along with nationalist commitment, constituted the line between selective and excessive westernization.

The Kemalist state, despite stigmatizing Edib herself, placed its bets on the new Turkish woman found in her novels, and began bringing her to life through selective westernization measures. Kemalists encouraged female students' athleticism and instituted girl scout troops who represented an upright, orderly, asexual mobility at national parades. The idealized masculine figure of the army officer, who no longer wore a fez, met his feminine counterpart in the unveiled schoolteacher ready to form Turkish children into figures of nationalist modernity. Legislating heterosexual monogamy, glorifying motherhood, and advancing asexual images of the modern Turkish woman in the newly heterosocial public sphere, Kemalists sought to "secure the sign of the modern and/ but chaste woman."[66] The gendered boundary between selective and excessive westernization, however, became even more perilous with the rise of a new irreverent politics of personal liberation and unbounded mobility, symbolized by "the flapper" and associated with the United States.

The flapper entered Turkish literature around the same time the United States became a central force in Turkish politics: after World War I. For many Turkish intellectuals, the mobile, active women of the United States and Turkish women educated like them were hardly laudable. Müfide Ferit Tek's 1924 *Pervaneler* (The moths) associated an American-style education with a misguided feminism (cast as near-lesbianism) of individualistic pleasure seeking. One of the signs of westoxication in the novel is ceaseless, energetic, but unproductive movement by these American-educated young Turkish women. Their constant involvement in tennis, rowing, dancing, bicycling, and other forms of exercise, contrasted with their counterparts in Turkish schools, symbolizes a mad, ambitious restlessness that eventually pulls them toward their "beloved" America like moths toward a flame.[67] Poet Ahmet Haşim described the United States as a "laughable" land of "women who ape men."[68] The education of Turkish girls in "the foreign school for girls situated on the Bosphorous" (i.e., the American College for Girls) disturbed him profoundly; he wrote an article criticizing the young women's apathetic dissection of the cats they had personally raised.[69] The majority of important authors of the early twentieth century, such as Mehmet Rauf, Hüseyin Rahmi Gürpınar, and Peyami Safa, consistently depicted American women (and their local copies) as lustful, overenergetic, and materialistic Amazons.[70]

The 1928 *Sodom ve Gomore* by Yakup Kadri Karaosmanoğlu epitomizes this post–World War I shift in the gender and severity of over-westernization as a literary discourse and the increasing presence of the United States in Turkish literature. Karaosmanoğlu, like Ottoman novelists Ahmed Mithat and Recaizade Mahmut Ekrem, epitomized the role of the novelist as public intellectual and held government positions as a Kemalist member of parliament and ambassador. Set in occupation-era Istanbul (1918–1923), his novel *Sodom ve Gomore* focuses on a segment of Istanbul bourgeoisie consorting and collaborating with the invading soldiers. Felatun and Bihruz had been comic though central figures; Ceylan was a tragic, though minor, character; Halide Edib's heroines were central and exemplary. Leyla, the main focus of *Sodom ve Gomore*, is central, tragic, and treacherous. A beautiful and fiery Turkish girl engaged to her traditionally inclined cousin Necdet, Leyla is an unabashed Anglophile at a time when Istanbul is teeming with British soldiers. A graduate of the American College for Girls, Leyla emulates American flappers by bobbing her hair and walking around in her riding outfit, sometimes going so far as to enter high society functions on horseback, wielding a whip like an Amazon.[71] Following several such outings, she becomes the lover of a handsome English captain. By depicting Leyla's athletic mobility as a precursor to her sexual "fall," the novel voices unresolved Kemalist fears in relation to Muslim women's increasing public visibility. The state cast unveiled, energetic, slim young women—symbolic opposites of the lounging, voluptuous, oversexed odalisques of Orientalist fantasy—as representatives of selective westernization and sought to desexualize them in the process. The novel shows how the newly imported figure of the American flapper—mobile, androgynous, *and* sexually active—threatened to overwhelm this fragile equilibrium.

Karaosmanoğlu's depictions of Leyla and her fiancé Necdet show a smart, beautiful, energetic girl in the throes of westoxication and a young man unable to take control of the situation. Leyla constantly appears to be giddy with unproductive motion, jumping from event to event unconsciously, as if suffering from a bout of "malaria."[72] She is always active but rarely aware. In contrast, Necdet, the young man from the first tram scene opening this chapter, appears passive, either "drifting" or motionless; yet he is full of torturous emotions and thoughts.[73] Just as Leyla's love for the West makes her wild and boyish, Necdet's persistent desire for Leyla feminizes and disempowers the young man. His wish to fall deeper and deeper into pain and dissipation with love is, according to Karaosmanoğlu, a disease that is found "mainly among fallen women."[74] Of course, suffering willingly for love and wandering wildly in search of it is also the central trope of Sufi allegories.[75] However, Leyla is decidedly not a symbol of God; she serves another, entirely secular lesson in *Sodom ve Gomore*. When the Allies leave, she ends up broken and abandoned, another tragic victim of over-westernization, as well as its treacherous antiheroine.

Karaosmanoğlu places part of the blame for Leyla's actions on her materialistic Anglophile father, who makes money from the invasion and is unwilling to exercise any authority over the officer courting his daughter.[76] In a clever historico-allegorical twist, we find out that Sami Bey is a retiree from the Ottoman Public Debt Administration, recalling the debt-ridden dandy of an earlier era and the ceding of economic control to Europe in 1881.[77] As such, Leyla's fall is predicated on her father's degeneracy, just as the nation's literal invasion is only the natural next step after its economic dependency. However, the author also blames the other man in Leyla's life for her fate. Necdet, Leyla's fiancé, is depicted as the victim of the kind of idealized, blind love found in traditional Turkish allegories, romanticizing suffering instead of rationally asserting a manly authority.

Like the works of Ahmed Mithat and Recaizade Ekrem, Karaosmanoğlu rewrites several key religious and folk texts in *Sodom ve Gomore*, the most obvious being the eponymous section of the Old Testament. Leyla's name also clearly alludes to the Near East's most famous allegorical Sufi love story: *Leyla ile Mecnun* (Layla and Majnun). In this story, the star-crossed lovers go through many allegorical tests to reach each other after Leyla, the girl, is forcibly betrothed to another. The boy then loses his self and his mind in lovesickness, earning the name Majnun-e Layla (Layla's lunatic). In the Sufi allegory, Mecnun's crazed behavior and his complete lack of ego represents the noblest truth of the human soul in perpetual longing for the ultimate Beloved, that is, God.[78] However, as in *Araba Sevdası*, in *Sodom ve Gomore* such idealized, irrational "love" and directionless wandering is neither to be celebrated nor trusted. Instead, it must be exchanged for a manly love for the pure, battered homeland and well-directed, rational movement. In fact, Necdet harms his fiancée by insisting on seeing her in allegorical terms. Instead of taking charge of the situation and severing her from her English "friends," he sees her as "an enchanted maiden taken prisoner by a dragon."[79] Stuck on Leyla, he is unable to abscond to Anatolia to join Mustafa Kemal's troops, betraying his country as well as dishonoring his name, which means "courage."

Necdet and Sami Bey are not the only Turkish men who refuse to see things clearly and act with authority to protect the female members of their household and, by extension, Anatolia. The novel depicts a gambler who lets his wife bed the invaders just so she will not interfere with his financial games, and a father who refuses to see that a young American lesbian has seduced his sixteen-year-old daughter, Nermin. Nermin, a family friend of Leyla's, also attends the American College for Girls but finds little joy in all the European men surrounding her. An American reporter described as "an incorrigible flapper" manages to seduce this young, restless teenager at a party while wild jazz music plays in the background (56). When the Independence War is won and the Europeans abandon their defiled female bounty and leave the country, all this young girl's parents get is a breathless letter celebrating her arrival in the New World with Miss Fanny Moore. Her father's denial of this fact and his conviction that little Nermin has been abducted by Protestant missionaries, who wish to convert her and raise her like an Armenian orphan, heralds how the older generation's knowledge of the United States as a missionary nation clashes with the rise of a new, jazz-infused, pleasure-focused, consumerist America.

Nermin, however, is a minor character, and the novel's Americans are consistently less harmful than its Europeans. The gentle seduction of Nermin through cuddles, dancing, and companionship pales in comparison with the sadomasochistic pleasure room a second English captain, a decadent homosexual, builds in a mansion he leases from an old, respectable Ottoman family. To add insult to injury, the room, now filled with whips, feathers, and vulgar statues, had originally been the family's *masjid*, or prayer room (102). In *Sodom ve Gomore*, most Europeans are coarse soldiers, freely looting the city and taking advantage of all it has to offer, sexually as well as materially. The Americans, on the other hand, are naïve progressives who are very proud of themselves for exploring "the Orient" and who study all that is around them, particularly the local Turks, as if attending "an educational zoo" (97). Thus even the most decadent Americans of the novel carry qualities of youthfulness and innocence. Fanny Moore, for example, appears to be joking good-humoredly even when she is quiet, and reminds one of "a naïve school girl" as well as a wild bird (65). Necdet finds the age of an American millionaire difficult to guess because he "carries two eyes expressing only simplicity and naiveté in the middle of the face of a hardened bandit" (208). These Americans' studious detachment and their double-edged interest in Turkey serve as an allegory for Wilsonian liberal progressivism, particularly recalling the survey missions sent to the area after World War I. Miss Moore's lesbianism, in contrast to the European males' heterosexual and homosexual sadism, symbolizes a form of soft perversity and gentle domination, although it certainly differs from the "benevolent supremacy" U.S. policy makers would be seeking to attain in the region.[80]

The slow and uneven shift in the moral geography of over-westernization from Europe to the United States, and from the United States as a missionary nation to the United States as sexually charged consumer paradise, continued between the wars. Interestingly, official American representatives in Turkey were aware of both the Turkish discourse of over-westernization and America's rising presence within it. A 1930 ethnographic study of Turkish petty government officials, shared with the State Department in 1932, reads like an allegorical novel, with its figure of an imagined composite Turkish official, Cevat, who is constructing new geographies of mobility and desire around Europe and America:

> [Cevat was afraid] the Ministry might begin to doubt his avowed nationalism and class him as pro-foreign. Nevertheless Cevat's secret desire was to be able to revisit Paris. It was something he did not for a moment believe would ever happen but it was a most pleasant topic on which to daydream and fancy. America, too, fascinated him. He had never known any Americans in Turkey—for Americans meant missionaries—and he had never read any book on that country. It was through the movies that he received most

of his ideas—luxurious night-clubs, beautiful women, limousines, jazz and easily acquired wealth.[81]

In the early twentieth century, America as a shiny new Western dreamscape, producing dizzying images of passion ("beautiful women") and mobility ("limousines"), still appeared as an afterthought to a better-known Europe. This new West became more fleshed out with each imported representation, and its shiny cultural exports eclipsed the older, familiar image of the missionaries. It would, however, take a couple more decades for America's "soft love" to mature as a literary theme in Turkey and for Turkish ambivalence toward the United States as "the lesser of two evils" (or, perhaps, the least debilitating of two loves) to become full-fledged distrust, awash in conspiracy theories.

AMERICAN ALLEGORIES I: THE COLD WAR PROTEST NOVEL

Until the end of World War II, Turkey followed a foreign policy of defensive neutrality and pragmatic collaboration, including with the Soviet Union. This period began Turkish–American rapprochement as bilateral relations slowly became neutral, and even took positive turns. State Department officials, public relations groups such as American Friends of Turkey, and sympathetic intellectuals from both countries cited Kemalist westernization efforts in order to boost U.S.–Turkish relations.[82] Selective reforms in women's rights and sociocultural developments, in particular, earned the young state a great deal of positive press in the United States. The success of authoritarian westernization as a diplomatic tool between the wars was perhaps best epitomized by the *Life* magazine headline from October 31, 1938: "Turkey's Kamal Ataturk is the World's Best Dictator."[83] Despite all this, the racialized figure of the "terrible Turk" continued to haunt American perceptions.[84]

It was only during the early Cold War that U.S. foreign policy and Turkish authoritarian westernization overlapped, eclipsing older civilizational figures. Stalin's expansionist rhetoric increased suspicions between Turkey and the Soviet Union after World War II, pushing Turkish policy makers toward the Western bloc. Kemalists loosened their grip on the political system, as necessitated by the 1948 Truman Doctrine, which promised aid to Turkey and Greece in response to the threat of Soviet aggression and subversion.[85] In May 1950, the country's first multiparty elections brought the pro-American and populist Democratic Party to power. Just as the United States slowly became the main representative of "the West" in Turkey, now with the added connotation of the West as the clear side to choose in the Cold War, the cognitive map of Turkey shifted for U.S. officials in the late 1940s and early 1950s.

Modernization theory and the doctrine of containment, the two central strategies the United States developed in response to the USSR, both helped improve the image of Turkey in the United States. Atatürk had been the first world leader to use the word "modernization" to indicate "a *directed* process of nation building" early in the century.[86] After World War II, a loose network of U.S.-based specialists built modernization theory largely on the historical example of Kemalist selective westernization, and figured Turkey as an intermediary model for the rest of the Middle East.[87] Underplaying racial and religious differences, modernization theory emphasized the possibility that non-Western nations could become "modern" by following the same "stages of growth" as the United States.[88] Accommodating Atatürk's top-down model of authoritarian westernization, theorists projected antidemocratic measures as intermediary necessities.[89] This Cold War revision of Turkish history circumvented the old Orientalist binary between (Islamic) despotism and (Western) modernity that had haunted earlier U.S. representations of the Atatürk revolution. Turkey's history—modernization before democratization—would even be used to justify support for friendly dictatorships throughout the so-called Third World.

At the same time, the binary opposition between Islam and Christendom U.S. policy makers had long employed receded in importance as the Cold War drew symbolic lines between "godless" communism and religion in general.[90] Official documents from the early Cold War inescapably referred to the country in the dyad "Greece and Turkey" in the model of the Truman Doctrine, marking a new moral geography. U.S. representatives in the country depicted Turks as eager students learning to be properly mobile (as opposed to provincial), connected to their American benefactors through affective ties of gratitude (figure 2.1).[91] Turkey's militarized border with Soviet Russia soon began to dominate popular American visions of Turkey. A 1958 *Time* article, depicting

FIGURE 2.1 This photograph from a 1948 congressional report on aid to Greece and Turkey depicts Turkish men as orderly and compliant students of U.S.-led modernization—a large contrast to pre–World War II images of Turks as rapacious barbarians undeserving of America's imperial stewardship (cf. Figure 1.3). The aid trucks symbolize the benevolence of the United States as well as the promise of mobility/progress through the building of asphalt roads. U.S. Congress, House Committee on Foreign Affairs, Fourth Report to Congress on Assistance to Greece and Turkey, Message from the President of the United States Transmitting the Fourth Report to Congress on Assistance to Greece and Turkey for the Period Ended June 30, 1948. Washington: [s.n.], 1948. Print. Illustration on page 34.

Turkey as a steadfast masculine ally in contrast to "hysterically 'anti-imperialist' Arab nations," began with the image of Turkish soldiers guarding the "frontier between Russia and the rest of the world."[92] A celebratory 1958 CBS documentary on Atatürk called *The Incredible Turk* similarly started with a point-of-view sequence encouraging viewers' identification with the young Turkish guards keeping watch over the Soviet border. Narrated by Walter Cronkite, the film implicitly challenged the figure of the terrible Turk with its title, and introduced Atatürk to a broader audience as a proto-hero of modernization theory.

As U.S. intellectuals, in collaboration with local scholars and politicians, were molding selective westernization into modernization theory,

Turkish intellectuals began reconsidering the place of the United States within the good/bad rubric of westernization. In the late 1940s and early 1950s, Turkey's power elite began to see the United States once again as the good West, a benevolent guide toward a properly Turkish modernization. This time, it seemed, America would not reject Turkey as its ward. Turkey's entry into NATO in 1952 implied that the country had finally become an equal member, a "part of the West."[93] U.S. representatives and Turkish policy makers argued that Turkey could even go beyond belonging in Pax America and become a small version of America itself. Referring to Kemalist strategic westernization as "Operation Bootstrap," scholars embraced the new nation within the mythology of the American Dream.[94] The United States aggressively advertised "the American way of life" for adoption in Turkish fairs.[95] In a public speech in 1957, President Celal Bayar promised to remake Turkey into a "Little America" within thirty years.[96]

If one of the most obvious effects of this early Cold War U.S.–Turkish alliance on Turkish culture was the rise of English-language education (chapter 3), one of its most visible effects on the Turkish landscape was the rise of a new system of movement and transportation. The early republic had built state-financed, state-owned railroads in keeping with its statist economic policy and its wish to avoid the mobility impasse of the late Ottoman Empire. Following the War of Independence (1919–1923), Kemalists immediately nationalized the existing foreign-owned lines and began an aggressive campaign to knit "a web of steel" around the motherland.[97] As soldiers, they had learned a lesson they sought to implement as statesmen: the unbalanced, unconnected, Western-ruled railway system had facilitated the country's invasion; national railroads were therefore a necessity of authoritarian westernization.[98] In 1948, the final foreign railroad line was nationalized. Yet, around the same time, Turkey's transportation policy took a U.S.-directed shift, intended to integrate the country into the capitalist system in line with the Marshall Plan. Under Democratic Party rule, supported by U.S. financial and technical assistance, a different network began to wrap around Anatolia: hard-surfaced asphalt roads for heavy vehicles. These highways and motor vehicles soon became some of the most visible symbols of U.S.-accented modernization.[99]

The early fifties were marked by a very heavy dependence on American aid, financing a boom in industrialization, infrastructure development, and agriculture.[100] By the end of the decade, the United States was firmly implemented as the new "West" in Turkish culture, becoming a model and conduit for selective westernization (particularly vis-à-vis agriculture, transportation, and defense systems), the key bearer of transculturation, and, increasingly, the focus of debates on the limits of westernization. As the boom of the early fifties, built on the flimsiest of foundations, morphed into spiraling inflation and stagnation, left-leaning authors led the way in denouncing the United States and her over-westernized local accomplices. As in the prewar period, much of this criticism was deeply gendered and sexualized: pundits criticized Turkish women's flirtations with visiting Americans and mercilessly mocked the government's policy of painting and renovating Istanbul's brothels and making them off limits to Turkish patrons during visits by U.S. naval vessels.[101] Critics complained that in an ostensibly statist economy, which barred foreign imports, literal American garbage (colorful cans, empty bottles, secondhand jeans discarded by military bases) decorated modest family living rooms and maidens' dowry chests.[102] Utilizing the myth of the Wild West, recently imported through movie westerns and comic book series, communist poet Nazım Hikmet depicted the Motherland itself as a naked woman, tied down by its supposed protectors to serve the lust of "Texan Sergeants."[103]

Like the tramcars of an earlier era, cars and tractors, symbols of U.S.-assisted westernization, came to be associated with over-westernization in literature and folk culture in the late 1950s and 1960s. In fiction, an ironic mode of international allegory, engaging roads and vehicles as tropes for failed progress, emerged.[104] The American-brand tractors pushed through the Marshall Plan, in particular, became potent symbols for literary protest. In short stories by Fahri Erdinç and Aziz Nesin, progress and movement stop short because the tractors, which the villagers name "the Marshall Mule," quickly become immobile due to the lack of "spare parts of civilization" in Turkey.[105] A 1963 consul report to the U.S. State Department singled out villagers around Izmir stoning "a large and luxurious appearing late model automobile" to provide an idea of the growing envy and resentment toward Americanized local wealth.[106] On January 6, 1969, leftist protestors associated with

Middle East Technical University in Ankara overturned and torched U.S. Ambassador Robert William Komer's diplomatic vehicle.[107]

If Karaosmanoğlu's *Sodom ve Gomore* is the seminal Kemalist allegorical novel, Fakir Baykurt's *Amerikan Sargısı* (The American bandage, 1967) epitomizes leftist Cold War allegory. A critique of U.S.-based modernization theory and attempts to turn Turkey into a compliant ward, the novel depicts how American aid—promising progress—ends up paralyzing an entire people. In this novel, movement becomes impossible because of the specific kind of "love" America claims to have for Turkey, built on self-congratulatory, universalizing assumptions about development and blindness to local conditions. The book focuses on American efforts to create a model village in Kızılöz, a relatively prosperous traditional agricultural community close to the nation's capital, Ankara. The model village project fails spectacularly, and the novel concludes with the villagers burning down its relics the night before a state official's photo-op visit. The locked coop filled with imported chickens that only lay empty eggs, the locked garden filled with pineapple trees that do not bear fruit, the model kitchen, which the village women refuse to use, all go up in flames. The ashes are then used to rebuild the hill the villagers had originally asked the Americans to level.

In *Amerikan Sargısı*, as in *Sodom ve Gomore*, westoxicated elite Turks invite the trouble in with hopes of benefiting financially and politically from the American aid. The Americans in *Amerikan Sargısı* also have the same condescending yet naïve attitude as those in *Sodom ve Gomore*: they are particularly interested in the "primitive" folk dances, architecture, and handicrafts of the villagers, which they believe resemble the artifacts of American "Indians."[108] In singling out the behavior of some of the aid workers for praise or censure, Baykurt parallels *The Ugly American* (1958) by Eugene Burdick and William Lederer. The villagers are particularly impressed with a young American called Bobby who learns the language and eats with relish the food prepared by the villagers. On the other hand, the book criticizes Americans who bring their own food, need translators, and assume an air of superiority.

As in *Sodom ve Gomore*, the arrival of the Westerners in *Amerikan Sargısı* is closely connected to gendered and sexualized excess at all levels of society. Already at the beginning of the novel, official American representatives and their upper-class Turkish accomplices seem given to philandering, supporting both wives and mistresses. Soon the villagers who serve the American project begin to act in degenerate ways, in accordance with their own cultural vices. We hear from Temeloş, the upright village guard and the hero of the novel, that one has begun to drink alcohol and another has married a much younger second wife, letting the first one till the fields. While the village women seem to have resisted the Americans' efforts to teach them how to cook, Temeloş is certain Turkish girls will soon begin to marry young Americans, too. The villagers are particularly distressed by the intimate use of toilet paper ("thin American papers") by the young village teacher, a modest young woman whose platonic friendship with Bobby raises eyebrows. The young teacher is closer as a type to Halide Edib's idealistic, chaste heroines, and even Temeloş condones their friendship. In fact, the book criticizes the mother who would rather marry her daughter to an unscrupulous, excessively westernized Turk than to an upright non-Muslim like Bobby. However, most characters do not share this generous attitude toward multicultural love. Soon rival villages begin to gossip that the foreigners are pouring all this money into Kızılöz because the village girls have been "rented" to Americans.

However, the most damaging love in the novel does not depend on the sexual threats of heterosexual contact and toilet paper, but the immobilizing, emasculating "love" and "friendship" of the United States. Baykurt, a graduate of the republican Village Institutes, is well versed in Anatolian dialects and folklore, and uses them to build up his Cold War allegory.[109] The characters consistently refer to Americans as "*Türk'ün Amerikan dostları*" (the Turk's American friends), even in the most violent moments of the novel; this lends the term "*dost*," which can mean a close friend or an illegitimate lover, an increasingly ominous cadence. "Türk-Amerikan Dostluk Bahçesi," the Garden of Turkish–American Friendship, filled with orderly rows of immaculately tended pineapple trees, is off limits to the villagers. Its gorgeous yet barren trees are guarded by one of their own, wearing American sneakers and enjoying an excellent salary. On the garden fence hangs an image of two disembodied hands frozen in a handshake; one sports a Turkish flag on its sleeve, the other an American one. Here Baykurt mobilizes a covert reference to the Turkish proverbial expression "*elini ver, kolunu kaptır*" (give your hand, lose your arm), meaning that showing understanding and friendship to a greedy person can lead to irreparable losses. Mashing the USAID hand-shake icon, designed in 1953 to symbolize "unity, goodwill, and coopera-tion," with Turkish folklore, Baykurt subverts it into a paralyzing grasp as opposed to a figure of mutual affection.[110]

The novel reaches its emotional climax when Temeloş tries to enter the Garden of Friendship in an attempt to understand why its stunningly healthy-looking trees do not bear fruit. The American-employed guard beats the old village guard under the handshake sign, damaging Temeloş's knees with his fancy sneakers and immobilizing him. After an under-staffed state hospital dismisses Temeloş, Bobby drives him to the Amer-ican Hospital in Ankara. There, Temeloş receives expert care and the eponymous "American bandage" of the novel. Temeloş had been one of the first to resist attempts to turn Kızılöz into a model village by using the Turkish proverbial expression, "We are among those who tend to our own wounds" to express that the village can take care of itself.[111] Follow-ing the beating, however, the old village guard becomes deathly ill and needs an American to literally tend to his wounds, due to the failed state health-care system. This American turns out to be a kind blonde nurse called Dorothy, who speaks minimal Turkish and loves to boast of her skills in applying bandages to wounds. She wraps Temeloş's wounded knee expertly. However, Temeloş has a panic attack when he sees that the bandage she has used bears the same image of the Turkish–American handshake guarding the friendship garden where he was beaten. To make matters worse, Dorothy takes particular pride in her ability to set the handshake side of the bandage to face the patients directly. Mad with frustration, Temeloş attacks the young nurse, who tries to calm him down, insisting in broken Turkish, between laughter and tears, "[C]an nobody wrap perfectly like me this bandage in this here Ankara, in this here Turkiye even, Temeloş."[112] Bobby enters the room just in time to help Temeloş undo the bandage and to drive him back to his village, saving him from the misplaced affection of the nurse. A few days later the whole village is liberated from the immobilizing bandage of American "friend-ship" by fire.

Mobility is carefully rationed throughout the novel. Selected youth are sent to the city to learn how to drive the new motorcycles, and there is talk of an educational trip all the way to the United States. However, at the end, Cold War attempts at progress mainly end up enforcing limits and policing boundaries. Only the exported prized American cows are allowed to enter the greenest meadow of Kızılöz; the chicken coop, like the garden of friendship, is locked and guarded. When the imported animals suddenly die, the villagers are certain it is because of homesickness—a projection of their own feelings of lack of control, paralysis, and displacement in their own lands. While Baykurt focuses on the villagers' lack of access to their own lands, we also get glimpses of the Turkish government selling control over larger swaths of country to the Americans in the form of mining rights. The villagers observe that their government seems to be completely under the sway of "the Turk's American friends," deprived of sovereignty in quite the same way they are. In this way, Temeloş's American bandage is a metaphor for the American Aid Mission to the Government of Turkey; it pretends to heal and mobilize, but ultimately binds the country and paralyzes its politics. Baykurt's American bandage allegorizes the inequality, despite all the rhetoric of love and friendship, of Turkey's Cold War relationship with the United States. The immobility (amid frantic activity) of Kızılöz is a metonym for the paralysis (amid all the talk of progress) in the Turkish Republic (figure 2.2).

Amerikan Sargısı is an allegory of collective hindsight; like *Sodom ve Gomore*, it was published over a decade after the era it seeks to represent, and it corresponds to an increasingly popular, leftist critique of U.S.–Turkish relations, capitalist modernization theory, and those overwesternized Turks responsible for its (mis)implementation. Thus it engages official history with its own mode of remembering. Although critics began to equate the Cold War alliance with the American mandate as early as 1948, in the sixties, discourse about the bandage/bondage of American aid intensified.[113] Modernization theory had overshadowed older racial/religious figures without eliminating them, and civilizational logic did infiltrate U.S. aid and NATO policies toward Turkey. Considered "a semi-Oriental country," Turkey received fewer funds and less autonomy than most European countries under the Marshall Plan.[114] Even the Truman Doctrine's formulation of "Greece and Turkey" announced the country's secondary status and, of course, NATO was no equal partnership. These realities, and the increasingly regressive policies of the Democratic Party exploiting religious sentiments, dampened celebrations of having finally become an equal member of the West in the 1960s, a decade that began with the country's first military coup.

FIGURE 2.2 This 1974 cover of the novel *American Sargısı* reflects Baykurt's vision of the immobilizing binds of America's postwar "love" for Turkey. The illustrator satirizes the new stereotype of Turkey as a beloved, youthful pupil of U.S.-led modernization (see figure 2.1), depicting the aid bandage as a swaddle and Temeloş as a smothered baby.

The 1960 crash of a U.S. military reconnaissance plane flying over Soviet Russia without the Turkish government's knowledge exemplified the problems of sovereignty associated with NATO membership. During the 1962 Cuban Missile Crisis, the USSR and the United States bargained behind closed doors over missiles in Turkey and Cuba, which were reduced to voiceless client states risking nuclear war on their soil.

The Cyprus crisis led to a further cooling of bilateral relationships. In June 1964, Turkish newspapers reported that President Lyndon Johnson had sent a strongly worded note of ultimatum against intervening in the island to Prime Minister İsmet İnönü.[115] The limiting language of the letter, believed to be insulting and emasculating this hero of the War of Independence, inflamed anti-American feelings across the country.[116] "Johnson, False Friend," read protest banners, reflecting the cynicism toward "the Turk's American friends" in the political arena.[117] Some authors also emphasized Johnson's Texas roots to connect his perceived bullying to the transculturated myth of the violent Wild West.[118]

The 1974 Turkish invasion of Cyprus in response to an ultranationalist Greek coup fully dismantled America's Greece and Turkey dyad and led to a series of U.S. embargoes. Throughout the 1970s, sectarian violence between the radical left and right in Turkey demonstrated the impact of the disappearing consensus on the official U.S.–Turkish alliance. On September 12, 1980, a military junta took over control of the government, marking the country's third military coup since the 1950 transition to multiparty diplomacy. The military government brutally suppressed dissent, particularly from the left. After three years, the junta returned power to civilian authorities, and newly elected Prime Minister Turgut Özal reformed the economy along free-market lines, placing the country squarely on the side of Reagan's United States economically, politically, and culturally. As the world economy entered its post-Keynesian phase and modernization theory transitioned into neoliberal development doctrine, Turkey became an early testing ground for structural adjustment policies.[119] A new kind of Turkish novel followed.

AMERICAN ALLEGORIES II: POST-COUP POSTMODERNISM

The coup of 1980 ushered in a new era of contradictions in Turkish society: a time of intense ideological suppression followed by a proliferation of civic discourses.[120] The coup debilitated the Turkish left and suppressed political dissent for decades to come with a new constitution, but economic restructuring, erratic democratization efforts, and the rise of large popular nonstate media outlets led to a growing civil society.[121] Issues the state media would have deemed too frivolous or deviant burst into the public sphere with the expansion of private media outlets and increasing tabloidization in the late 1980s and 1990s. A new feminist movement rose to question the sexual puritanism of Kemalist selective westernization; the LGBT rights movement was born; religion became a formidable force in politics. Though the final decades of the twentieth century were marred by Kurdish separatism, terrorism, and state brutality, for the first time since the founding of the republic, officials began to acknowledge the existence of ethnic and religious minorities within the nation.[122]

Turgut Özal as prime minister (1983–1989) and president (1989–1993) accelerated the cultural exchange between the United States and Turkey, connecting the Anatolian hinterland to Istanbul and the world.[123] Unlike Turkey's early twentieth-century elite, Özal had no training in the European intellectual tradition. Born to a devout, part-Kurdish family from Malatya in eastern Anatolia, he had grown up during the Cold War and worked at the World Bank. His "West" was the United States.[124] Under his rule, Turkey allowed the United States to attack Iraq from local military bases during the first Gulf War (1990–1991), marking the government's willingness to play the "good Muslim" in America's new Middle Eastern ventures. The increasing visibility of Islam in the public sphere was only matched by the proliferation of American imports. As American media products streamed into modest homes, new types of hybrid music, such as *arabesk*, became ubiquitous in the cities.[125] A popular 1992 book summarized this Eastern-accented wild westernization under Özal with its title: *Teksas-Malatya* (Texas-Malatya).[126] "A synthesis has been realized between the West and Islam," declared Özal triumphantly.[127] However premature the celebration, the eighties and nineties were indeed a time of intense vernacular transculturation and of "broadening the [discursive] road," effects of which resonated in Turkish literature.[128]

The junta's forceful depoliticization of Turkish letters led to new subgenres of postmodern literature in the 1980s and 1990s. "Practice of tendentious literature," literary critic Azade Seyhan points out, "is aesthetically risky business": aiming to educate and inculcate, much early republican and postwar political writing had alternated between protesting and preaching.[129] Barring a few exceptions, which stretched Western genres by incorporating folk forms, leftist novels of the early Cold

War had also remained stymied in their style and language. The shift away from realist literature of social responsibility gave a boost to what Börte Sagaster has identified as the "extra-canon" in Turkish literature, which refused to serve as handmaiden to the state's selective westernization projects and was equally suspicious of the ideological doctrines of the right and the left.[130] In the hands of a new generation of authors such as Latife Tekin, Bilge Karasu, Nazlı Eray, Aslı Erdoğan, and Orhan Pamuk, the Turkish novel matured into something strange and beautiful in the final decades of the twentieth century, shedding its long history of self-imposed realism.[131] Reconciled with its traditional mystical roots, combining a progressive political sensibility with fine-tuned attention to the changes wrought by vernacular transculturation, the Turkish novel emerged as a formidable literary force after the coup. Yet, if novelist Orhan Pamuk's 2006 Nobel Prize win was a testament to the cultural successes of the Turkish novel under intense wild westernization, the nationalist controversies surrounding it and the rise of a new type of ultranationalist mass literature in the early twenty-first century showed that the debate on over-westernization was far from over.

From Orhan Pamuk's popular 1994 novel *Yeni Hayat* (The new life), we learn two central facts about life in post-coup Turkey: it is ruled by the motorway and fueled by conspiracy theories. Both of these elements had been present in realist fictions of the early Cold War era. The *tomofil*, the automobile in Temeloş's mistaken pronunciation, had already entered the villagers' symbolic lexicon in the form of tractors, cars, and motorcycles in *Amerikan Sargısı*. Villagers were constantly speculating about why the Americans would come all the way to the village and pour so much money into this project. What is new in *Yeni Hayat* is the triumphant return of the supernatural and the irrational into the cultural atmosphere of urban Turkey, and a deeply ambivalent politics of remembering and forgetting. Among other things, *Yeni Hayat* is a work of hindsight about the postwar switch from state-run railroads to an exponentially more dangerous, gasoline-fueled highway system. It is an allegory about the post-1980 move toward a neoliberal consumption economy and the sense of psychic discontinuity and melancholy it sparked in many Turks. It is a dark postmodern story about unrequited love and a mystical quest—an honest homage to the Sufi literary tradition marginalized by selective westernization projects. Most importantly, it may be Turkey's first best-selling novel to mock efforts to draw the limits of westernization.

The protagonist and first-person narrator of *Yeni Hayat* is a young, rational Istanbul-born engineering student called Osman, whose life changes because of a book he has read titled *Yeni Hayat*. Seeing *Yeni Hayat* in the hands of a beautiful student at his university, Canan, Osman buys a copy and finishes it in one night. He immediately falls under its spell, reading and copying the text furiously, waiting for a "New Life" and the mysterious figure of an Angel who will take him there. He is, however, even more in love with Canan, who remains in love with Mehmet, her boyfriend and the first discoverer of the book. A conspiracy against the book surfaces when Mehmet is shot and narrowly escapes with his life, disappearing into Anatolia. Canan starts seeking her lover; in turn, Osman, in search of Canan, the Angel, and the New Life, launches into frenzied adventures recalling the mad Mecnun. Spiraling into frantic and irrational movement, Osman imagines he will run into Canan again if he is, for example, "the first person off the ferry" and doesn't "step on the cracks in the sidewalk."[132] When obsessive-compulsive wishful thinking fails, Osman takes long, hypnotic bus journeys across Anatolia, searching for Canan as well as a certain "threshold" guarded by the Angel.[133] The threshold, he decides, must become luminous at the moment of accidents. Access to it, therefore, becomes just a matter of randomly boarding and traveling in buses, since the Turkish motorway (unlike the railroad) is so deadly.[134] In *Yeni Hayat* and in contemporary Turkey, "Buses have a way of burning," as a minor character notes with a shrug.[135]

Following an accident, Osman runs into Canan, who is seeking the same threshold and looking for Mehmet. They begin to travel together, but Osman cannot win Canan's heart or body, and remains full of jealousy for Mehmet. The two take on fake identities and penetrate an Anatolian general merchandise dealers' (*bayiiler*) convention, where they learn about a "counter-conspiracy" against the book.[136] The counter-conspiracy is, in fact, an "all-out battle against printed matter" and "against foreign cultures that annihilate us, against the newfangled stuff that comes from the West," as a dealer puts it.[137] A patriarchal old lawyer called Dr. Fine is the brains behind the operation; he runs a countrywide network of dealers who refuse to carry most of the Western products that have streamed into the country after the free-market reforms. Dr. Fine makes exceptions for watches, guns, and buses, but is particularly repulsed by "soulless" printed books and "the timetable for trains" (159). Osman and Canan, using fake identities, penetrate the inner circle of Dr. Fine and discover that this grand conspiracy theorist is, in fact, Mehmet's father. He has turned against the book because of his son's enchantment with it, and he has had its author killed.

Osman reads the reports of Dr. Fine's private spies and discovers that one of these men has attempted to kill Mehmet without Dr. Fine's approval. Escaping with his life, Mehmet has faked his death in a bus accident. Unbeknownst to his father, who believes him dead, Mehmet has taken on Osman's identity and lives in a sleepy Anatolian town, spending his time copying the book. Osman finds out that he knows the author of *Yeni Hayat* personally, as well. Rıfkı Ray, who has published the book under a pseudonym, is none other than Uncle Rıfkı, an old friend of Osman's deceased father, and like him, a retiree from the State Railroads Administration. As children, Osman and Mehmet were both avid fans of the comic book series Uncle Rıfkı wrote to teach Turkish children to appreciate their own culture. The books featured Turkish kids having adventures in the historical United States, fighting off land conspiracies and helping the good Americans build their transcontinental railroad. Having grown up with Uncle Rıfkı's imagination, they had both found his book for grown-ups, *Yeni Hayat*, deeply compelling. In fact, it seemed as if the book was not only speaking to them but also about them. Unlike his comic books, however, Uncle Rıfkı regretted this book, which had backfired, leading young Turks' lives "off track." Before his death, he had supported the government's ban on the book. Toward the end of the novel, Osman locates and shoots Mehmet with a gun secured from Dr. Fine; Canan marries a well-adjusted doctor called Mehmet, another devotee of the book, and moves to Germany. Osman learns of Dr. Fine's death at the hands of the CIA. He himself dies in a bus accident, after having realized he was a character in a book called *Yeni Hayat*, written by his father's old friend, Uncle Rıfkı.

In its themes, imagery, and language, *Yeni Hayat* is very much a postmodern, post-coup book. Its details are carefully chosen to mark the era as post-1980s Turkey: the dealers' convention is held at Kenan Evren High

School, named after the general who led the coup. A young boy at the convention introduces himself as Michael Jackson (87). The book is also a post-1980 book in its refusal to draw the line between selective and excessive westernizations. Although the novel's drama rests on Uncle Rıfkı's and Dr. Fine's passionate pursuit of these boundaries in ink and blood, the narrator never lets us settle on what constitutes over-westernization and what imports are acceptable. Despite being cast as opposing actors in "the great conspiracy" and "the great counter-conspiracy," both Uncle Rıfkı and Dr. Fine are failed selective westernizers. They are father figures who try to control the future of Turkey vis-à-vis the West, and their deaths imply the futility of such boundary drawing.

Uncle Rıfkı is thoroughly committed to the Kemalist railroad policy and deeply dismayed by the postwar switch to the more dangerous highway system. In the comics he has written for children, he seeks out a synthesis of Western rationality, Islamic values, and Kemalism by placing plucky young Turkish heroes in nineteenth-century American settings. His allegorical stories such as *Nebi in Nebraska* and *Pertev and Peter* seek to influence Turkish children who love American comic books so they will also come to cherish "the ethics and national values that our forefathers have bequeathed to us" (118). In the former comic, Nebi is appointed by the sultan to represent Muslim children at the 1893 Chicago World's Fair and combines forces with a Native American child to save native lands from a conspiracy of "white men who have their eyes on the lands" (116). In the latter, Pertev from Istanbul and Peter from Boston have many adventures around the building of the world's first true transcontinental railroad between 1863 and 1869. Like *Nebi in Nebraska*, which allegorizes the American mandate over Turkey, *Pertev and Peter* recalls the transportation policies of early republican Turkey. "Should the railroad proposition fail," Peter worries in one bubble, "the development of our country will be curtailed, and what people call accident will be a matter of fate" (120). Uncle Rıfkı also claims selective westernization as a specifically Turkish gift to the world. In another bubble, Peter from Boston saves the day by giving "an Ataturk-style speech on secularization, enlightened by the ideas of Westernization which he has learned from Pertev," the Turkish boy (119). Turkey thus ironically westernizes the United States through a local proxy. (Of course, considering how heavily

U.S. modernization theory drew upon the Kemalist precedent, the proposition that westernization is a uniquely Turkish gift to the United States is not all that wrong-headed.)

While we do not have access to Uncle Rıfkı's book for adults, *Yeni Hayat* (unless, of course, it is the book we are holding in our hands), it seems to build on a similar synthesis between the East and the West, incorporating works that include Dante's *La Vita Nuova*, Ib'n Arabi's mystical tomes, Rilke's poetry, selections from the Turkish Ministry of Education's world classics series, as well as translated pop culture books on ornithology and geniuses. However, unlike Uncle Rıfkı's straightforwardly allegorical works, *Yeni Hayat* is a new kind of allegorical book—perhaps a postmodern one—that drives its young readers insane and sets them on impossible quests. Tellingly, it is Uncle Rıfkı's selectively westernized comics that lead to the rapture of young adults, who believe *Yeni Hayat* is addressing them because they recognize in it things both familiar and uncanny.

Those against the book, led by Dr. Fine, are also authoritarian westernizers, although they disagree with Uncle Rıfkı on what constitutes excessive westernization. While Uncle Rıfkı is interested in ideologies of mobility, Dr. Fine focuses on matter and time, fighting objects that have streamed into the country after the post-coup switch to a free-market economy. "Dull and flat stuff that was displayed in odorless, colorless stores," according to Dr. Fine, damages Turks' sense of time and erases Turkish collective memory (127). Thus, Dr. Fine and his dealers refuse to carry the new American exports in their dusty stores, selling only old goods produced by the pre-1980s state or Cold War era Soviet and East German products. According to Dr. Fine, mass printed matter similarly displaces the handwritten tomes filled with congealed time and human effort; thus, though a few exceptions can be made for education, most printed works, particularly those "soulless" texts like *Yeni Hayat*, must be banned and their authors and readers shot.

However, like all selective westernizers, Dr. Fine resorts to various nonsensical mental acrobatics in explaining why watches and buses and guns are allowable but trains are not. Trains, according to Dr. Fine, are unacceptable due to their timetables, which clash with the timetable for prayers, despite the fact that few policies represent Kemalist statism better than the early republic's public transportation policy. Similarly,

Dr. Fine accepts buses because their accident-prone and unpredictable schedules restore a sense of subjective time, although, as noted, few changes in Turkish daily life are more linked to the United States than postwar Turkey's disaster-ridden, inefficient, and polluting motorway policy.

Uncle Rıfkı and Dr. Fine are not alone in their use of bizarre boundaries and methods to fix selective westernization. The Turkish state in *Yeni Hayat* also seems utterly confused as to the boundaries of acceptable change. The minor state representatives in the book are all quite lost and helpless, unsure of their principles, and unable to stop either the great conspiracy or the great counter-conspiracy. The recirculation of *Yeni Hayat* by unscrupulous police seeking a profit after the ban is a case in point. The nonsense missive the governor of a small town proudly asks Osman to review before the dealers' convention is another one. The statement vows to protect "the statue of Atatürk" along with "the sheiks," even though the Kemalist regime banned sheikhs and their orders, and Islamic orthodoxy frowns upon three-dimensional, representational art apotheosizing humans. The town stork and "conscientious firefighters" are listed in one breath as the national treasures to be protected from the visitors (103). "Who is the angel?" rambles the statement, "And who has the temerity to put the angel up for ridicule on TV? . . . Was it for this that Atatürk chased out the Greek army?" Unlike in *Sodom ve Gomore*, this passionate historical reference to the War of Independence falls flat, made into gibberish by all that came before.

The novel clearly carries a wounded sense of being on the periphery, of being left out, and of being moved by forces outside of its characters' control, but there is no clear solution, no Rakım to follow as an example. The attempts to define westernization persistently backfire, leading young people off track, as Uncle Rıfkı's book does, or make them turn to violence, as Dr. Fine's organization advocates. Characters outside the conspiracies are no more commendable. They sense a conspiracy having to do with the United States, but are simply unhappily resigned to whatever happens. One utilitarian bystander explains his stance:

Every rock you lift, there they are, the Americans. Sure it's sad to realize we will never be ourselves again but mature assessment may save us from disaster. So our sons and grandsons no longer understand us, so what? Civilizations come and civilizations go. (95)

In its sexual politics, too, *Yeni Hayat* blurs the conventions of selective and excessive westernization. The narrator refuses to blame Canan for Osman's troubles, although Osman admits that his life had gone off track "on account of love not the book" (204). In fact, there is little difference between love and the book, as both are opaque seductive forces intimately connected to Osman's own imagination. Inspired by Dante's Beatrice and by the Beloved of Sufi tales, Canan seems to be an allegorical figure—yet what she symbolizes is difficult to fix. As Osman notes early on, Canan's name not only means soul mate, but also implies "God" in Sufi literature (39). Yet we see a picture of her as a little girl wearing an angel's costume, "whose every detail down to the tiny wings was appropriated from the West" (36). Of course, Dante himself was inspired by the Sufi tradition, particularly the trope of the *miraj*—Prophet Muhammad's symbolic night journey to the heavens.[138] Pamuk uses such cycles of transculturation and indigenization to further complicate the selective/excessive westernization dichotomy.

Canan, as a character, is so idealized by Osman as to be incredibly vague. She is soulful and kind; she wears long skirts that remind Osman of an idealistic young teacher; yet she is far from the properly westernized woman found in Halide Edib's novels, given her extensive roaming and her extramarital relationship with Mehmet. Osman's and Mehmet's names also insist on some kind of allegorical puzzle. Osman's name is both a play on Orhan (as in Orhan Pamuk) and on *Osmanlı İmparatorluğu* (the Ottoman Empire, in Turkish); Mehmet is the Turkish form of Muhammad. Yet any attempt to arrive at a clear allegorical formula based on these facts will fail to capture the complexities of the novel. As such, Orhan Pamuk's *Yeni Hayat* fits what Neil Larsen has identified as the postmodern tradition of allegory in the Third World novel, with its "characters whose national-allegorical representativity is so complicated and ironized as to be made virtually impossible."[139] In other words, it is both what Fredric Jameson has identified as a national allegory and one among a series of Turkish novels whose protagonists rebel against the figurative impetus of state nationalism, as Sibel Irzık theorizes.

Literary selective westernization (and, as its centerpiece, the Turkish novel) started as a movement to secure boundaries between useful mobility and aimless mobility, between appropriate gender relations and over-westernized sexualities and irrational loves, and between the novel as the bearer of a disenchanted worldview and mystical allegory. The postmodern novel and traditional Sufi literature, on the other hand, share an interest in the dissolution of boundaries between self and other, author and protagonist, utilitarian movement and passivity. *Yeni Hayat*, like the eponymous text at its center, stems from simplistic national allegories of Turkish literature just as Uncle Rıfkı's complex book stems from his allegorical comics. Yet, unlike its forebears, it refuses to recommend a metanarrative as cure for the troubles of wild-westernized Turkey. The novel contains countless conspiracies and counter-conspiracies, but refuses either to take them seriously or to dismiss them entirely. It depicts characters in endless movement but opens up only the vaguest possibilities of compromise-filled progress. Love rules the book through and through, yet it is neither romanticized nor decried. The novel's language mixes the mundane and the sublime; its imagery combines the realities of life on the periphery of the market economy with age-old Sufi sensibilities. It is not clear that *Yeni Hayat* (whether by Orhan Pamuk or by Uncle Rıfkı) can even be called a novel. This is especially true if we take Osman at his word:

> So, Reader, place your faith neither in a character like me, who is not all that sensitive, nor in my anguish and the violence of the story I have to tell; but believe that the world is a cruel place. Besides, this newfangled plaything called the novel, which is the greatest invention of Western culture, is none of our culture's business.[140]

The 2006 Nobel Prize committee agreed with Orhan Pamuk on one thing: he had transformed this Western invention beyond recognition. As one committee member put it, Pamuk had "stolen" the novel from Westerners and had transformed it into "something different from what [they] had ever seen before."[141] As the novel had been the poster child of Turkish selective westernization and nationalism, worldwide success in this genre by a Turk should have pleased nationalists. Orhan Pamuk's

2006 Nobel win, however, was met with grumbles instead of nationalist celebration in Turkey.

Never a proponent of literature *engagée*, Orhan Pamuk had become controversial in Turkey a year earlier due to comments he had made to the Western press regarding mass murders of Kurds and Armenians.[142] A hate campaign began, bolstered by a notorious court case accusing him of "insulting Turkishness" based on a 2005 article of the Turkish penal code. Critics attacked him for his public comments as well as his books, decrying him as "an Orientalist" who "plays for the West."[143] His opponents accused him of supporting "imperialist forces who want to undermine the country and divide it," utilizing historical memories of the post–World War I Sèvres Treaty and the American mandate.[144] Like Halide Edib, Pamuk was accused of being a decadent, westoxicated crypto-Jew, out of touch with the sentiments of "real" Turks. Conspiracy theories spread like wildfire, and extremists threatened to annihilate his books, in a strange case of life replicating art. Socioeconomic changes of the 1980s had made Orhan Pamuk's novels possible both in theme and style, but his Nobel win coincided with increased mistrust of neoliberalism and rising anti-Western sentiments in Turkey, fueled by the 2003 U.S. invasion of Iraq and endless bottlenecks in Turkey's application for membership in the European Union. Orhan Pamuk became a *cause célèbre* in the West at the wrong time, and the famous novelist came to be read as a westoxicated figure reminiscent of the protagonists of so many Turkish novels.

As Pamuk was being attacked for his alleged over-westernization, a new kind of novel banking on rising anti-Americanism was on the rise in Turkey: ultranationalist mass-market books attempting to redraw the boundaries of westernization in form and content had begun appearing on bookstore shelves. Orhan Pamuk's postmodern success notwithstanding, best-sellers like *Metal Fırtına* (The metal storm, 2004), which envisions an American invasion of Turkey, showed that the debate on the limits of westernization in Turkey was far from over. These novels resemble nationalist realist fiction of the early republican era in their obsession with mobility, sexualized treachery, and over-westernization. However, beyond simply echoing Kemalist history writing, they merge the past with the near future and allegorical figures with real-life characters, like so many *Sodom ve Gomores* on steroids.

Metal Fırtına, a fast-paced action novel, features real-life American personalities like George W. Bush and Donald Rumsfeld as characters and advances a preexisting popular conspiracy theory: that the United States will invade Turkey for its generous boron reserves. In the novel, this plot is revealed when an intrepid Turkish spy discovers a folder with pages of information on the boron reserves in Turkey, which the U.S. government has identified as the energy source of the future. Also included in the folder is the copy of a contract in which the U.S. government sells the rights to extract the boron in Turkey to Ornicron, a Texas-based mining firm, for 99 years, as of December 2007. There are also documents implying ties with evangelical missionary groups and suggesting that once the United States gets what it wants, the rest of the land will be divided between Armenians, Kurds, and Greeks. The spy muses on the implications of the plan:

> Countries, religious organizations, lobbies were involved in this. Soon after a shock invasion, Anatolia would be posited as a holy land to be rescued from "barbarian" Turks, and the American Army would be the hero of a belated Crusade. In fact, had not President Bush said, "we have begun a Crusade" after the attacks of 9/11? Afghanistan, Iraq and now, finally, Turkey! Except, the difference in the case of Turkey was that it would be directly under the rule of America.[145]

This historical nightmare/fantasy of Turkey becoming a colony of the United States, aided by forces from within and without, echoes the popular mythology of the American mandate, explored in chapter 1. *Metal Fırtına* also mimics Mustafa Kemal's *Nutuk* in its obsession with nonfiction evidence and reference to primary documents, combined with a hyperbolic tone. The novel mobilizes its readers against the imagined U.S. invasion with short, action-packed chapters that echo Hollywood blockbusters, just as the republican Turkish novels sought to employ formal selective westernization (i.e., the progress-driven form of the novel) to develop the discourse of over-westernization. Like them, the novel colors westoxication in the language of gender, sexuality, class, and ethnicity, and depicts decadent Istanbulites as groupies of the U.S. invasion.

Unlike *Yeni Hayat*, and like the early republican novels, *Metal Fırtına* clearly views mobility as a matter of power and love as a superficial distraction. The elite underground Turkish forces, of which the intrepid spy is a member, who help liberate Turkey are forbidden to marry and must undergo strenuous training. This training ends when they shoot the puppies they have raised with their own hands. (It is highly unlikely that the authors are familiar with Ahmet Haşim's early twentieth-century criticism of the dissection of pets as a sign of westoxication at the American College for Girls.)

However suspect its ideology and amateurish its style, the novel does constitute a formal innovation; its vision of an alternative near future has no precedent in Turkey.[146] As the passage quoted above shows, the novel also pushes the boundaries of realism; it cites real people and events and hails the reader in a clear colloquial tone reminiscent of the patronizing Ahmed Mithat. Yet the novel's formal innovations do not stem from its denial of metanarratives and the idea of Truth. Instead, the text posits itself as truth. Like *Yeni Hayat*, *Metal Fırtına* is a novel of conspiracy theories, except, in this case, the novel upholds them. Like Orhan Pamuk, its authors question the label "novel," yet they do so for different reasons. "From our point of view," the authors were quoted as saying, "it's a philosophical and scientific calculation. It's more than a novel."[147]

More than a novel: this is what the Turkish novel has been since its very beginnings. The novel was imported as a tool of selective westernization into the Ottoman Empire and thus became symbolically connected to the idea of "the West" (in both good and bad connotations) from the beginning. The allegorical discourse of over-westernization, with its double themes of love and mobility, constituted a new problem and creative possibility for the Turkish novel, becoming its driving force in the late nineteenth century. Over-westernization gained new cadences throughout the twentieth century, absorbing changes to gender norms and the rise of the United States as a world power. Accelerated transculturation sparked a renaissance for the Turkish novel, both toward the end of the nineteenth century and after the coup of 1980. This has led to critically acclaimed, formally and thematically innovative texts. In the early twenty-first century, Orhan Pamuk won the Nobel Prize for his complex novels that jumbled the genre, even as hyperrealist and ultranationalist novels like *Metal Fırtına* pushed against genre boundaries for different reasons.

In Turkey, the local manifestation of national allegory has meant that novelists have long operated as political figures and novels as semi-official historical commentaries. Figures of over-westernization criss-cross between state histories like Kemal's *Nutuk* and literary texts like *Sodom ve Gomore*. The novel, however, has exceeded both history writing and authoritarian westernization. First written by intellectuals with ties to the state, the Turkish novel might have started out as a project of selective westernization, yet it inevitably diverged from the state's goals. Instead, even pre-republican novels such as *Araba Sevdası* reveal cracks in the state's ability to determine the limits of westernization. Turkish novelists have mobilized alternative cultural memories, challenging (as in *Amerikan Sargısı*) or deconstructing (as in *Yeni Hayat*) the allegorical figures of love and mobility official U.S. and Turkish policies have sought to fix. Literature owes this power to its ability to incorporate folk forms and to both represent and be transformed by vernacular transcultura-tion, explored in depth in the next chapter.

Under-Westernization

Humoring English

Wild Westernization and Anti-American Folklore

During the first months of 2009, I received several forwarded emails with
a link to a webpage titled "Türk Olmak" (Being Turkish).[1] The site featured random humorous photographs: signs with false translations,
funny misspellings, and instances of everyday wit. One image featured
the back of a black car with a makeshift bumper sticker placed above the
name of the car model ("Caddy"), spelling "Kara Caddy." This sticker sub-
verted the English name of a German-made vehicle with a bilingual pun:
Kara means black in Turkish, and the car model, Caddy, is a near homo-
phone of the Turkish word *kedi*, meaning cat. Its owner had rechristened
this car "Black Cat." This improvised bumper sticker references the local
truck, minibus, and taxi driver (*şöför*) tradition of humorous and/or am-
orous vehicle writings, but with a signal difference: only individuals
who are familiar with the English pronunciation of the letters c-a-d-d-y
will get this joke, because the same letters will read as nonsense to any
monolingual Turk. This is bilingual Turkish humor, or "Turklish" humor, consisting of a variety of folkloric and vernacular genres and subgenres, such as riddles, jokes, false translations, mock lyrics to popular
songs, and even lengthy love stories.

Often dependent on homophonic puns and substitutions (e.g., caddy/
kedi), such texts require various degrees of familiarity with the English
and Turkish languages, as well as with Turkish and Anglo-American

cultures, for comprehension. Their humor depends, in part, on "rebellion against linguistic conformity," that is, against linguistic rules and conventions, including those that require individuals to use a single language in any one communication.[2] However, each item can also be politically potent in other ways. Currently, no car produced in Turkey has a Turkish brand name, despite the many multinational automobile factories operating in the country. By rechristening this car in Turklish, the owner publicly claims a linguistic ground that has been lost along with Turkey's first "Turkish" car, built in 1961 and called Devrim (Revolution).[3] This reclaiming of the road should resonate in a country in which (auto) mobility has historically been inflected by ideas of both selective and excessive westernization, as explored in depth in chapter 2.

The website of the famous Association for the Defense of the French Language also includes pictures of English-language signs peppering the French urban landscape; however, their site is not titled playfully ("being French"), but catastrophically as *"Musée des horreurs"* (Museum of horrors).[4] Such linguistic nationalism is also present in Turkey. The state-sponsored Turkish Language Association (TLA), for example, is committed to protecting "the integrity of Turkish" and discouraging Turklish. However, the compilation of jokes like "Kara Caddy" on an Internet site called "Being Turkish," and the 2006 publication of a popular humorous best-seller on Turkish vernacular culture with the Turklish title *The Türkler* ("The" Turks), both point to an alternative relation between English and national identity.[5] What does "being Turkish" have to do with publicly playing with English? How do we theorize the complex mixture of nationalist affect, linguistic merging, and bicultural fluency displayed by such texts? What drives the Kara Caddy?

Taking its cue from Linda Dégh's groundbreaking study of folklore and popular media, this chapter builds on a broad archive of published and online texts, bolstered by texts I have collected and conversations I have had with Turks who use bilingual humor.[6] I chronicle the rise of Turklish humor, summarize the political discussions around language and folklore in Turkey, and examine the uses of bilingual humor at a time of increasing tensions with the United States. As with history writing and the novel, language and folklore became targets and tools of selective westernization in Kemalist Turkey; yet they have proven even more difficult to control. Despite the state's continued investment in it, folk humor does not represent pure, "authentic" Turkishness. Instead, everyday folk culture is prone to cycles of transculturation and indigenization. Authored collectively, disseminated informally, and existing in multiple versions, folklore is often more difficult to police than official, elite, or mass media texts, and may harbor "hidden transcripts" at odds with hegemonic ideologies.[7] These unique qualities of vernacular humor make it an alternative, indispensable archive for considering the intersections of culture and politics.

U.S. representatives in Turkey have historically encouraged the circulation of American media and boosted English language education in the country. Between the wars, the United States even refused to pursue copyright regulations for American comic books to prevent Turks from adopting "cultural influences which they find more readily available instead."[8] During the Cold War, American representatives read the rising Turkish interest in American cultural products and English as signs of the proper shifting of civilizational loyalties from France to the United States (and, of course, away from the Soviet Union). This constituted a central truism of the so-called American century as "a particular logic of the circulation of capital, signs, texts, and cultural goods," which associated the spread of American popular culture with political gains.[9] The absorption of English into the Turkish vernacular, however, has not meant a wholesale adoption of mainstream American culture. As in "Kara Caddy," the humor of Turklish often stems from the incongruous interaction of indigenized cultural components with elements that carry symbolic associations with "the West." Nor does the use of Turklish necessarily imply consent to U.S. foreign policy goals for the region. As I explore later in this chapter, most recently, secularist activists have been using bilingual humor to challenge American constructions of Turkey as a "moderate Muslim" ally in the War on Terror.

An embrace, however ambivalent, of English and U.S. popular culture became central to the practice of certain gendered and classed forms of Turkishness in the twentieth century. Vernacular Turklish texts reveal a collective willingness to "signify" or "talk back" to an American-accented global media culture that seems bewilderingly near but frustratingly unidirectional. A big part of this enterprise is the rewriting of American tropes, including the figure of the Wild West, in order to underline the violent aspects of U.S. cultural expansion. Such humor regularly employs "uncivilized" stock characters, such as Temel the Fisherman, whose animalistic masculinity challenges both authoritarian state projects and U.S. dominance. Combining hegemonic and counter-hegemonic elements, bilingual humor also reinforces class divides between those who can joke in English/Turklish and those presumed to resemble the under-westernized stock figures from such jokes.

ENCOUNTERING THE OTHER'S LANGUAGE: FROM ARABIC TO ENGLISH

Encounters with a foreign language have long been a significant part of folklore worldwide. Transnational folk humor contains many examples of numbskull jests and anecdotes, in which the presence of a foreign language drives the plot. These simple tales often depend on a single narrative motif marked by cultural and linguistic ruptures in communication, "absurd misunderstandings," or outright deceptions.[10] In fact, almost all previously recorded instances of foreign-language humor imply miscommunication and belittle the presumptuous act of wanting to learn a foreign language. In the Indo-European motif K317.1, for example, the stereotypical fool is tricked into buying two jars of live black wasps as interpreters of a foreign language.[11] In motif K137.2, the numbskull ends up purchasing a parrot familiar with only two foreign-language words, believing it is a fluent speaker of a foreign language he himself does not know. In other tales, insufficient competency in foreign language causes innocent travelers to incriminate themselves as robbers (Aarne-Thompson-Uther Tale Type [ATU] 1697) or mix up polite words with insults (ATU 1322, Motif j1802; ATU 1699).[12] The wish to learn a foreign language can even lead to outright dismemberment: in motif K825, authorities trick petty criminals into holding out their tongues, promising to teach them a foreign language this way. Then they chop the tongues off.[13]

Pre-republican Turkish jocular tradition was equally resistant if not openly antagonistic toward foreigners and the idea of communication in a foreign language. An early tale printed in a sixteenth-century Ottoman manuscript features the classic jocular character Nasreddin Hodja questioning the possibilities for communication with non-Turks:

> Hodja was appointed as an ambassador to Arabia. He took an assistant with him and left. There, at the home of an Arab sheikh dur-

ing a banquet, Hodja suddenly farted very loudly. When they finally left the house, the assistant said, "Oh Hodja, what did you do? You embarrassed us, made us blush with shame!" Hodja replied, "Come on now! How can the Arabs understand a Turkish fart?!"[14]

As folklorists and humor scholars have argued, no matter how "timeless" or "universal" jokes seem, they must be historicized.[15] Although themes, tropes, and even narrative structures often cross temporal and geographical boundaries, a joke can only be understood within its context. David Viktoroff notes, "One never laughs alone—laughter is always the laughter of a particular social group."[16] A North American in the early twenty-first century can certainly appreciate the punch line of this five-hundred-year-old joke. However, in order to fully understand Hodja's gaseous defiance, we must connect it to the many and multilayered Turkish anxieties about language, beginning with the relation of Turkish to Arabic and Persian under Ottoman rule.

As early as the eleventh-century Seljuk dynasty, Turkish intellectuals declared the nomadic Turkish they brought from the steppes of Central Asia to Asia Minor to be poor and embarrassing when compared with the great Persian and Arabic literary traditions. Famous Seljuk poets apologized copiously for having to write in Turkish. Arabic and Persian education soon became the sine qua non of social elevation. The Turkish elements in Ottoman Turkish melted into these two languages, disappearing under not only Persian and Arabic lexical loans, but also actual grammatical structures.[17] The two languages had so saturated the language of elite Turks by the seventeenth century that the Turks of the Ottoman Empire had become a diglossic community. The educated elite called themselves Ottomans and spoke and wrote in "Ottoman"—a language so complex that sometimes the present tense suffix -*dir* was the only Turkic element in these texts.[18] The uneducated or undereducated "Turks" (the word itself operated as an insult implying an uncouth peasant) spoke and generated a lively folklore in a "crude" Turkish that is intelligible today. This diglossic situation sparked its own bilingual humor, reflected in oral traditions like the Turkish shadow puppet theater. Humor in Ottoman Turkish shadow puppetry built on the distinction between the long-winded Ottoman of the educated subjects and the vernacular Turkish spoken on the streets by setting the urbane character

Hacıvat against the crude Karagöz, a man of the people. Karagöz's humorous misunderstandings of Hacıvat's Persian- and Arabic-infused language often led to the latter receiving a sound beating from the former. Karagöz also mocked Hacıvat's genteel speech by replying to his flowery platitudes in rhyming vulgarities.[19]

By equating loud anal emissions with oral communication, the Hodja joke brings language down from its association with the head and rational intercourse and toward the grotesque lower body.[20] It expresses disdain for the civilized opulence of the feast, the untold delicacies of which Hodja's body quickly transforms into a familiar gaseous product. It reinforces ethnic boundaries by suggesting that this gas itself will be as unintelligible to the sophisticated Arab as the latter's opulence was indigestible for the Turk, expressing pride through folksy crudeness. As such, the joke refers to an already established hierarchy between the lowly Turkish and the elegant Arabic language, defiantly reversing the power dynamic, making the head the butt (of the joke).

In contrast to Arabic and Persian, the Ottoman Turkish relation to Western languages developed later, within the context of a balkanizing empire threatened by European invasion in the nineteenth century. In the 1820s, with Arabic and Persian serving as standards in basic Ottoman education, no Muslim Turk spoke a European language. This is not an exaggeration: until the beginning of the Greek rebellion in 1821, the Ottoman authorities had relied almost exclusively on the empire's Christian minorities to translate communications with Europe. The Ottoman word for translator, from the Arabic *turjuman* (translator), itself had become "entangled in histories of betrayal."[21] When the so-called "dragoman crisis" of the early 1820s left the government scrambling for official interpreters, the state could not find a single Muslim Turk with sufficient knowledge of any Western language.[22] In response to the crisis and the growing necessity of communication with an increasingly powerful Europe, Sultan Mahmut II founded the Translation Bureau in April 1821. Initially a minor office, the bureau became a significant cultural force, generating a local intellectual elite by the mid-nineteenth century.[23]

In the age of European imperialism and scientific racism, mistrust of Western institutions and cultural influence repeatedly clashed with the advantages foreign-language fluency and a secular education could

provide, reflecting a constant negotiation of the linguistic boundaries between selective and excessive westernization. Even when members of
the Turkish elite placed their sons at foreign-run educational institutions
in the hope of easing their social climb, their presence led to agitation. In
the 1880s and 1890s, Sultan Abdulhamid II forced Turkish students at
foreign schools to leave them. Turkish students at the French-language
Galatasaray Lyceum rebelled on their own accord against the school
administration, with the accusation that their native language was being slighted. Students in the military and medical schools also peri-
odically demanded that the language of instruction be changed from
French to Turkish.[24] The few Muslim girls educated in Western languages, like the Turkish intellectual Halide Edib, also risked the stigma
of "over-westernization."

The "Sick Man of Europe"—as the Brits dubbed the Ottoman
Empire—died in 1923, speaking late Ottoman and writing in the Perso-
Arabic alphabet. Between 1923 and 1948, Mustafa Kemal Atatürk and his
nationalist cadre successfully executed a series of reform laws related to
language, including the translation of the call to prayer into Turkish from
Arabic; the Law of Surnames, which mandated all citizens to adopt
Turkish-language last names; and the replacement of Arabic numerals
with their Western equivalents. The 1928 alphabet reform, which instituted a new Latin-based Turkish alphabet to replace the Perso-Arabic
alphabet, however, was the most massive of such reforms, making possible the eradication of hundreds of Persian and Arabic words and the
construction of a new Turkish language for the new nation. On October 1, 1928, foreign-language education in Persian and Arabic ended for
good. In 1929, it became illegal to write Turkish in the Arabic script except for scholarly purposes. The Turkish Language Association (TLA),
founded in 1932, guided the further "purification" of the language, purging dictionaries of words of Arabic or Persian origin and publishing lists
of new "pure" (öz) Turkish words for adoption. Currently, most Turks
know little or no Arabic except for a few basic Qur'anic *suras* (verses)
memorized for use in the daily prayers. In the spirit of Hodja, they could
not understand an Arabic fart.

The alphabet revolution had a salubrious effect on Turkish–American
relations, strained as they were by decades of racist propaganda about
the "terrible Turk" and the attendant U.S. failure to sign the Lausanne

Treaty recognizing the Republic of Turkey. Atatürk's strategic western-izing reforms generally received positive coverage in the U.S. media. Pun-dits saw the alphabet reform in particular as a welcome civilizational shift, bringing Turkey closer to the United States and confirming West-ern, even specifically American, cultural superiority.[25] In January 1929, *National Geographic* magazine—the bible of the liberal American internationalist—published a charming narrative of a once moribund land that had exchanged "the sword" for "the pen" in search of "enlight-enment." The author, Maynard Owen Williams, expressed his appre-ciation of the resulting "less forbidding" environment for the Western eye. For Williams, the alphabet reform and other selective westerniza-tion measures functioned as signs that Turkey, once "nominated as an American mandate," was now proving an eager pupil, "adopting changes which no foreign tutor would dare impose."[26] The public celebration of the language revolution in such middlebrow American media matched the approving tone of classified reports by American diplomats working in Turkey in the late 1920s and early 1930s.[27] For these representatives, Kemal's speedy execution of these reforms demonstrated a proper coun-terbalance to the "lethargic nature of the Turk."[28]

The links between Western-language fluency and treason in Turk-ish cultural history and memory, developed in the ethnically fractured Ottoman Empire, however, continued to haunt the new republic's selec-tive westernization projects. For three months in 1924, the Turkish gov-ernment hosted American philosopher and educational reformer John Dewey, who presented the state with a report containing suggestions for Turkish education. Among the suggestions was greater cooperation with foreign schools, like Robert College and the American College for Girls, which were already in Turkey.[29] The same year, however, Müfide Ferid Tek's allegorical novel *Pervaneler* warned readers that while Turks may enter American-run schools, they will not leave them as Turks.[30] Under the 1924 Law of Education, French, English, and German replaced Ara-bic and Persian as the primary foreign languages in Turkish schools.[31] The percentage of Muslim Turkish students among all students in for-eign schools also rose to 51 percent in 1926, from practically none in 1890. The Kemalist government, however, rejected Halide Edib's plans to se-cure U.S. aid for a new chain of American colleges in Anatolia.[32] When three Turkish girls studying at the Bursa American College for Girls allegedly converted to Christianity in 1928, they sparked a nationalist hysteria.[33] A series of inspections and new regulations followed. While most American schools were allowed to operate with some changes to their curriculum and hiring practices, the government also authorized the establishment of new English-language schools "to save Turkish children from having to attend foreign institutions to learn foreign languages," applying selective westernization to control over-westernization once again.[34]

Although Americans saw their alphabet in Kemalist reform, actual U.S. influence on Turkish language policy remained limited until the end of World War II. Education in Western languages stayed the prerogative of a handpicked few: the urban elite and Anatolian youth who passed the competitive state exams and studied in Europe on government funds for the purpose of uplifting the nation upon their return. These chosen citizens predominantly learned French or German. Even when the university reform of 1933 made knowledge of a European language a prerequisite for study at a university, French continued to dominate the curriculum. English as a foreign language (EFL) education constituted only about 10 percent of foreign-language instruction in 1938, trailing behind both French (70 percent) and German (20 percent).[35] Famous Turkish humorist Aziz Nesin (1915–1995) recalled in 1968:

> When I was a child, people in the mighty city of Istanbul would point with their fingers at anyone who could speak English. . . . Whenever the pupils were divided into groups for the various foreign languages, there would not be a single person wanting to register for English. English instruction had been introduced in schools, but no teachers could be found for this language.[36]

English, therefore, had little influence on Turkish until the end of World War II, after which it began to dominate foreign-language education, on the heels of a "golden" age in Turkish–American relations. The reasons for this sea change include the fading of French cultural influence in the Middle East after World War II, Turkey's close alliance with the United States due to the implementation of the Truman Doctrine and the Marshall Plan, the opportunities of the Fulbright Act, the stationing of NATO forces in Turkey, and the mobilization of Peace Corps youths as English teachers in even the remotest Turkish provinces.[37] Working in tandem with such government-sponsored policies were bilateral friendship associations, which sought to counter the possibilities of a Turkish turn toward communism with cultural events and language classes. In the 1953–1954 educational year, English overtook French for the first time.[38]

The Cold War alliance, also called the "strategic partnership," would be strained several times throughout the mid- and late twentieth century. However, even serious quakes in foreign policy had little influence on the rise of English as a foreign language in Turkey. The number of middle school and high school students learning English increased fifty-sevenfold between 1950 and 1985.[39] The same period generated the first examples of Turklish humor I was able to collect. In fact, the first use of the term *Türkilizce* (Turklish) can be traced to the mid-1970s.[40] After the coup of 1980, under Turgut Özal's leadership, American cultural products began flooding the country, further increasing the presence of English in the Turkish milieu. Currently, English education is widespread in Turkish private primary schools, private and state-run secondary schools, and institutions of higher education, including the many English-medium state universities and private universities, which do not just teach English as a foreign language but also conduct education in English. The number of schools and universities in which the medium of instruction is predominantly English is increasing. Since 1998, four hours of English to five hours of Turkish language education has been compulsory in sixth, seventh, and eighth grades, even in regular state schools.[41]

With English having taken over from Arabic, Persian, and French as the privileged intruder into the vernacular, modern jokes about Anglo-American linguistic and material dominance echo the insolence Hodja expressed toward the opulent Arab sheik centuries ago. Temel, an ethnic Laz fisherman from the Black Sea region of Turkey, is a wise fool character like Nasreddin Hodja and, unlike Hodja, is a very common protagonist in many modern language jokes. The trope of flatulence as communicative challenge, for example, appears in the following Temel joke, collected in 1995:

Temel buys himself a cell phone. He proudly places it on the table where he is holding a meeting with a Japanese and an American businessman. During the meeting, a phone rings and the American begins talking into his hand, showing off and putting on airs [*hava atmak*, lit. throwing air]. Suddenly the Japanese man's telephone rings, and he begins talking into his own mouth, putting on airs, saying a computer chip he had planted inside a tooth allows for communication. Temel, who is upset at this situation, farts very loudly at some point. When the American and the Japanese man ask what happened, he answers, "I've just sent a fax."[42]

This joke comes from an era in which communication is controlled not only by language skills but also via technology. On this front, too, Turks seem to be trailing behind not only the United States but also a supposedly non-Western nation like Japan. The inclusion of Japan breaks the binaries of the West and the East, but leaves the logic of selective westernization intact. Turks have long coveted Japan's success in attaining Western status. Writing as early as 1923, Ziya Gökalp complained, "Japan is accepted as a European power, but we are still regarded as an Asiatic nation."[43] In the Information Age, marked by a decentralization of symbolic modernity, Temel can only "throw air" by literally passing gas, like Hodja did in the age of Arab cultural dominance.

FROM HUMOR ABOUT LANGUAGE TO BILINGUAL HUMOR

Like Ottoman Turkish attitudes toward Arabic and French, modern Turkish attitudes toward English are complex, tinged with envy and anxiety, admiration and disdain. Language jokes, therefore, constitute a fertile medium for the expression of complex cultural transcripts about the intrusion of English and American culture into the modern Turkish milieu. In one category are jokes that refuse to acknowledge and simply ridicule the foreign signs. In another are jokes that engage (or "humor") the foreign language, creating hybrids that require various levels of bilingual competency for comprehension. The trope of testing appears frequently in both kinds of jokes, expressing anxieties connected to educational (and, therefore, financial) success in a globalizing, neoliberal world. In the first instance, foreign-language tests are rejected and testers outwitted. In more complex jokes, on the other hand, the humor itself functions as a bilingual and bicultural literacy test.

Many Turkish-language jokes demonstrate an outright resistance to education in the new lingua franca, and even to communication with those who have English as their native tongue. In one joke, Temel complains to his English teacher, "What kind of thing is this, you write this word as 'come,' you read it as 'kam,' but how do you understand that it means *gel* ['come' in Turkish]?"[44] In another tale, Temel seems even more hostile. Rowing his boat, he refuses to save a drowning tourist, responding to his cries of "Help!" with a snide, "[Y]ou should have learned to swim instead of learning English." In both of these jokes, Turkish serves as the norm and English is something that is always learned—a nonsensical, elite luxury. Characteristically, Temel speaks with a very peculiar Black Sea region accent in these jokes, which reminds the hearer or reader that he holds a marginalized position even vis-à-vis standard Turkish.

Temel's class-based and ethnic liminality allows the joke teller to enjoy two laughs in one—the first at Temel's expense and a larger one with him at the expense of the overcivilized, effete West. Temel's ignorance makes him a butt of the jokes to a certain extent; he refuses to understand that different languages simply have different signifiers for similar signifieds, and he believes anyone speaking English must have learned it while neglecting more essential life skills such as swimming. Yet Temel is also the hero of the jokes, the mouthpiece of folksy rebellion. Unlike the joke teller, he can refuse both the primacy and the necessity of English in a cultural environment that presents English competency as the apex of educational achievement and a necessary life skill.

Other texts demonstrate an outright resistance to the idea of being tested for foreign-language knowledge. For example, Temel, when asked how many "l's" there are in the English language song "Happy Birthday," replies there are ten "l's" and explains his ridiculous answer by singing, "*lal lal lal la lal la.*"[45] Although this again creates an opportunity to laugh at Temel's ignorance, such instances of nonsense verbal play can also be interpreted as a way of protesting the obvious arbitrariness of a new language that has come to saturate the cultural environment in postwar, particularly post-1980s, Turkey. Here musical play operates like the gas in the previous Hodja and Temel jokes, equating the foreign language with noncommunicative ramblings that merely resemble language. The protagonist uses traditional folkloric wit to overcome the newly instituted linguistic literacy test. The question remains unanswered and the testers receive a mocking for glorifying an unfamiliar set of signs over local ones.

Folkloric humor featuring the outright rejection of foreign languages is a cross-cultural phenomenon. Yet equally important and perhaps richer as a source for analysis are bilingual texts, like "Kara Caddy," which engage the foreign language at different levels, through puns and homophonic substitutions. Although important intellectual foundations exist within studies of diasporic and borderlands (particularly Latinx) communities, bilingual folklore remains under-collected and -analyzed in transnational American studies.[46] Even in folkloristics, there is a surprising dearth of research on bilingual humor, especially on linguistic mixing between languages from noncontiguous areas and within nonimmigrant communities. Hasan El-Shamy's work, reporting instances of bilingual humor from the Middle East and North Africa under new motif classifications, including X1915, "Humor based on cross-lingual puns (phonetic similarities between words of different languages)," and Z96, "Cross-lingual puns (based on phonetic similarities)," unfortunately remains an exception.[47]

Bilingual folklore involving English is quite common among many age groups, and equally understudied, in Turkey. One example involves the following riddling question, which was circulating in Istanbul's private primary schools in the early 1990s:

—*Türkiye'nin en çok araba olan şehri hangisidir?*
[What city in Turkey has the most automobiles?]
—*Kars.* [Pronounced "cars."]

As a riddle based on punning and wordplay, this item can be classified further as belonging to the folkloric subgenre "conundrum."[48] Its humor depends on a bilingual pun on the eastern Anatolian city of Kars and the plural noun meaning automobiles in English. The riddle is tricky not just due to linguistic complexity, but also for sociohistorical reasons: despite a rich history, Kars is not one of the most industrialized and populous cities in the republic. Situated on Turkey's northeastern border, it has benefited little from republican selective westernization. Thus the humorous incongruity here depends on the strong association of cars with modernity and Turkey's eastern regions with inadequate modernization.

Another particularly popular joke includes the question, *"Erkek erkeğe yenen yemeğe ne denir?"* (What does one call the food that is eaten among men?) and the answer *"menemen"* (a type of omelet), which builds a complex bilingual pun on the English word "men" and the Turkish suffix "e" (-to), resulting in a cross-lingual phrase which means "men-to-men," i.e., among men. I have heard this item multiple times from both men and women since the 1990s, and finally even saw it as a viral Internet meme on social media in 2016. Since menemen is a very easy dish to make, this joke comments on Turkish men's stereotypically inadequate cooking abilities, both mocking and celebrating local hypermasculinity. The humor also stems from the incongruity of associating a very humble, traditional dish with a cosmopolitan language.

Although the figurative binary opposition between the East/provincial (Kars; menemen) and the West/global (cars; "men") drives the incongruity and the humor, undetected palimpsestic processes of hybridization and indigenization also undergird these texts. Structurally, such joking questions, as opposed to true riddles, are a relatively new development for Turkish vernacular culture: in 1973, folklorist İlhan Başgöz estimated that direct questions formed only about 0.5 percent of all traditional Turkish riddles, and noted that most of these are "religious test questions."[49] The stripped-down question/answer format, therefore, carries a history of vernacular transculturation, connected to the rise of the so-called "urban joke" as a simplified, sharpened, formulaic item available for commercialization.[50] As Wickberg demonstrates, this structural shift was closely tied to the rise of professional joke writers ("gag men") in the early twentieth-century United States.[51] As the twentieth century progressed, riddling questions posed in direct sentences became increasingly common in Turkey as well, disseminated in humor sections of popular newspapers, mass-market joke books, and orally in social settings.[52] In both texts cited above, the joking question format has become largely indigenized and no longer appears "tethered to an imaginary master signifier called America," while the English content furthers symbolic connections to the United States as a foil to the local.[53] This complex interaction of cross-cultural merging and symbolic differentiation in even the most basic text reveals the irony of any search for ethno-national purity in folklore.

Selective westernization, designed to control the sociocultural, can easily unleash unexpected, "wild" developments. Diachronically and cross-culturally, a great deal of language play has followed on the heels of standardized language education. As the bulk of Ottoman education was based on Arabic and Persian, the literate classes generated a kind of bilingual humor by concocting fake Ottoman phrases, placing everyday Turkish words into elevated Persian and Arabic grammar and syntax.[54] As the nineteenth century progressed, French–Turkish hybrids came to feature as well.[55] The 1896 novel *Araba Sevdası*, for example, depicts humorous misunderstandings between the dandy Bihruz and his acquaintances, due to the former's insistence on speaking *Turkçais*.[56] Karagöz shadow puppetry and Ottoman humor magazines also regularly lampooned French linguistic influence on the upper classes.[57] Turklish humor, similarly, both stems from a post–World War II educational system that mandates English-language education and comments on it.

In Europe, and to a lesser extent in the United States, Latin historically embodied the role of arbitrary language forced upon young people in the name of education, thus becoming the focus of much bilingual folklore. American humorist Willard R. Espy recorded the following item in his 1972 collection titled *The Game of Words*, stating that he learned it "while struggling with Latin verbs" in college. He and his schoolmates passed the note "from hand to hand," along with the witty comment that the script on it was found "in diggings in Roman ruins":

Civili derego fortibus inero
Demes nobus demes trux.

When sounded out, this sophisticated ancient text turns out to be nothing but a casual chat between two country bumpkins about passing vehicles:

"See Willy, dere dey go, forty buses in a row."
"Dem is no buses, dem is trucks."[58]

This item, like a great deal of Turklish folklore, builds on the incongruity of a "high" foreign language with the low vernacular in both form and content. Containing serious-sounding words like "civili," "demes," and "fortibus," the Latin surface text appears both civil and political. The homophonic "redneck" translation, on the other hand, depicts rural simpletons who are simply impressed by the large number of vehicles passing their town. What's more, these men do not even know what kind of vehicles they are observing. Here the rednecks function as the other to the Western modern, as Temel does in Turkish jokes, creating a type of humor that exploits working-class masculinities to attack an overcivilized, unpractical foreign culture.

This is a _macaronic_ text, defined broadly as "language, especially burlesque verse, containing words or inflections from one language introduced into the context of another."[59] Unlike simple bilingual puns (e.g., Kars/cars), which may be transmitted orally, this type of macaronic depends on the homophonic translation of written language (e.g., Demes → "them is"). In his influential _The Dialogic Imagination_, Bakhtin defined Italian Renaissance macaronics as "complex linguistic satire," mocking the purified high Latin of the learned.[60] Such linguistic merging spans eras and continents, with different histories connected to the politics of encounter and the features of the languages interacting.[61] The following English/Turkish macaronic was reprinted in the business section of the popular newspaper _Hürriyet_ under the title "İngilizce Oku, Türkçe Anla" [Read it in English, understand it in Turkish]. The hypothetical dialogue (i.e., the surface text) looks like gibberish English in print. However, it reads meaningfully in Turkish due to the near irrelevance of vowel length in the language:

—I run each teen me?
Ayran içtin mi?
[Did you drink _ayran_?]
—A wet each teem.
Evet içtim.
[Yes, I did.]
—I run each make is tea your sun each.
Ayran içmek istiyorsan iç.
[If you want to drink _ayran_, drink it.]
—Higher them in each team.
Hayır demin içtim.

[No, I've just had some.]

—Catch bar duck each teen?

Kaç bardak içtin?

[How many glasses have you had?]

—On bar duck each team

On bardak içtim.

[I had ten glasses.]

—Why high one why!

Vay hayvan vay!

[Wow, you animal!][62]

While this text does not require advanced English comprehension skills—in fact, such skills might get in the way of solving the puzzle, as is usual with Turklish folklore—it does require one to be familiar with English pronunciation rules. The humor builds on homophonic substitution, which completely eliminates the English signified and uses the surface appearance and sounds of English to signify the Turkish meaning and as a symbolic resource. Like English-language macaronics mimicking Latin, the incongruity is between the perceived cultural capital of a "higher" language and the actual meaning of the text, which turns out to be a quotidian dialogue about having a traditional yogurt drink (*ayran*) in the everyday vernacular. In true Rabelaisian fashion, the gut replaces the brain.[63] The reader is left to imagine the indigestion that will likely follow the second interlocutor's ingestion of ten glasses of cultured milk, with echoes of Nasreddin Hodja's defiantly gassy behavior at the Arab sheikh's banquet.

As Bakhtin demonstrated, the carnivalesque does not stop at the belly. One can even collect a great deal of "adult" Turklish. Perhaps the most famous risqué bilingual conundrum consists of the question, "*En şanslı Ce hangisidir?*" (Which is the luckiest "*Ce*"?), and the answer, "Ambulance." This item requires one to pronounce the English word as if it were a Turkish word, sounding out all the syllables. The final sound "ce" (/dʒ/, as in jungle) is how the letter "c," the third in the Turkish alphabet, is pronounced phonetically in Turkish, as opposed to its English pronunciation (siː). Broken down into phonetic segments ("am-bulan-ce"), this English word means "vagina-finding-ce" in Turkish, that is, a letter "c" that finds vaginas. While hard to grasp for the monolingual English speaker, this hybrid joke is so well known that the second definition of "ambulance" in the popular collaborative hypertext dictionary *Ekşi Sözlük* refers to it.[64] The first posting wryly notes that ambulance is "English for *ambulans*," using a Turkish word that is obviously a loan from English.

Another popular item reverses the semiotic order, similarly building on the near irrelevance of vowel length to meaning in the Turkish language. A joke teller may state his favorite Turkish number is "seksen bir," which means eighty-one, but is pronounced perilously close to "sex and beer." In this case, the text is to be read in Turkish and understood in English. Like "am-bulan-ce," this homophonic translation converts a perfectly innocent phrase in one language into a risqué one in another (or a combination of the two), just by switching the parameters through which the spoken sounds are to be interpreted. Similarly, the transition is from high to low, from the numerical brain to the animal appetites. The linguistic merging and the bawdy tone of these texts, as well as the subtle histories of indigenization alongside continuing symbolic links to "the West," epitomize vernacular transculturation, or wild westernization.

A professional humorist specializing in word play, Espy called macaronics "nonsense" and stated that the aim of his collection was to foreground the importance of "irrelevance" in modern life.[65] Nonsense, however, is not a politically empty category. As folklorist Alan Dundes has asserted, "[N]o genre of folklore is so trivial or so insignificant that it cannot provide important data for the study of worldview."[66] The generation of "nonsense" and gibberish is, in fact, a method by which these wild-westernized texts transcend dismissal and rejection as the sole mechanisms of bilingual humor. The performer of bilingual puns and macaronic translations humors the foreign language, actively connecting it to his or her native language through sound play. Unlike folktales based on the rejection of linguistic contact, such folklore allows for a merging and a negotiation between the two languages, even if it usually privileges the native tongue as the ultimate signified.

Bilingual folklore in contemporary Turkey consists of an impressive variety of genres and subgenres, marking a widespread, if uneven, familiarity with English and American popular culture. In addition to riddles, narrative jokes, and macaronics, *calques* (loan translations), false translations, and literal translations of Turkish proverbs and proverbial phrases are popular and widely disseminated. This variety makes it possible to appreciate many Turklish jokes without a full grasp of English. Others, however, require multiple, deep linguistic and cultural competencies. In addition to intensified English-language education in private schools, the increasing availability of Internet access in Turkey has further facilitated the semantic and structural complexity of Turklish folklore. Like faxing, email forwarding and social media–based sharing allow for the dissemination of larger vernacular texts more quickly and broadly.[67] An example of Turklish digital lore is the following short story; currently transmitted via email and social media among young Turks, this item circulated via fax in the 1990s.

This story, based on the plot of star-crossed lovers common to Turkish melodramas, utilizes English translations of well-known Turkish proverbial phrases to such an extent that it is impossible to appreciate without a solid knowledge of the English language, Turkish language, Turkish folklore, and Turkish popular culture. Like the riddling questions, this item screens for a specific bilingual identity that is neither purely Turkish nor purely English speaking. In fact, the Internet user who posted it on a social networking site introduced it with the boast "only the Turkish people can understand the following translations :))," in English.[68] Of course, she or he meant "only Turkish people who are competent in English." One can easily imagine a young primary school student weaned on riddling questions graduating to such advanced bilingual folklore, implying an ongoing (privileged) community. This makes such tales *esoteric* items intended for communication within social groups, rather than material to be shared with outsiders.[69] In order to demonstrate the complexity of contemporary Turklish humor, I am reproducing this text in full below, with the original punctuation and footnoted explanations:

Hasan was a very heavy headed[a] boy. His father was a middle situationed[b] man. To make his son readin good schools he did everything

a. Heavy-headed: A literal translation of *ağırbaşlı* in Turkish, this folk metaphor implies a calm, stable character.
b. Middle class, with implications of having a fixed income.

coming from his hand.[c] *He took everything to eye.*[d] *His mother was
a house woman. Every job used to come from her hand. In making
food there was no one on top of her. The taste of the observations (gö-
zleme) she made caused you to eat your fingers. This woman made
her hair a brush for her son. When Hasan became sick, she cried her
two eyes two fountains.*[e] *When Hasan finished lycee he wanted to
be a tooth doctor, and he entered the university exams and won
Tootherness School. In the school he met Jale. Hasan was hit to Jale
in first look but Jale was not hit to him in the first look. However her
blood boiled to him. A few weeks later they cooked the job.*[f] *Jale's
father was a money-father. He turned the corner many years ago by
making dreamy export.*[g] *But Jale was not like her father. She was a
very low hearted girl.*[h] *Her father was wanting to make her marry to
his soldierness friend s son Abdurrahim. Abdurrahim finished first
school and didn t read later.*[i] *He became a rough uncle. He started
to turn dirty jobs when he was a crazy blooded man. He was his
mother s eye. He said, 'HIK' and he fell from his father s nose. So
three under, five up he was like his father.*[j] *When he saw Jale, he put
eye to her. His inside went. His mouth got watered. His eyes opened
like a fortune stone.*[k] *To be able to see Jale, Hasan's inside was eat-
ing his inside.*[l] *Finally, together they went to a park. When they were*

c. The verbs "to read" and "to attend school" are identical in Turkish. The sentence implies that the father did everything possible to make sure his son got a good education, despite
his limited income.

d. The father put his mind to it and decided to overcome any difficulties that may
arise.

e. The mother was a competent housewife and an expert cook. The *gözlemes* (a kind of
Turkish pastry) she made were irresistible. She worked very hard to ensure her son's happi-
ness and cried a lot whenever he became sick.

f. "To be hit to someone" is Turkish slang for falling in love with them. Jale's "blood boil-
ing" to Hasan means she warmed up to him. "They cooked the job," means—to use another
slang term—they "hooked up."

g. Jale's father was very wealthy. He struck it rich many years ago through unethical
business practices.

h. Low-hearted: *alçakgönüllü*, meaning modest.

i. Her father wanted Jale to marry the son of an old army friend, Abdurrahim. Abdurrahim received only a primary school education.

j. He became a bully and a crook when he was a young man. He was a crook and re-
sembled his father greatly. So, more or less, he was like his father.

k. This series of proverbial phrases all indicate intense sexual and romantic interest.

l. Hasan was distressed.

wrinkling in the park, Abdurrahim saw them. First he pulled a deep inside.[m] *And then his eyes turned.*[n] *He couldn t control himself. He wanted to send them to the village with wood, but he collected himself. He decided to leave them head to head. At that moment the devil poked him. He fit to the devil, pulled his gun and fired.*[o] *However, a man passing stayed under lead rain and poorman went to who hit. He planted the horseshoes.*[p] *Then the mirrorless came. They took all of them under eye. Jale s inside was blood crying. The man died eye seeing seeing. And so, this job finished in the black arm (karakol).*[q]

On the most basic level, the humor in this tale depends on innocent linguistic incongruity—the direct translation of proverbial phrases or folk metaphors into a foreign language.[70] Access to the pleasures of the text requires the reader to translate the badly translated phrases back into Turkish, sometimes one suffix at a time (e.g., tooth-er-ness → diş-çi-lik). This is a very common method for creating Turklish humor. *Ekşi Sözlük*, for example, contains sixty-eight pages of Turklish humor under the heading "türkçeden ingilizceye direkt çeviri" (Direct translation from Turkish to English).[71] Such items, no matter their content, are ultimately jokes about language. Instead of translation as treason, here we find translation as public play, a mode of humoring the other's language, as well as challenging it.

Access to laughter in this case requires immense bicultural fluency as well. The humor reward hinges on one's familiarity with the old Turkish melodramas that came to saturate TV screens after the end of Turkey's import-substitution economy. Following the liberalization of the economy after the 1980 coup, new private TV channels needed cheap material for their round-the-clock schedules. They began buying in bulk

m. "Wrinkling," *kırıştırmak* in Turkish slang, means "making out" when translated into Anglo-American slang. To pull an inside: to sigh.

n. He became uncontrollably mad.

o. The village with wood: hell. Head to head: in each other's company. The devil poked him: the devil tempted him. He obeyed the devil, took out his gun, and fired.

p. Lead rain: crossfire. To go to "who hit": to get accidentally killed. To plant the horseshoes: to die.

q. The mirrorless: the police, in Turkish slang. To be taken under eye: to be placed in jail or custody. To have one's inside blood crying: to be incredibly sad and distressed. Eye seeing seeing: out in the open. The "black arm" is a literal translation of *karakol*, meaning jail, broken into two syllables: "kara" (black) and "kol" (arm).

and screening old Turkish movies from the 1960s and 1970s. The youth growing up in the 1980s and 1990s (my generation) developed an ironic appreciation for these "arabesk" Turkish movies, with their star-crossed lovers, improbable twists of fate, and classed battles of the sexes.[72] This story parodies such movies, juxtaposing the global with the local, or more accurately, juxtaposing the English language that retains its symbolic foreignness with the indigenized plotline. (After all, these old movies, cast as hopelessly provincial in this Turklish tale, were themselves products of transculturation, influenced by Egyptian, Indian, and Hollywood cinema.)[73] Access to the pleasures of the text, therefore, requires not only serious competency in the English and Turkish languages, but considerable familiarity with the post-1980s Turkish milieu.

The text also screens against individuals who are familiar with classical Turkish melodrama but may not maintain an ironic distance from it—an inter-cultural bifurcation imagined along class lines. In fact, the narrative repeatedly reinforces classed rifts through the satirization of the conventions of Turkish melodrama, the promotion of companionate marriage among compatibly educated youth, and the presence of an undereducated villain with a long, traditional Muslim name. Their given names immediately mark Jale as high society, Hasan as middle class, and Abdurrahim as working class even before the narrative provides any details. The inadequately modernized Abdurrahim cannot handle the fact that Jale and Hasan are in love and making out in the public space of a park. However, he is also unable to police the boundaries of Jale's sexuality, and, instead, ends up shooting an innocent bystander. Tellingly, Abdurrahim ends up in jail. This text, like much Turklish humor, operates as boundary maintenance, both between Turks and native speakers of English and among Turks. We are subtly assured that, unlike Hasan, Jale, and us, Abdurrahim, the ignorant, hypermasculine thug, would not have the linguistic and cultural competency to understand it. As Ayşe Öncü has observed, Turkish women's emancipation under Kemalism has not just been classed—excluding large groups of women—but is in fact "largely a function of class inequalities," marked by the advancement of women from elite backgrounds over rural, working-class men.[74] Here, Jale's emancipation as a post-Kemalist sexual subject is made possible by the very presence of Abdurrahim, whose libido is criminalized as out-of-bounds. For all its linguistic defiance, Turklish humor proliferates and operates in a country marked by continuing anxieties about both the upper and lower limits of westernization.

SELECTIVE VS. WILD WESTERNIZATION: THE CASE OF HODJA AND TEMEL

As U.S. representatives in Turkey also noted, the Turkish state began to use folklore as a tool for authoritarian westernization in the early twentieth century. The young republic launched a countrywide effort to collect and preserve folk literature, showcasing the government's dedication to ethnic nationalism and to a Western-style modernity marked by appreciation for "vanishing" folk cultures.[75] The Kemalist press also employed Nasreddin Hodja to ridicule opponents of the alphabet reform.[76] Such measures built on the theories of Ziya Gökalp (1876–1924), the ideological father of Turkish nationalism. As a selective westernizer, Gökalp believed Turkish culture must "go to the people and at the same time towards the West."[77] He glorified folklore as a representative of national identity and a fount of authentic Turkish culture, and used it to spread his ideas about Turkism and civilization. In other words, he believed folklore had an important role in keeping selective westernization from becoming excessive westernization. Like most of his contemporaries, Gökalp conceived the limits of westernization along gendered and sexualized lines. For example, he advocated versifying Hodja jokes for "women and children" and cleansing the Hodja corpus from "immoral" and "foreign" jokes.[78] His views coincided with a broad, largely unofficial cultural cleansing project in the late Ottoman Empire, suppressing sexually explicit material in literature and popular culture (e.g., Karagöz plays), in response to Orientalist depictions of Middle Eastern Muslims as sexual degenerates.[79]

Throughout the twentieth century, the state and the Kemalist elite followed Gökalp's lead and attempted to sanitize and promote select folkloric texts to boost the imagined community of the nation and cultural diplomacy.[80] The different contemporary manifestations of the two Turkish jocular heroes introduced earlier, Nasreddin Hodja and Temel, exemplify the impact of such authoritarian westernization projects. Many of the complex folklore texts that engage English feature Temel courting English-speaking tourists, visiting America, becoming Americanized, or rejecting stereotypical elements of American culture. These jokes range from relatively innocuous bumpkin jokes to sexually explicit tales. In one joke, Temel goes to America and decides he will try the "hot dog" from a stand. Upon receiving the snack, he grumbles, "Damn it, look what part of the dog they gave me!"[81] In another joke, Temel in the United States notices a woman who has fallen into a garbage can, legs up in the air. He shakes his head with a sense of cultural superiority, "These Americans are so wasteful. This woman could have been used some more!"[82] While the Temel corpus is filled with such cross-cultural, bilingual, and vulgar jokes, there are no reported instances of Nasreddin Hodja interacting with Americans or any other Westerners.[83] This is a strange discrepancy, since Temel and Nasreddin Hodja share many traits. Both are dominant *focusees*, that is, folkloric characters "serving as the focus for the attribution of narratives," and both are fairly flexible: in their narratives they can act as fools, tricksters, or wise men.[84] What then has kept Hodja away from tricking imperialist Westerners the way he is constantly depicted as tricking Tamerlane, the fourteenth-century Mongol conqueror?[85] Why can Temel travel with such ease in the United States, while Hodja has no contact even with Europe?

As JoAnn Conrad has noted, folkloristics as a field in Turkey is dominated by "a very active, vocal group of Turkish nationalists" and receives funding from the Turkish Ministry of Culture and Tourism.[86] Throughout the twentieth century, Turkish folklorists and state-identified nationalist intellectuals invested Hodja with a moral and representative purpose, and cleansed the tradition from sexually transgressive tales. Multiple Turkish folklorists have built their careers on Hodja's supposed moral character and have attempted to turn him into a figure of Turkish purity. Şükrü Elçin, for example, made a point of eliminating obscene narratives from manuscripts he transcribed for scholarly publication in the 1970s.[87] Şükrü Kurgan published an article on discerning "authentic" Hodja jokes, stating that if his wife cheats on Hodja in a joke, this tale is not "Sunni Muslim," thus not Hodja's.[88] Saim Sakaoğlu has similarly aimed to declassify many collected anecdotes as "foreign" and inauthentic in his essay on vulgarity in Nasreddin Hodja jokes.[89]

The laundering of Hodja, supported by state institutions and publications, has had real effects at the quotidian level, as obscene Hodja jokes have become unimaginable for many outside academia. Most Turkish people would be surprised to learn that the Nasreddin Hodja corpus originally included a great number of obscene tales, including the first known tale in print, which featured a Hodja who casually talked about his penis and testes.[90] These tales remain unknown to the overwhelming majority of the population due to the state's attempts to figure Hodja as a "folk philosopher" and old-fashioned moralizer.[91] The squeaky clean Hodja who reaches Turks through Ministry of Culture–approved reading primers can hardly be said to be a part of a living vernacular tradition. The purging of the corpus has reduced the number of tales known to urban Turks, leading to comments like, "[T]here are very few Hodja jokes compared to Temel ones."[92]

To counter Western stereotypes of Turks as rapacious barbarians, the state has attempted to refigure Hodja as a "cultural ambassador" and "national jocular monument."[93] Although selective westernizers have succeeded in arresting the Nasreddin Hodja tradition in Turkey and almost completely erasing the cultural memory of the vulgar trickster, the benefits of such a project are debatable. Just as enjoyment of American cultural products does not necessarily indicate pro-U.S. views, there is no evidence that appreciating aspects of Turkish folklore leads to pro-Turkish policies. Charles Richard Crane of the King-Crane Commission, which toured the Middle East after World War I, as explored in chapter 1, was apparently quite fond of Nasreddin Hodja jokes and enjoyed telling them to other senior U.S. figures. Woodrow Wilson was particularly impressed with his retelling of a joke in which Hodja tries to save the reflection of the moon from a well. When Hodja finally falls on his back, he sees the moon in the sky and sighs, "I worked a long time, but I finally saved the poor moon." For Crane and Wilson, this joke symbolized their efforts to save the world at the Paris Peace Conference.[94] It is unlikely that Wilson's identification with a bit of Turkish folklore mitigated his unwillingness to help the "terrible Turk." One even wonders whether his fondness for Nasreddin Hodja differed all that much from his well-known penchant for jokes featuring simple-minded "darkies."[95]

The intense nationalist emphasis on Hodja limits intellectual freedom, making it difficult for scholars to report obscene Hodja jokes from the manuscript tradition. When İlhan Başgöz, arguably Turkey's most distinguished folklorist, reported a vulgar Hodja joke found in an early manuscript as part of his presentation to the Fifth International

Turkish Folklore Congress in 1996, for example, he was booed off the stage as the audience protested, "This is not our Hodja!"[96] Ironically, my informants agree that Hodja is not fully theirs, though for different reasons. In their responses, most noted their preference for telling and hearing Temel jokes, depicting Nasreddin Hodja as too moralistic, old-fashioned, and "for kids."[97] A twenty-six-year-old English teacher from Istanbul, for example, asserted in English that Hodja is "lame," because he "always has something to teach," and that she prefers Temel jokes since they tend to be "more obscene" and more "up to date."[98] Similarly, a Turkish graduate student living in Connecticut argued that Hodja tales were not very funny even though they may be wise and meaningful (*anlamlı*), and she and her friends are more likely to share Temel jokes, which have "popular versions adapted to modern life."[99] An older informant voiced a similar opinion, calling Hodja tales more "classical" and noting that she and her friends preferred to tell Temel jokes because they are "modern" and more varied.[100] Nor is the telling of Temel jokes a pastime among the privileged alone: according to one estimate, 90 percent of all current Turkish jokes, including those told among working-class Turkish immigrants in Europe, are Temel jokes.[101]

The state's investment in Hodja has frozen the corpus and diminished its popular utility in the modern world. As vernacular transculturation with the United States increased after the mid-twentieth century, Nasreddin Hodja simply did not keep up with the changes. In contrast to the nationalist investment in Hodja limiting the tales officially attributed to the focusee, the cycle of Temel jokes is expanding, perhaps ironically due to the lack of attention paid to it by folklorists. Temel, ignored by nationalist folklore scholars, serves as a transnational and multicultural fool and trickster, employing crude body humor and obscenity as well as Turklish as rhetorical weapons. Despite appearances, selective westernizers have not been able to tame folklore: Temel has simply taken over Hodja's role. What we find in this contemporary Temel corpus is a serious engagement with a globalizing world in which the English language and American figures, including the mythology of the Wild West, prevail.

The Wild West began to dominate Turkish figurations of America in the 1950s. The motif entered Turkish popular culture through the movie western (called *kovboy filmi* or cowboy movie), including spaghetti westerns produced in Italy in the mid-1960s and local productions. In the

1970s, the state media corporation began broadcasting classic westerns from the only channel available in the country on Sunday mornings, developing a fan base—the joke goes—of "dads."[102] Perhaps even more influential were cheap comic book series such as the Belgian *Red Kit* (orig. Lucky Luke), and the Italian *Tommiks* (orig. Capitan Miki) and *Teksas* (orig. Il Grande Blek), which began local publication in the 1950s. The *Teksas* series is likely responsible for the strong overlap between Texas and the Wild West in the Turkish imagination. This connotation also got a boost from President Lyndon Johnson, a Texan whose opposition to Turkey's Cyprus policy angered nationalists in the 1960s. Texas thus became a local metonym for the Wild West, and began to symbolize imperial bullying and impunity in Turkish culture as the century progressed. In the 1980s and 1990s, for example, leftist and nationalist media mocked Özal's fondness for *Red Kit* comics as a symbol of his uncritical alliance with President Ronald Reagan, depicted as a stereotypical American cowboy.[103] In the new millennium, the motif incorporated George W. Bush as another expansionist "Texan."

Temel, a sexist, under-educated, marginal character and hardly a representative Turk with his Laz accent, has taken on the role of speaking Turklish back to this local figuration of the United States. More than one joke depicts Temel as an actual cowboy, conquering America and Americans, rewriting the power dynamic in irreverent, if violent, Turklish, or, as in the following case, in perfect English:

> *Temel barda oturuyormuş, yanında da sıska bir adam varmış. İçeriye silahlı bir adam girmiş. Temel'in yanındaki sıska adamın kafasına bir elma koyup silahını çekmiş ve elmayı parçalamış. -I'm Pekos Bill, demiş. Daha sonra bir başka adam gelmiş. Sıskayı duvara dayamış, başına küçük bir bardak koymuş, bardağı vurmuş. -I'm Red Kit, demiş. Bu sefer Temel adamı çekmiş, başına şişe koymuş, adamı alnından vurmuş. -I'm sorry, demiş.*

Temel was sitting at a bar, right next to him was a skinny guy. A man with a gun came inside. He put an apple on the head of the skinny guy, fired and blew up the apple to pieces. He said, "I'm Pekos Bill." A while later another man came in. He pushed the skinny guy against the wall, placed a tiny glass on his head and shot the glass. He said, "I'm Red Kit." This time Temel pulled the

guy aside, placed a bottle on his head, and shot him on the fore-
head. He said, "I'm sorry."[104]

Such jokes use the figure of the Wild West to mark the globalized world
as an essentially violent place, where anyone, even a poser with a gun,
can effectively bully the weak. Temel, unlike the famous American cowboys he tries to copy, is unable to assert his identity and declare his name
after showcasing his marksmanship. Instead, he ends up murdering an
innocent civilian, materializing the violence that had haunted the cowboys' game all along. The joke ends with the same phrase that ended the
1896 novel *Araba Sevdası* (The carriage affair), but in the new lingua
franca: the baffled *"pardon"* of the turn-of-the-century dandy has become Temel's truncated "I'm sorry." As with the westoxicated dandy,
our identification with the inadequately westernized Temel becomes
strained, and not just because he is a poor shooter. The joke suggests dangers in playing cowboy, especially for country bumpkins like Temel. Yet it
also appears to humor U.S. hegemony. Its anticlimactic and dark ending
carries a kind of cynicism, "a mode of dampening the emotional impact
of anxieties through either a humorous or a world-weary response to
them."[105] Like the bystander in Orhan Pamuk's *Yeni Hayat* (1996), who
shrugs "civilizations come and civilizations go" in response to the accelerating spread of American culture, the joke makes us ask whether getting a
gun and learning English is the only thing left to do in a violent, American-
accented world. The only other unclaimed subject position seems to be
that of "the skinny guy," next to whom Temel stands at the beginning of
the joke, almost indistinguishable from his future victim.

In another narrative joke, Wild Western violence proves a bit more
productive. This complex text reached a female informant in 2006 in an
email forwarded from an old colleague.[106] This particular informant had
a very limited knowledge of English, suggesting (again) that advanced English skills are not required for many types of Turklish humor. Inserting
homophonic translations inside a mock tall tale, this joke posits Temel
as practically responsible for naming American states and cities:

Temel ve Dursun bir gün ellerinde sazla Amerikaya giderler. Bay-
agi dolastiktan sonra yorulurlar ve uyurlar. Sabah kalktiklarinda
etraflarinda bir sürü kizilderili görürler, çok korkarlar. Temel

Dursun'a "Dur bunlar hayatta saz görmemistir, bi saz çalayim da kaçsinlar" der. Temel'in sazi çalmasiyla kizilderililer hizla kaçarlar. Dursun "vaay sen bunlari sadece bir sazla kaçirdin . . . o zaman buranin adi TEKSAZ olsun" der. Ertesi gün uyurlar; uyandiklarinda gene karsilarinda kizilderilileri görürler. Bu sefer Temel "dur baska bi yöntemim var" der ve güçlü bir sesle osurur. Ve adamlar kaçmaya baslarlar. Dursun da "mademki adamlari osurup ta kaçirttin buranin adi LAZVEGAZ olsun" der. Ertesi gün dolastiktan sonra tekrar uyurlar; sabah kalktiklarinda etraflarinda gene kizilderilileri görürler. Bu sefer Dursun "bi de ben saz çalayim de korkup kaçsinlar" der. Dursun sazi çalar ama kizilderililer korkmaz ve sazi Dursun'un götüne sokarlar. Temel de "ehe . . . bu sazi senin ötüne soktular o zaman buranin adi ARKANSAZ olsun." der

One day Temel and [his friend] Dursun take their saz [traditional string instrument] and go to America. After walking around they get tired and go to sleep. When they wake up in the morning, they see that they are surrounded by Indians and become really afraid. Temel says to Dursun, "Hold on, I bet these guys have never seen a saz in their lives, they will run away if I play it." As soon as Temel begins to play, the Indians run away. Dursun says, "Wow, you managed to scare them away with tek saz [a single saz]. . . . So let's name this place TEKSAZ [Texas]." Next day, they go to sleep, and they see that they are surrounded by Indians again when they wake up. Temel says, "Hold on, I have another idea" and farts very loudly. The men begin to run away again. Dursun says, "Since you managed to scare these men away by farting, let this place be called LAZVEGAZ [the Laz and gas, implying Las Vegas]." The next day, after traveling some more, they sleep and find that the Indians have surrounded them once again. This time Dursun says, "This time, let me play the saz, so they'll be afraid and run away." Dursun plays the saz but the Indians aren't scared. So they take the saz and stick it up Dursun's ass. Temel says, "Heh, they stuck that saz up your ass, so this place must be called ARKANSAZ ['your behind is a saz' in Turkish, referring to Arkansas]."

This joke refigures Temel as the half-savage, half-civilized leatherstocking character, built up by U.S. popular culture and disseminated the world over via Hollywood movies and comic books. It underlines the epistemological violence of the United States, the myths and symbols of which have infiltrated the very guts of Turkish folklore. However, in this tale, unlike Nasreddin Hodja's ephemeral fart, Temel's bodily emissions are depicted as lastingly productive—they practically create cross-lingual folk etymologies for American cities and states. The joke, in fact, proposes a complete mock cosmogony, challenging the American myth of westward expansion and the familiar trope of noble frontiersmen bravely defending themselves against savage Indians and bringing settlements and language (i.e., civilization) to the wilderness. Like the natives, who get tired of playing the intruders' game and literally penetrate Dursun with his own saz, Temel penetrates through American mythology, allowing us to remember how multicultural the names and histories of places like "Texas" really are, Manifest Destiny notwithstanding.

Despite expressions of folksy superiority over the United States, the joke mocks official linguistic nationalisms and selective westernization as well. It is well known that in the service of the Kemalist state, plenty of nationalist intellectuals generated such faux etymologies during the early twentieth century under the "Sun Language Theory," based on the idea that Turkish is the oldest language in the world, out of which all world languages emerged.[107] Humorist Aziz Nesin reported how, in the 1930s, his history teacher insisted that ancient Turks had migrated to the Western hemisphere and were responsible for the naming of several famous natural landmarks. According to this theory, the Amazon was named after these ancient Turks exclaiming *"Amma uzun!"* ("How very long!"), and Niagara Falls was christened by their observation, *"Ne yaygara!"* ("What commotion!").[108] Although easy to mock in retrospect, proponents of such etymologies were quite serious: in fact, theories proving the Turkish origins of foreign languages helped smooth nationalist feathers at a time of intense selective westernization, casting borrowing from Westerners as a mere reclaiming of origins.[109] The Temel joke takes this a step further: it collects "psychological compensations" for the intrusion of English into Turkish and American stock figures into Turkish popular culture, even as it mocks official linguistic nationalisms that seek to control vernacular communication.[110] The joke, however, also builds on hegemonic ideas regarding power differentials between the penetrated and the penetratee, perpetuating a dangerous logic of violence and sexuality that saturates Turkish vernacular culture, explored in depth in chapter 4.

USES OF TURKLISH HUMOR: BETWEEN AMERICANIZATION AND ANTI-AMERICANISM

From the Turklish tale of star-crossed lovers to Temel's adventures in name coining, the fact that such a complex and vibrant bilingual folklore tradition exists among contemporary Turks is in itself fascinating. But what does it signify? According to some theorists, such bilingual texts always indicate a kind of unilateral violence, marking the presence of "linguistic imperialism." Robert Philipson famously promoted this view in his 1992 book *Linguistic Imperialism*, stating, "English intrudes on all the languages that it comes into contact with," and depicting the phenomenon in confrontational terms.[111] Although contested by sociolinguists proposing alternative theories of "transculturation" and "appropriation," which emphasize local meanings and uses for foreign cultural exports, the language of cultural imperialism and the attending tropes of aggression and injury also permeate popular discussions on Turklish. In addition, these discussions are colored by the gendered and sexualized discourse of westoxication.

When a new group of Ottoman officials began to learn French and sent their children to study in the European capitals at the request of the state in the nineteenth century, critics complained, with a bilingual pun, that most of them came back "syphilized, not civilized."[112] During the Cold War, Turkish pundits argued that trainees sent to the United States under the auspices of the Marshall Plan were prioritizing their own enjoyment at the expense of strategic information gathering and national priorities.[113] Even folklore expresses such gendered and sexualized worries about over-westernization. In one popular joke, a young boy sent to England to learn English squanders all his money and time at parties, and returns home having learned nothing. When the proud father asks the boy to demonstrate his English fluency by telling guests what a "tree" is, the boy makes up the word "*dan.*" When one of the guests asks him what a forest is, he starts singing, "*Dan dandan dandan dan dan dan*" in a folkloric rhythm and belly dancing.

For some, the problem lies not in refusing to learn English, but in learning it all too well. In contemporary Turkey, nationalist parties argue that, as the education of young affluent Turks continues to be conducted in the English language, Turkey may find itself in the unpleasant situation of the Ottoman Empire, as a diglossic nation fractured along class lines. Pundits apocalyptically point out that education in a foreign language, as opposed to foreign-language education, was also the method used in the missionary schools during the final period of the Ottoman Empire.[114] Once again, the language of treason and conspiracy is in the air as nationalist histories and popular memories of elite westoxication are projected onto the contemporary moment. A recent polemic against higher education in English, for example, argued that the practice will lead to the rise of a treacherous generation, a generation that "feels sorry for not having been born American, may express hate for the Turkish letters such as ç, ğ, ı, ş, ö, ü in our alphabet, may cooperate with foreigners in unprincipled ways [kişiliksiz çizgide] or be prone to brain drain."[115] Here references to a yearning to become American, or, barring that, to shamefully serve Americans, demonstrate how the popular history of the American mandate continues to color discussions over foreign language in Turkey. The Turkish letters cited are, of course, not "Turkish" in any essential sense, but products of Kemalist westernization, which the American press once celebrated as U.S.-inspired.

Such unequivocal statements, then, cannot quite explain the popular appeal and the diverse uses of Turklish humor. In the twenty-first century, bilingual humor even uncannily pervades public campaigns against Turklish. "Türkçe'ye OK atma, TAMAM mi?" ("Do not throw arrows at Turkish, okay?") pleads one campaign poster, using a bilingual pun on the Turkish word for arrow (ok) and the English abbreviation for okay.[116] This item continues the metaphors of violence regarding the intrusion of English into Turkish. Yet here the discourse of over-westernization operates alongside a Turklish pun, marking an appropriation that exceeds theories of cultural imperialism. Moreover, tamam, the term the poster recommends as the proper Turkish substitute for "OK," is of Arabic origin, and is thus not "pure" Turkish either. Like the "Turkish" letters listed above, this text unintentionally demonstrates how language and folklore shift through cycles of hybridization and indigenization. These changes are certainly connected to power asymmetries between and within states, but they are difficult to manage through politics in the narrow sense.

Bilingual vernacular humor performed in contemporary Turkish public forums is a complex hybrid that does not fit into the tidy binary categories of Americanized versus anti-American. In fact, as Rob Kroes reminds us, histories of vernacular transculturation are inseparable from histories of anti-American sentiment "in many places of the world that have experienced the intrusion of forms of American power, soft or not so soft, overt or covert."[117] The earliest samples of Turklish folklore I have collected date back to the late 1960s—a time of rising anti-American sentiment among university youth who also constituted the first Turkish generation to be educated primarily in English as opposed to French.[118] A middle-aged Turkish-American informant reported learning the following items of bilingual folklore in Ankara during breaks at the law school in the late 1960s:

A. Morning morning where are you going? I am going to my circle.
   Translation: Sabah sabah nereye gidiyorsun? Daireme gidiyorum. [Where are you going so early in the morning? I am going to my flat.][119]
B. I am banana narrow rope.
   Translation: I am = *ben*, banana = *muz*, narrow = *dar*, rope = *ip[im]*
   Ben muzdaripim.
   [I am suffering.]

It is interesting that these early items of Turklish humor depend mostly on false translations, resembling texts that might be encountered in a language classroom. They do not contain the structural complexities and political bite of later bilingual humor. My informant, however, noted that while she had been learning English since middle school, like many of her peers, she was critical of the unequal NATO alliance between Turkey and the United States:

Some [of us] had meetings and used to chant "Yankee go home" referring to USA. They were also very disenchanted with the present government then. . . . Turkish youth felt than [*sic*] that we were a very strong ally of USA, and we were always slighted and not respected by USA. Now, I feel a similar sentiment rising.[120]

The coexistence of bilingual folklore with rising criticism of U.S. policies (and pro-American Turkish governments) is not an oxymoron. Though American missionaries, U.S. cultural diplomacy initiatives, and bilateral friendship associations have long considered English education as a tool for nurturing America's image in the world, the connection between English fluency and pro-American feelings is uncertain. Rising English-language proficiency does not necessarily imply increasing appreciation for U.S. foreign policy in Turkey. A 2000 study of 308 Turkish high school students, for example, did not reveal positive emotions about Americans to be an important motivating factor for learning English.[121] Throughout the twentieth century and into the early twenty-first, Turkish uneasiness about U.S. political, military, and economic power developed alongside the saturation of the cultural environment with American cultural products and Anglo-Americanisms.

Like middle-aged respondents relating their complex connection to Turklish and the United States in the late 1960s and early 1970s, my younger informants in the first decade of the twenty-first century were likely to be critical toward the official U.S.-Turkish alliance and even more comfortable with English. Many noted that they felt slighted by the United States. A graduate student studying in the United States explained, "Turkey acts like the puppet of America, or as if it were America's toy. And America doesn't even care about us."[122] A young English teacher in Turkey expressed the same sentiments eloquently in Turklish, complete with emoticons, "Well like any right minded turk, i feel like we r begging at their feet :)). . . . *köpekleri olduk zaten şu anda. her bişeyimize onlar karar veriyorlar* [Right now we totally turned into their dogs anyway. They get to decide everything we do]."[123]

The role of the 2003 U.S. invasion of Iraq in boosting such sentiments cannot be underestimated. Most Turks adamantly opposed the invasion and were upset (and concerned) by this unprovoked attack on a neighboring state. In July 2003, U.S. forces arrested and hooded a group of Turkish special forces officers in Iraq, further enraging nationalists. Another blow came in April 2004, when then U.S. Secretary of State Colin

Powell referred to Turkey as a moderate "Republic of Islam" during a visit and projected the country as a model for the rest of the Middle East.[124] Although the ruling AKP government seemed comfortable with this figuration, its opponents decried the newly invented term "moderate Islam" (translated as mild, or compliant *ılımlı* Islam) for its connotations of servility and for undermining Kemalist secularism.[125] As in the 1960s, many Turks began to feel the Turkish government was submitting to an unequal alliance, accepting yet another American label that limited its sovereignty. Moreover, unlike Cold War modernization theory, which had rhetorically exalted Kemalist secularism despite America's weaponization of political Islam against socialist nationalisms across the Middle East, this time the label seemed to be encouraging not just submission but also backwardness.

The depiction of the Turkish government as the "dog," the "toy," or the "puppet" of the U.S. implies a sense of silent weakness coupled with intense intimacy. In the shadow of the Iraq War, my informants felt that the communication had been constant but one-sided—America did not listen to Turks or to Turkish; the puppet/dog/toy could not speak or was not understood. Instead, Turkey's political leaders were simply bowing down to the United States, playing the "moderate" Muslim. A 2003 political cartoon published on the cover of the popular weekly humor magazine *Penguen* reflected these sentiments perfectly (figure 3.1). Employing both Turkish and English, it featured a headscarf-wearing Prime Minister Recep Tayyip Erdoğan explaining to a baffled George Bush that unless the latter denounces him by saying "I divorce thee!" (*boş ol!*) three times, tradition calls for the relationship to continue.

The tropes of gender and sexuality connect this twenty-first-century bilingual cartoon to the over-westernized Ottoman dandy, the sexist attacks on Halide Edib, and the outcries over the hosting of American sailors in Turkish brothels in the 1960s. The depiction of Erdoğan as a bashful, "covered" woman in an Islamic marriage with George W. Bush signifies an undignified political liaison. As Erdoğan leans into Bush, the latter, wearing cowboy boots under his crisp business suit, remains behind his desk, rigid and inaccessible. Like the cowboy boots stacked in front of the Turkish prime minister's face, Bush's inability to understand Erdoğan's Turkish implies a barrier, a one-sided and unequal relationship between the two countries. (As many Turks know, Erdoğan also

FIGURE 3.1 Political cartoon printed as cover of *Penguen* magazine in 2003. Image courtesy of *Penguen* and Bahadır Baruter.
Erdoğan [in Turkish]: This is our tradition. Whatever you do, unless you say "I Divorce Thee" (*boş ol*) three times, our relationship will continue.
Bush [in English]: What? What is *boş ol*?

cannot speak English in real life.) The rhetorical figure of the orthodox Islamic marriage codes for a closeness coexisting with sheer gendered and sexualized inequality. According to popular perception, the rules of an Islamic marriage allow the male to rule over the female and give him the right to commence or end the essentially unequal, though intimate, relationship through the use of language (e.g., "I divorce thee!"). Bilingual humor embodies and complicates this idea of uneven communication and hierarchical companionship, both humoring and challenging English.

Politically unpredictable, Turklish humor mocks official linguistic nationalisms by "claiming Texas," even as it enacts a kind of populist linguistic nationalism. Bilingual humor clashes with state nationalism due to its linguistic hybridity and risqué themes; yet it is also part of "a powerful global backlash against the spirit of American nationalism that shapes and animates U.S. foreign policy," which itself builds upon the symbolism of the Wild West.[126] Scholars of postcolonialism have noted the increasing gap between the affects and practices of nationalism and governing apparatuses of nation-states in the neoliberal era.[127] In Turkey, too, political scientist Doğan Gürpınar in 2006 identified the rise of a civic nationalism distinct from Kemalist "fetishism of the Turkish state" as the final culmination of the "westernization of nationalism."[128] Although Gürpınar uses the term *batılılaşma* (westernization) to explain both Kemalist nation-state consolidation and unofficial nationalisms, Turklish humor highlights the distinction between authoritarian westernization and vernacular transculturation. Turklish jokes that rewrite American figures, linguistic nationalisms that utilize bilingual puns, and the vernacular nature of both herald the rise of a new nationalism—a civic, popular, but not necessarily progressive, wild-westernized nationalism that differs from joke-purifying, state-focused Kemalism. Exploring this difference can help us better theorize the complex connections between increasing transcultural contact and rising anti-American sentiment across the world.

WILD WESTERNIZATION AS TRANSNATIONAL SIGNIFYIN(G)

Every study of political humor is bound to run into the question of impact. How does such humor function? What are its political trajectories? For studies of transnational bilingual humor, the questions become further complicated in scale. While all bilingual humor implies a kind of talking back, the political effects of any specific text will depend on the emotions it evokes in its recipients. Some Turklish is simply there for novelty in advertising. The market owner who puts up a sign saying "Acil Sandwich" (Emergency sandwich) or the water-vendor who advertises as the "Crazy Sucu" (Crazy water-vendor)—both samples from the website "Being Turkish"—are mainly trying to sell goods, using the symbolic connections between English and the culture of speedy consumption. Some bilingual jokes may function as an outlet for anxieties that might otherwise have turned political; in the words of Roland Barthes, they might simply "inoculate" the system against protest.[129] Others, like Temel's "I'm sorry," may evoke apolitical world-weariness. However, bilingual humor can also undermine official policies and mobilize the opposition.

While it is impossible to gauge the influence of one cartoon or a single joke, let alone fix its ultimate meaning, the cumulative effect of shared vernacular disdain can be striking. Research suggests that, over time, the presence of an active humor cluster within a community can make certain thoughts and actions—whether progressive or conservative—more acceptable, making the field of collective action more hospitable.[130] A version of the cartoon featuring the headscarf-wearing Erdoğan and Bush in cowboy boots, for example, was printed in a booklet in protest of George W. Bush's June 2004 visit to Turkey for a NATO summit.[131] On the day of Bush's arrival, 40,000 protestors gathered in Istanbul to chant, among other slogans, "Yankees go home!"[132] In 2008, a banner featuring Erdoğan wearing a headscarf made out of an American flag made news, marking the use of this trope in the streets.[133]

Such images were used to protest the shift from a Kemalist, French-style secularism (laïcité) suppressing public religiosity to an American-style secularism embracing and encouraging public piety—a transformation that began during the Cold War and peaked under the AKP.[134] Key scholars of modernization theory, including Lerner, Lewis, and Berkes, had long equated modernity with the secularization of social life, assuming a figurative secular West as model. Kemalist selective westernization, a central building block of modernization theory, was also forged on this basic template. Though scholarship on modernity/modernization has moved on from these assumptions regarding the connections between secularism, "the West," and modernity, popular figures of civilization remain yoked to performative secularism in Turkey as well as abroad. In the first decade of the new century, these normative understandings became fodder for attacks on AKP leaders' public religiosity (signified by their headscarf-wearing wives, their Islamic rhetoric, and their propensity for public prayer) and its overlap with America's post-9/11 concoction, "moderate Islam."

Secularist criticism of the AKP's "moderate" Muslims identified a political culture that is inadequately westernized in some areas (e.g., dress, foreign-language competency, religious display) and too westoxicated in others (e.g., the push for privatization, consumerism, continuing an asymmetrical political alliance with the United States). What Özyürek has called the secularist Turkish "nostalgia for the modern," therefore, is not just a domestic reaction against the increasing visibility of religious modes of self-presentation: it specifically critiques a U.S.-inflected neoliberalism that combines consumer capitalism with public piety.[135] In this instance and during the 2013 Gezi protests, the protestors projected themselves as properly modern figures in opposition to the ruling party, using normative understandings of secular modernity alongside Turklish humor to attack what they saw as a backward and authoritarian government serving the United States.[136] In such cases, it appears as if bilingual folklore can function not merely as a safety valve, but as "dress rehearsal" for open political rebellion.[137]

While Turklish humor may help mobilize political sentiments, its complex linguistic politics also comes at a cost: the requirement of English proficiency. Certainly the wide variety of folkloric texts showcased here demonstrates that the population generating and disseminating Turklish folklore transcends Turks who are fluent in English. Worldwide, even individuals with a limited understanding of English regularly partake in minor acts of code switching.[138] However, as long as high-quality EFL education remains the purview of the elite, Turklish remains tarred with inequalities. For all its potentially counter-hegemonic qualities, such folklore exploits and reinforces classed divides between those who can produce and consume bilingual humor and those who cannot, those who utilize uncivilized figures of masculinity and femininity as the driving force of their humor and those who are believed to naturally embody these figures, and anybody on the receiving end of penetrative "tendentious" jokes.[139]

In a 1945 essay called "Funny but Not Vulgar," English author George Orwell famously wrote, "Every joke is a tiny revolution."[140] Orwell also argued that the truly funny had to be "vulgar" to some degree, so as to shock sensibilities. In 1611, Shakespeare's haunting character Caliban memorably proclaimed to his protocolonialist master Prospero, "You taught me language, and my profit on't / Is, I know how to curse."[141] Bilingual Turkish humor can be read in the light of these statements as potentially revolutionary, jolting, and subversive, as well as with the understanding that not all humor is progressive. The Turklish casting of the United States as the land of violent dumb white cowboys is both inaccurate and disconcerting.[142] The use of "Texas" as the local metonym for U.S. imperialism ignores both the complex regionalisms that structure U.S. politics and the actual multiethnic diversity of that state. In fact, the figure of "the Texan" in contemporary Turkish vernacular has become the equivalent of the terrible Turk of early twentieth-century American discourse—a rapacious boor with way too much power. Such discursive constructions may successfully mobilize popular affects, but also foreclose important discussions about foreign policy.

Given the sexist and intolerant tone of so much bilingual humor, we should also ask, in the spirit of Audre Lorde, whether the master's tools can dismantle the master's house.[143] Can one reject U.S. cultural imperialism by speaking like an "American" and acting like a figurative cowboy? It is obvious that the linguistic intrusion is reversed when Temel names Las Vegas after his bodily emissions, or when the Internet harbors stories ostensibly in English but unintelligible to native speakers of English. But is the hierarchy challenged or simply reified when Temel not only claims Texas but also straps on a gun? Isn't the use of machismo to counteract a national feeling of disempowerment particularly problematic, considering theories that argue machismo has historically functioned as an imperial "bribe," a compensation prize for the colonized male?[144] At least for now, my research suggests that many Turks, male and female, prefer humoring English to silence. In this, they resemble other non-Westerners, whose increasing engagement with English combines a practical acknowledgment of the intrusion of a foreign tongue with the desire to claim some control over it.[145]

Despite its troubled economy, the United States remains the wealthiest and most powerful nation-state in the history of the world. Its settler colonial history means it will not easily face dissolution, unlike the Ottoman Empire in the nineteenth century.[146] However, America's extraterritorial, "informal" empire, built on economic supremacy and ideological hegemony, does appear troubled. Like the late Ottoman Empire, the American empire of the early twenty-first century seems overstretched and unable to police the multilingual multitude. Worldwide, Anglo-Americans are cast as defiantly monolingual as well as ignorant of basic geopolitical facts. While there are many bilingual and multilingual Americans, this persistent stereotype does not exactly clash with statistics, given what Doris Sommer has called the "white-out policy for 'foreign' speech" of darker peoples.[147] Consider the dangers of speaking Arabic on a plane in the post-9/11 United States. Now consider also how easily a group of Arabic-speaking graffiti artists were able to "hack" the popular TV series *Homeland* in 2015, making the producers air Arabic graffiti criticizing the show's premises.[148] Turkish-Americans are also well aware of this knowledge/power dynamic, which comes with both risks and benefits. One adult Turklish joke I collected in the United States depicted an American real estate agent overhearing a wife tell her husband "Muvaffak bu mutfak cok ufak" (Muvaffak, this kitchen is too small) in the house they are viewing, with its plethora of "fak" (/fʌk/) sounds. "What a fucking language!" exclaims the agent on learning they are speaking Turkish.[149] Here the American both lacks access to important information related to his or her livelihood and looks down on the "uncivilized" sounds coming from the couple.

This weakness, known commonly enough to make Anglo-American monolingualism the target of jokes, suggests a complex, exoteric use for bilingual Turkish humor on the Internet. Turklish texts disseminated digitally are unintelligible to Americans, although they will probably and ironically fit into the statistics theorists of cultural imperialism cite regarding the dominance of English online. One can, therefore, imagine the statement that framed the bilingual story of the star-crossed lovers ("only the Turkish people can understand the following translations") being silently repeated at the beginning of almost every item I have collected. What is the use of a "translation" into English that remains unintelligible to native speakers of English? A kind of nonterritorial, popular nationalism and a hermeneutic challenge is issued to Anglo-Americans in every utterance of Turklish, especially in complex, online texts of Turklish humor, peppered with fake translations of traditional folk metaphors. This utter denial of hermeneutic access despite easy technological and financial access challenges the semantic powers of the American hegemon, reminding one of the "intelligence failures" that continue to advertise the empire's weaknesses to the world.

While most Americans cannot understand anti-American jokes in foreign languages denotatively, their linguistic opacity can function as a connotative dare. During the Cold War, Americans inadvertently experienced the political chaos another nation's folklore can generate when "translated" into English. In 1956, the Soviet premier Nikita Khrushchev famously used a Russian proverb that Americans interpreted as overly belligerent in English translation: "We will bury you." Proverbs and proverbial expressions are notoriously difficult to translate and study due to their employment of culturally specific metaphors; influential folklorist Archer Taylor has even joked that a monograph is called for with every proverb use.[150] This particular statement was apparently meant to imply that communism is bound to outlast capitalism, as dictated by Marxist dialectics. Khrushchev meant, according to linguistic experts, "we will attend your funeral," not "we shall cause your funeral."[151] But could the American people really be sure of what threats hid between those strange signifiers? (Was the Turkish couple in the joke really talking about a small kitchen?) We cannot underestimate how uncomfortable such ambiguity can be to monolingual subjects weaned on a transparent, commonsense notion of *parole*. Everyday encounters with U.S. cultural exports and bilingual humor disrupt the pleasant illusion of linguistic transparency for many people across the world. Anglo-Americans, on the other hand, may have to go out of their way to get such training.

In the 2006 box office hit *Borat: Cultural Learnings of America for Make Benefit Glorious Nation of Kazakhstan*, comedian Sacha Baron Cohen posed as a clueless foreign journalist and used the kind of insecurity a foreigner's clumsy English can spark to great comic and political effect. Speaking to a group of ultranationalist rodeo-goers and acting as a misguided Kazakh journalist, the comedian proclaimed that he supports George W. Bush's "War of Terror."[152] With a single "wrong" preposition, Cohen rewrote the notorious War on Terror trope the

Bush administration had spent five years building, bolstering, and disseminating across the globe—all while posing as the stereotypical, uncivilized foreigner who wishes he could learn from Americans. That small preposition and Cohen's subversion of the uncivilized foreigner stereotype should remind us that successfully talking back to any kind of hegemonic entity often involves a kind of doublespeak.

We can imagine the exoteric use of Turklish humor as a transnational version of "signifyin(g)," which Henry Louis Gates Jr. outlines in the context of African-American literature. Associated with the folkloric trickster figure, signifyin(g) involves black artists "repeating received tropes and narrative strategies with a difference" in order to subvert established meanings.[153] Cohen's calling the trope of the War on Terror America's "war of terror," and Temel's ridiculing of the American Dream through the bilingual conversion of the vapid glamour of Las Vegas into pure "gas," show that such transgressive signifyin(g) on hegemonic U.S. figures can be found far beyond the borders of the United States. According to Inderpal Grewal, individuals who do not reside in the United States can still show a great deal of dexterity with the codes of mainstream American culture.[154] In contrast to perceived Anglo-American ignorance of other languages and cultures, many foreigners are conversant with English and American mass culture, and regularly engage in the kind of "cross-cultural revisionism" minorities in the United States have been practicing for centuries.[155]

Hidden transcripts at odds with authoritarian westernization and the official U.S.–Turkish alliance proliferate in the lowly, hybrid domain of the vernacular. Like Cohen, an educated British Jew who adopts the mask of the ignorant, sexist Easterner to unmask the supposedly "civilized," performers of Turklish humor often employ the hypervirile fool Temel to talk back to the United States. Mobilizing narratives of rough-hewn masculinity, bilingual humor "degrades and materializes" the supposedly high language of the Westerner.[156] Embodying wild westernization, Turklish folklore challenges the state's joke- and language-purifying westernization projects. Turklish signifyin(g) also confronts the imperialist figurative impulse that shoves other countries into templates defined by U.S. foreign policy goals. Its acerbity depends on stock characters who function as both mouthpiece and foil to the self: the use of English allows for the projection of a properly modern Turkish identity even while mobilizing figures of folksy rebellion against America and her local allies. Thus Turklish becomes a double-edged sword, reinforcing certain ethnic, regional, and class hierarchies, while challenging others. As explored in the next chapter, it only takes a shift in register (from the humorous to the sensational) for this comic, hypersexual, undercivilized local type to become the very figure of queer criminality.

CHAPTER FOUR

Figuring Sexualities

Inadequate Westernization and Rights Activism

On the evening of July 8, 2008, Istanbulites and tourists filled Hagia Irene, a museum and former Eastern Orthodox church, for a concert by the gay Canadian-American singer Rufus Wainwright—a top-billed event in the 15th International Istanbul Jazz Festival. Between songs, Wainwright chatted casually with the audience. Talking about how much he liked Istanbul, he mentioned the colorful, shifting decorative nightlights on the Bosphorus Bridge connecting the European and Asian sides of the city. "You have a very gay bridge," he joked. "It's lighted pink. . . ." The urbane, English-speaking audience of concertgoers laughed knowingly. The Ministry of Culture and Tourism under the ruling Justice and Development Party (AKP) had installed the lights as part of a controversial, large-scale urban beautification project in 2007. A few days later, Nur Çintay, a columnist in the left-leaning newspaper *Radikal*, objected to Wainwright's joke with a wink and a nudge. She was not offended by the word "gay"; she had felt it was too generous. Instead, she suggested a different, local metaphor:

> Rufus was being polite, of course. Wouldn't it be a compliment to call this bridge's shiny, iridescent, flamboyant, kitsch, cheap nightclub [*pavyon*] existence "gay"? Wasn't there supposed to be a high level of aesthetic appreciation and concern for design in gay culture?

I, for one, see the Bosphorus Bridge more as a *travesti* than as gay. A sad travesti, with the make-up falling off of her/his face, wearing garish colors, attempting to appear like someone s/he isn't.[1]

Travesti is a popular cultural category that includes any sex worker who was assigned male at birth and wears feminine attire while working. Individuals marked as travesti may self-identify in any number of ways (e.g., men, women, homosexuals, trans, gay, *lubunya*, or travesti) or not identify based on gender/sexuality at all. As a category that combines socioeconomic class with public gender performance, travesti does not have a modern Western equivalent.[2] However, Çintay's comparison of travesti to gay offers clues as to how this identity category relates to a civilizational spectrum in Turkey. The assumption is that both gay men and travesti were assigned male at birth and have sex with men, but the commonality ends there. The former identity is legitimate, even cool. Travesti, on the other hand, are a "sad" mistake. According to this formulation, they are both too masculine—unable to pass as respectable women—and too feminine, failing to look like proper (gay) men. In the end, though, their real problem is tackiness, a classed concept. In contemporary Turkey, where class is both racialized and regionalized, travesti symbolize the unwelcome presence of the country's Eastern/Kurdish/rural hinterlands in its shiny Western cities, where fancy jazz concerts are held.[3]

The travesti versus gay bridge joke must have resonated with *Radikal*'s editors. That Saturday, the newspaper took the discussion further by preparing a special section asking top architects and designers what they thought of Wainwright's comments. Those who agreed to comment mostly concurred that the lighted bridge seemed garish. Being called "gay" would be a compliment, they agreed, because "gay culture carries elements of creativity and being avant-garde."[4] The AKP had attempted to modernize the bridge with its urban renewal project but, instead, produced a cheap, arabesk light show, like the dashboard of a Turkish night taxi. The unspoken implication was that travesti constitute a similar embarrassment to modern Turkey under Western eyes—a symbol of inadequate westernization.

Çintay mocked those who refused to take the question seriously, as well as those who took it too seriously and attempted to defend the bridge's honor. The latter were represented by a hypothetical ignorant nationalist yelling, "Whaaaat! Did this unfamiliar infidel call our bridge a f*ggot [*ibne*]?!"[5] She also briefly noted that she had received complaints from several readers who found her earlier comments about travesti "transphobic." Without exactly apologizing, she said she hadn't meant to offend anyone. That she might be accused of "homophobia" was the furthest thing from her mind. By mocking vulgar heterosexist nationalisms, such as those explored in chapter 3, and entertaining these newly imported political categories, Çintay emphasized her and her newspaper's commitment to a cosmopolitan liberalism. Yet she still reserved their right to deploy joking figures of speech based on cultural capital.

Çintay and her colleagues were not the first to juxtapose travesti with gay men and find the latter a big improvement on the former. In the 1990s, activists, journalists, and tourists all played anthropologist and clairvoyant in response to the proliferation of this new sexual identity category in Turkey. A standard analysis would start with broad ethnographic observations in which the author noted the coexistence of gender-inversive and role-dependent identities along with the Western "egalitarian" model of homosexuality in the country. Then came the peek into the future, predicting a decline in local identities like travesti and heralding a new era of well-adjusted, Western-style Turkish gays and lesbians, leading to a successful, mainstream political movement.[6] Even though they did not always use the Turkish term for westernization (*batılılaşma*), such pieces held up an idealized West as a model when criticizing Turkey's "inadequate modernization." Mehmet Ümit Necef's 1992 article "Turkey on the Brink of Modernity," for example, embodies this evolutionary narrative in its title. According to Necef, "in many of its social, economic, and cultural traits Turkey still resembles early nineteenth century Europe." The future then is clear: Turkish queers will become fully modern (read: Western) in over a century or so.[7]

Scholarship has become considerably more nuanced in the last decade; however, Çintay's travesti versus gay quip suggests the interpretation of travesti identity as a metonym of Turkey's inadequate modernization/westernization survived into the early twenty-first century, even in the left-wing media. As James G. Carrier reminds us, "[O]ccidentalisms and Orientalisms serve not just to draw a line between societies but also to draw a line within them."[8] There is no evidence that the rise of gay has meant the decline of travesti. In fact, both identities have become more

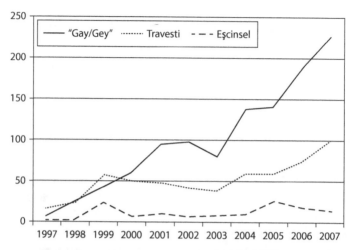

FIGURE 4.1 The number of times the words "gay" or "gey" and "travesti" are used in comparison to "eşcinsel" (homosexual) in the popular mainstream newspaper *Hürriyet*, marking the increasing visibility of new categories of male sexuality since the 1990s. Media attention suggests the rise of gay has not meant the decline of travesti; in fact, both identities have become more visible, if not more common, around the same time.

visible in popular media through the turn of the new millennium (figure 4.1). However, as this chapter suggests, such evolutionary narratives about various identity categories have impacted lives and politics on the ground.

Building on bilingual historical research and textual analysis, bolstered by interviews and conversations conducted in Istanbul in the summers of 2007, 2008, and 2012, this chapter explores three male sexual identities, or figures, situated on civilizational webs of signification:

1. Gey identity, spelled with an *a* or an *e*, associated with "the West" and high class status.
2. Travesti identity, associated with inadequate westernization and urban abjection, imposed on and sometimes adopted by supposedly working-class people who were assigned male at birth, wear feminine attire in public, and work as sex workers.
3. The "active" [*aktif*] partner, referring to the masculine, supposedly working-class lovers of gay men and travesti. This is a nonidentity associated with inadequate westernization. The term I use here comes

from vernacular Turkish culture, and the category includes "rent boys," who have sex with gay men, as well as "hetero-flexible" clients of travesti.[9]

I chose these local categories not because they comprehensively describe all queer identities and behaviors in Turkey; even apart from the obvious omission of cisgender women, they do not. My focus here is not on the "reality" of contemporary Turkish sexual desires and experiences.[10] Instead, I am interested in rhetorical articulation of gendered/sexualized figures and how individuals maneuver within them. Even though women became central to discourse about the limits of westernization early in the twentieth century (chapter 2), masculinities have remained a key node for imagining Turkish modernity.[11] The late twentieth and early twenty-first centuries have seen a proliferation of civilizational discourse around these three "male" identity categories. The first three chapters of the book have explored how debates over the limits of westernization operate through figures of gender and sexuality. Here I demonstrate how moral geographies of the East and the West function as narrative resources in the construction of gendered and sexualized identities. There is nothing inevitable about identifying as a subject based on sexual preference and/ or gender performance—declarations and projections of sexual identity are necessarily historical and political.[12] Instead of correcting identities or vaguely celebrating "authentic" queer multiplicities, this chapter asks about representations of self and other, relationality, and "friction."[13] Who claims these figures, for whom, and under what circumstances? When are they celebrated? Which ones are decried, how, and why?

Although modernization/westernization has failed to convert travesti and "active" men into geys, "westernization" can help explain the two popular, and apparently contradictory, discourses regarding male non-heteronormativities in Turkey: the idea that they have been exported from the West and the idea that they are atavistic leftovers from Turkey's past (or Turkey's eastern regions, where the premodern past presumably still thrives). This is because westernization is not a singular variable. Vernacular transculturation has shifted and continues to shift the meanings of contemporary Turkish queer identities by expanding the categories and narratives available for individual and communal adaption. However, state-led authoritarian westernization has influenced sexual identity categories in the country as extensively as any cultural flow or me-diascape.[14] The Turkish military abides by the gender-inversive model of homosexuality in recruiting for service, excluding only "feminine" men who can prove they are "passive" in intercourse. The government, on the other hand, strategically espouses the egalitarian model in its communications with Western powers. In addition, a privatized form of selective westernization, in which activists with cultural capital launch projects of education and uplift, sometimes using Western funds, has also influenced representations of Turkish queer subjectivities.

As Joseph A. Massad has argued, Western views of Middle Eastern sexualities underwent a significant change in the twentieth century: Victorian depictions of the Islamic world as exceptionally promiscuous became partially replaced by liberal and neoliberal constructions of the same cultures as sexually repressed, close(te)d, and stifling.[15] The racialized hypermasculine figure of "the Islamic terrorist," coding for a potent combination of homophobia and unacceptable queerness (e.g., propensity for pederasty, polygamy, rape, bestiality), came to be contrasted with properly patriotic Western queers assimilating into white heteronormative structures via kinship, commerce, and citizenship networks.[16] These updated stereotypes gave the United States and Western Europe another rhetorical tool—in addition to the oppressed "Muslim woman"—to figure the Muslim world as barbaric and oppressive, bolstering a new era of unending military interventions across the Middle East, South and Central Asia, and North Africa.

In Turkey, these changes hybridized with connotations of gey and *lesbiyen* (lesbian) identities as Western/modern/upper class. Thus, during the 1990s and early 2000s, various Turkish governments came to view the increasing public visibility of local LGBT organizations as an acceptable compromise on the road to Western goodwill. In the first era of AKP rule (2002–2007), a coalition with liberals around efforts to join the European Union made this Islamically oriented party the primary force for selective westernization in the country. At this point, the AKP's selective westernization policies and some activist groups' tactics temporarily overlapped as LGBT organizations gained some legitimacy, visibility, and influence. At the same time, the state, opinion leaders, and even many scholars and activists came to increasingly marginalize working-class, non-gey-identified male sexualities and identities. The racialized and classed sexual identities that did not fit into Western categories, or that were not identities at all, became sources of civilizational anxiety and the target of criminalizing discourses.

Although the demarcation of sexual identities is a cultural (and not biological) phenomenon, figurative representations have real consequences for bodies on the ground. The limits of westernization, far from being a set of ethereal debates, can justify certain types of dispossession and killing. In this chapter, I identify and explore three crisis points around these limits: the apparent rise in murders of gey men by sexual partners who do not identify as gey; the resigning of veteran travesti activists from Turkey's first LGBT rights organization; and continuing rifts between liberal and socialist activists over alliances with Western institutions. The first crisis moment demonstrates how ideas about the West and the East operate as figurative resources for thinking about local bodies and desires. The second crisis moment, incorporating both the symbolic marginalization of travesti in activist discourses and their actual persecution by the state, demonstrates the effects of state and elite selective westernization projects on those deemed inadequately modern. Finally, the third crisis moment shows how rising anti-American sentiments and increasing disaffection with neoliberal economics may be impacting local gender/sexual rights tactics and outcomes in Turkey.

Individuals and groups sometimes, but not always, differentiate between Europe and America in their construction of "the West." Moreover, discursive iterations may or may not map onto actual involvement by political entities. In general, European institutions, including embassies and private foundations, have been more directly involved in Turkish LGBT projects than organizations from the United States. Similarly, rights activism in the late twentieth and early twenty-first centuries got its largest boost from consecutive government attempts to join the European Union. The United States, however, remains an important narrative resource due to perceptions of it as the home of a capitalism-friendly gay identity. At least one American scholar has found herself in the uncomfortable position of being seen as a "calling card" for imagined American funds during her fieldwork in eastern Turkey—funds the activists imagined would be abundant enough to pay for gender confirmation surgeries, multiple long-term salaries, and luxurious office spaces.[17] On the other side of the political spectrum, I found that queer socialist activists ritualistically malign the United States, their attacks contrasting with the U.S. government's general lack of involvement in Turkish LGBT issues.[18] In addition, U.S. scientific organizations, such as the American Psychiatric Association, and vocal activist groups play important roles in how elite Turks like Çintay have come to figure properly modern Turkish sexual identities. As such, the overwhelming cultural presence of America in post-1980s Turkey often complicates the dearth of direct U.S. involvement in Turkish LGBTQ issues. Thus, as with other discursive fields, figuring America and figuring properly westernized Turkishness operate in tandem when it comes to sexual identities.

HOMOSEXUAL HOMICIDES? CATEGORIES IN FLUX

> There is a belief in the West that Turkey oppresses gay men, that this country is like Iran where gay men are not allowed to do anything. I would like the Europeans and Americans to know that gay life in Istanbul is very comfortable. It is very comfortable being gay in Istanbul. We have our cafés, our bars, we just had a pride march, although I wasn't there. . . . In Turkey, unless you are effeminate, low class and crass, you can live really well as a gay man. Especially in Istanbul. Istanbul is now like "little Amsterdam."[19]

It is the summer of 2007, and I am sitting at Hot Spot, located in Beyoğlu, a bustling neighborhood on the European side of Istanbul.[20] I am chatting with Mert, a twenty-seven-year-old fitness instructor and café manager, and Kenan, a middle-aged tourism professional, about the joys of "gay life" in Turkey. Mert volunteers these positive comments almost immediately upon hearing I live in the United States. His comments demonstrate how the rhetorical West functions not only as a narrative resource for transnational identity formation but also as a point of comparison. In the words of Rob Kroes, this is America as *"tertium comparationis*, a significant other whose difference provides people elsewhere with the terms for internal struggles and debates concerning national identities and destinies."[21]

At this point, Kenan interrupts, saying, "What do you mean little Amsterdam? I've been there; I've been to Europe! Istanbul is much better than Amsterdam!"[22] Sitting at this chic café/bar, surrounded by hip gay men and women, including young same-sex couples cuddling and kissing, I can only nod. Any Westerner would have believed Istanbul to be quite gay-friendly if they happened to be around Beyoğlu on the first of July 2007 and witnessed the peaceful and colorful pride parade with its marchers completely unharassed by the police or the onlookers. (The same AKP government had brutally suppressed the workers' day parade a couple of months earlier.) However, just a few minutes more into the conversation, Mert's tone and message to Westerners changes completely. He lowers his voice and says:

> Tell the Westerners to not come to Turkey before making a good friend, you know, before contacting us. The Westerners will not be able to tell who they are, so the tourists should go to clubs and cafés with us first. We can point those guys out and slowly the Westerners will be able tell, too, so they can protect themselves.

Who is this "them"? Not gangs of youthful Islamic radicals or an undercover police force. . . . Homosexual acts are legal in Turkey. Mert is asking me to warn Western gays about Turkish men who will sleep with them. Americans, unskilled in the national middle-class pastime of telling properly westernized "white Turks" from under-westernized "black Turks" and Kurds, will need a guide like Mert.[23] Although Mert doesn't use these transculturated vernacular categories, he echoes their implicit civilizational logic with his us/them binary. These boundaries are real to many young people. Even the locally edited *Istanbul Gay Guide* replicates them: "Do not go with local people (especially with bisexual men) to their places, and prefer public venues such as hamams or saunas instead, if your hotel is not suitable."[24] Otherwise, the thinking goes, Westerners will risk sleeping with the wrong type of Turk, a "hetero-flexible," non-gey-identified man, and endanger their lives and property.

The rise of Turkish "gey" identities, both symbolically connected to the West and localized by transculturation, is by now a familiar story to scholars of sexuality.[25] Coinciding chronically with the rise of gey/gay, however, is a newly visible hate crime that appears both homosexual and homophobic: non-gey-identified men murdering their sexual partners.

While it is hard to find statistics for gay men as opposed to travesti, we know that at least fifteen gay men and travesti were reported murdered between January and October 2007 alone.[26] Forty-five gay men and travesti were killed between 2007 and 2010. For the three years leading up to the summer of 2012, the reported number is over forty murders.[27] Despite the sensational media attention paid to so-called "gay honor crimes" in the Western media, sexual partners and clients, not family members, commit a large number of these murders. Media and activist narratives around these murders reveal categories in flux. They also demonstrate how local interpretations of sexual desire and identities intersect with debates around the limits of westernization.

On March 9, 2007, prominent Turkish businessman Saim Kayhan-mete was found dead in his Izmir house, dressed in women's lingerie. There was a seventeen-centimeter slash across his throat; the murderer had also stabbed him repeatedly in the heart. The police soon tracked a twenty-five-year-old construction worker named Fikret Oruk through an Internet-based investigation. Oruk and Kayhanmete had met online on a gay dating site. Oruk was jailed and pleaded guilty. According to his testimony, he had become "enraged," "lost his mind," and murdered Kayhanmete when the latter "offered to have sex."[28] This is, of course, the familiar narrative of "homosexual panic" used as a mitigating excuse by murderers of gay men in the United States as well.[29] Oruk, however, seemed to have gone online with the specific purpose of talking to homosexual men, and it was probably the nature of this online flirtation that had made Kayhanmete invite the young man over to his home. Oruk had willingly entered the personal space of a man he knew to be interested in sex with men. Even more strangely, the two men had shared a romantic candlelit dinner right before the murder. In fact, there had been plenty of opportunities for Oruk to feel his heterosexuality was somehow threatened; this had been a drawn-out engagement, not something that could lead to the kind of sudden shock Oruk asserted he had felt. Soon, Oruk was identified as a part-time male sex worker with a history of meeting male clients online and engaging in intercourse with them for money.[30] He certainly had had plenty of opportunities to "panic."

According to Judith Butler, human bodies have a persistent materiality, but bodies and their acts never become intelligible and accessible outside the cultural register in which they are experienced.[31] Kayhanmete's murder and the following trial unleashed an open-ended public discussion of sexualized identity categories in Turkey; the words *eşcinsel* or *homoseksüel* (alternative translations of the English word "homosexual"), gay or gey (from the English "gay"), *metroseksüel* (from the English "metrosexual"), and *erkeklik* (manhood/masculinity) came up and were projected in various combinations onto the murderer and the victim. Kayhanmete's wife, a physician, insisted that her husband had not been gay but a metroseksüel—a "complete man," who nevertheless did his own laundry and cared about his appearance.[32] Reminiscent of the boundary-maintenance role English/Turklish can play in Turkey (chapter 3), she was careful in her choice of newly imported Western words. After deploying the term metroseksüel, she added, "to use a term that is fashionable these days." Embodying the enlightened, properly westernized, professional Turkish woman, Tülay Kayhanmete told the media that she would have gotten a divorce had she suspected her husband was gay. They had a happy marriage, she insisted. The media added that the two had a son together, reinforcing a mutually exclusive binary opposition between heterosexual and homosexual practices. News reports noted that, as an educated, "modern" woman, Tülay Kayhanmete would have had no financial necessity and experienced no traditional family pressures to stay in an "unsatisfactory" marriage.

We do not know how (or if) Saim Kayhanmete self-identified based on sexual object choice and/or gender performance; however, the mainstream media highlighted his use of feminine nicknames, such as Kleopatra, on the dating site where he met Oruk. Following the murder, an openly gay singer called Osman Koç, who moderated the site, came out of the woodwork and insisted he was a friend of Kayhanmete's and could help the police track Oruk. Tülay Kayhanmete was enraged at what she saw as a self-marketing move, denying any connection between her late husband and the flamboyantly gay singer. While the verdict on Kayhanmete's sexuality ranged from gay to metrosexual, media identified the murderer as a "normal," if criminal, heterosexual man. Although several pundits suggested he was a closeted, self-hating homosexual who had turned murderous because of some underlying insecurity about his sexual identity, most articles simply and unreflectively echoed Oruk's claims to heterosexuality and defined him not as a homosexual sex worker but as "a man who has sex with homosexuals for money."[33]

The Kayhanmete murder reflected the deadly side of a general lack of consensus on what makes a man queer in Turkish culture. The simultaneous existence within one sociocultural milieu of different sexual identity categories and different meanings for sexual acts is, of course, by no means unique to contemporary Turkey. Theorist Eve Kosofsky Sedgwick has famously pointed to "the unrationalized coexistence of different models" of homosexuality in the contemporary West.[34] Sexuality is thoroughly embedded in culture, which is not a fixed system, but endlessly deferred practices of meaning making marked by asymmetries.[35] Meanings of all sex acts are both synchronically contentious and also shift in time. In fact, one can argue that as "an especially dense transfer point for relations of power," sexuality is always a site for struggle over meaning—it certainly has been in the so-called modern era.[36] As the slippages between gay and metrosexual in the Kayhanmete case show, meanings of sex/gender acts are closely tied to linguistic categories that are available in a given cultural milieu and the ways in which certain subject positions are made discursively "viable" or "intelligible."[37]

Historians of sexuality identify several models through which same-sex erotic behavior has been understood in world cultures, such as age-differentiated, role-specific, gender-inversive, and modern "egalitarian" homosexuality, all deeply embedded in culture, and thus structures of power.[38] Like most of the world, Turkish culture has long-standing categorizations regarding role-differentiated sexual relations and "alternative gender statuses."[39] Gendered age- and role-differentiated models of sexuality largely overlap, especially in parts of the world where sexual acts and related taxonomies have been scripted on a "man/non-man" dichotomy hinging on the role played during penetration.[40] Unlike the egalitarian model of homosexuality, which posits that all males who are sexually attracted to males are gay—a simplification even in the contemporary West—Turkish folk categories for male homosexuality, *ibne* and *kulampara*, refer to the "passive" and "active" positions, respectively.[41] Throughout most of Ottoman history, literary texts, dream interpretations, and medical tomes cast what we would now consider "same-sex" intercourse as a normal, if adulterous, part of men's lives. Not only did the active versus passive distinction constitute "the principal line of demarcation," it historically mattered more than the sex of the partner.[42] Perceptions of abnormality and deviance, when present at all, targeted the adult male who went against his high status by seeking the passive role in intercourse.[43] Of course, such taxonomies, including those posed by scholars based on available philological data, inevitably attempt to control the amorphous chaos of human acts and affects, producing and ordering even as they describe and explain. However, they do provide us with a glimpse of how individuals may be hailed (or not hailed) as sexual subjects at any given time.

In the nineteenth century, selective westernization began to transform these sexual norms and taxonomies. The Ottoman cultural elite initiated an unofficial heterosexualizing project in response to increasing circulation of European travelogues, which used sexual excess (in the form of polygamy and sodomy) as a metaphor for broader cultural and political inferiority. This led to a tacit suppression of discourse on men's sexual attraction to young men and boys, which was reflected, among other cultural nodes, in the rise of the realist novel in opposition to allegorical, homoerotic *divan* literature (chapter 2).[44] Operating under the same modernizing logic, the Kemalist government of the new Turkish state aimed to install marital monogamy and heterosexuality as norms through legal and cultural measures in the early twentieth century. As a transcultural contact zone with an extraordinarily diverse population, and as the seat of two decadent "Eastern" empires, Istanbul had played a key role in Western visions of the licentious Orient; when Atatürk moved the capital to the relatively homogenous Ankara in 1923, he combined geostrategic considerations with an intersectional proclamation of ethnic and sexual purity.[45] Under his rule, Kemalists encouraged the public mixing of the sexes through state-sponsored dances and reduced opportunities for private homosexual contact by banning Sufi brotherhoods and polygamous marriages, the latter responsible for scandalous Western fantasies of the Sapphic harem.[46] The alphabet revolution of 1928 and reforms replacing Arabic and Persian education with French, German, and (eventually) English restricted new generations' access to vast forests of homoerotic Ottoman writing. However, the state did not make any explicit laws regarding queer practices and identities; instead, marital heteronormativity was simply assumed to be a part of Turkish modernization—to be quietly embodied by all citizens.[47]

Given this general legislative silence, public intellectuals associated with the Kemalist government, such as Yakup Kadri Karaosmanoğlu, played a significant pedagogical role in demonstrating the sexual limits of westernization. Karaosmanoğlu's canonical novel *Sodom ve Gomore* (1928) condemned homosexuality through allegorical figures, linking its Turkish manifestations to both over-westernization and inadequate modernization. As explored in chapter 2, the novel denounces a wes-toxicated Turkish girl who falls for the charms of an American flapper. However, it also bemoans uneducated, virile Turkish men who consort with, and likely have sex with, a decadent homosexual British officer for money. American representatives in Turkey shared this ideological connection between proper westernization and heterosexual monog-amy. In the early republican era, U.S. diplomatic personnel interpreted Atatürk's apparent sexual appetites as indexes for measuring the sincer-ity of his authoritarian westernization projects. Sympathetic officials dismissed whispers of homosexuality; others presented his womaniz-ing as proof that his Western-style modernization efforts were superfi-cial ruses, and that he remained a polygamist Oriental at heart.[48]

Vernacular transculturation also led to shifts in the meanings of sexual acts and related identity categories, accelerating in the late twentieth century. Kemalists had normalized marital heterosexuality quietly. In the late 1960s, the Turkish translation of the term "homo-sexual" (eşcinsel) began to appear more and more often in mainstream newspapers. Throughout the 1970s and early 1980s, the mainstream press regularly used the word, *eşcinseller* (homosexuals), to depict individuals who would later be classified as gay and trans.[49] Although the 1970s saw initial attempts by queer communities to organize politically, the prolif-eration of public discourse around sexual identity categories came mostly in the mid-1980s.[50] In his bizarrely homophobic book *Eşcinsellik ve Yabancılaşma* (Homosexuality and alienation), the famous Marxist politician Doğu Perinçek located the origins of homosexuality in men's alienation from biological reproduction through class stratification, and blamed the 1980 coup for suppressing legitimate leftist movements and boosting homosexuality.[51] Indeed, we can date the rise of Turkish queer movements to the post-coup era, but for three different, overlapping reasons. First, under the three years of junta rule, the state began ac-tively targeting and harassing Turkish queers in unprecedented ways, persecuting travesti sex workers and homosexual men associated with the queer subculture, banning "effeminate" actors and singers from appearing on state television, and suspending gender confirmation surgeries. This harassment emphasized the need for more substantive organization around LGBT rights. Second, the end of martial law and the increase in private media channels after 1983, along with intensified cultural contact with the United States and Western Europe, expanded vernacular discourse on sexual identities, broadening possible modes of identification and political activism. Travesti gained visibility in private media channels looking for sensational material to boost ratings, in stark contrast to the notorious silence of state media on issues related to sexuality.[52] Finally, the suppression of the left—with all its sexist and homophobic blind spots—did indeed eventually open the political arena to social movements that advanced a different relation to the body and sexuality, including post-Kemalist feminism. In the last decade and a half of the twentieth century, increasing numbers of Turkish men began to call themselves gey, forming a new, self-differentiating community.[53]

A rhetorical movement toward cisgender identity and egalitarian modes of sexual performance differentiates Turkish gey identity from "traditional" formations.[54] Gey in Istanbul, however, does not mean the same as gay in San Francisco. As David Halperin notes, meanings of contemporary categories of sexuality and identity result from a "cumulative process of historical overlay and accretion."[55] Transculturation has led to the hybridization of this category with vernacular understandings of the active/passive binary, as well as with local East/West symbolism. In other words, the rise of gey does not mark Turkey's transition toward an idealized model of sexual identity through westernization; instead, "gay" has become localized through the intersectional kaleidoscope of batılılaşma—a gendered and classed network of Occidentalisms that remains largely illegible to the so-called West. Media, friends, and families reflect this by reading Turkish men's gender performance and sexual habits intersectionally, considering class, ethnicity, and region of origin in order to place individuals and their acts on a figurative spectrum of "modernity." Kayhanmete's westernized class status made it okay for him to have some metrosexual habits; his family did not assume these behaviors implied a deviation from the sexual norm, because upper-class men in Turkey have greater leeway in their gender performance. On the other hand, Oruk's working-class rural background granted him a larger acceptable scope of sexual object choice. A working-class man with a normatively masculine self-presentation can be read as "a man who has sex with homosexuals" because of the assumption that he cannot afford other modes of sexual release.

Studies of male sexuality across the world reveal such "situational" explanations for non-gay-identified homosexual behavior to be common. In the United States, popular explanations cite "exceptional" cases of sex segregation found in prisons, the military, and boarding schools, as well as racial and ethnic differences (e.g., the much sensationalized phenomenon of "the down low"), even though sex among straight-identified men is also a common white, middle-class phenomenon.[56] Studies of Muslim-majority countries often point to the practice of *purdah*, the segregation of men and women who are not close relatives and would be allowed to marry each other.[57] Such rhetoric naturalizes gay-identification as the norm. It projects "culture" as the explanation for nonwhite, non-Western penetrative flexibility—but not for white male sexual practices that elude the gay label.[58] It bolsters white, middle-class, Western privilege by projecting a racialized masculinity with an aggressive penetrative drive onto the civilizational other, e.g., the perverse "Islamic terrorist" who responds best to sexualized torture.[59] Similar assumptions also propel a great deal of sex tourism to the so-called Third World, marking a potent node of racial desire and fear around supposedly hyperphallic non-white masculinities.[60]

In Turkey, elite explanations of behavioral bisexuality do include ideas about reduced opportunities for heterosexual contact among the more conservative working classes, but these can be mapped onto a larger regionalized and racialized East/West binary. Gey is a civilizational identity in contemporary Turkey, an ideological performance symbolically aligned with modernity/the West. According to Faces, a young urban professional, figuring oneself gey involves a commitment to a cultured way of living: "As a gay, I am interested in certain fields of art, I act in amateur plays, I participate in tours, I try to take photographs and enjoy every moment of life.... It is not very meaningful for me to be known as gay just because of my sexual object choice. I try to reflect this through my style of living too."[61] These words echo Çintay's description of "gay culture" as one committed to high aesthetics and urbane living, suggesting that transculturated discourses become identities through everyday practices that transcend or bolster the sexual. In order to be safe, Faces tries to not associate with men who do not accept "the gay life," marked as enlightened, artistic, and liberating. Other gay men, in contrast, may seek out "real men," new immigrants from eastern Turkey who are expected to take the "active" role during sex, with an exoticizing desire.[62] According to *Istanbul Gay Guide*, for example, "Kurdish-oriented [*sic*] men are popular attraction group among some local gay men in big cities, similar to the interest for Latin guys in Western countries."[63]

Although sexual identities in Turkey fall along racialized class lines in many instances, this category adaptation does not happen without tensions, frictions, and struggles. Media representations of murders like that of Kayhanmete show how sexual intimacy can throw identity categories into chaos and lead to a scramble for redefinition. Such anxieties feed narratives of violence and conflict on the ground. My gey-identified interlocutors argue that poor and working-class men may feel their identities are threatened if the sex seems too "gay," that is, too reciprocal or too affectionate. Upper-middle-class men often look down on such low-income youth as self-hating homosexuals, warn each other about sleeping with certain individuals, and disseminate vernacular narratives of revenge. Kenan, for example, tells of an upper-class HIV+ physician, who has sex only with young men from shantytowns (*gecekondu*) with the intention of infecting them—a chilling and telling urban legend.[64] Gey-identified men also differentiate between rent boys who try to "better" themselves by increasing their sociocultural capital through long-term interactions with educated lovers, and those that hold on to their "ghetto" identity and only care about short-term gain.[65] In this formulation, a "good rent boy" is one who has a high likelihood of becoming a gey man, with all the class-based and westernized connotations of this identity.

Don Kulick, in his ethnography of Brazilian travesti sex workers, argues that travestis' masculine boyfriends are "perched precariously on the edge of two conflated but conflicting understandings of homosexuality that coexist in Brazil": the Western egalitarian model and the role-dependent gender-inversive model.[66] Maneuvering within similar transcultural webs that precede them, non-gey-identified Turkish men who sleep with men actively manipulate available models. Published interviews with active-identified Turkish men are very limited in number and mainly focus on rent boys, thus (perhaps incorrectly) upholding the connection between "active" denials of homosexuality and working-class backgrounds. In his 1998 study, Ali Kemal Yılmaz briefly interviews a sex worker who indignantly asks, "[D]o I look like a homosexual?" when asked about his sexual orientation.[67] This interviewee notes that he prefers women and travesti, but has sex with gey men for money. In a 2002 interview, a twenty-five-year-old unemployed Turkish man states that he regularly goes to gey bars and meets men for the purpose of intercourse, but adds, "I'm not a homosexual, I just have sex with homosexuals."[68] When the interviewer asks him whether he sees the men he sleeps with "as women," he explains, "Yes, but not completely. I had meant that I am active."[69] "Active" men's voices also emerge in murder trials, where we find similar role-dependent denials of homosexuality.[70] These records suggest some men may push their masculine gender performance all the way to murder in an attempt to negate the Western model of mutual homosexuality.[71]

Many Turkish men who have sex with men but do not identify as gey may also perform a tough hypervirility in public in order to contest this label. The two working-class rent boys I met during my fieldwork in 2007 tried to flirt with me in the presence of gey-identified men. As a part of his gender/sexual performance, one even attempted to put his arm around me and ask me out. (In addition to embodying a figure of aggressive heterosexual masculinity for my benefit, this demonstration might have doubled as an advertisement directed at the gey men in my company.) Thus, some Turkish men who are committed to a role– and gender performance–defined vision of sexual identity may engage in multiple public and private strategies to fight the suggestion that penetrating a gey man makes them one. In this project of self-figuration, they have a strange ally: the Turkish military.

The Turkish state has adopted different biopolitical strategies regarding Turkish male homosexualities in the twentieth century. The most visible and widest-ranging official strategy, however, involves banning homosexuals from the army. The Turkish military still uses DSM-II (*Diagnostic and Statistical Manual of Mental Disorders*), dating from 1968, casting homosexuality as a form of mental illness, whereas the Turkish medical community uses the current DSM (DSM-V, 2013), as does the United States. This might seem like a perfect example of "the *multitemporal heterogeneity* of each nation"—a result of cultural hybridity.[72] However, this particular multitemporality is no mere superstructural effect of transcultural contact, or an outcome of Turkey's "uneven" westernization. The Turkish military, the second largest in NATO, is extremely "modern" technologically, if "deeply mired in archaisms" in many other ways.[73] Heterogeneity here results from the state's sovereign right to pick and choose the terms of its biopolitical control of the population.[74] In other words, it is an exception consistent with the logics of selective westernization, a central mode of governmentality in the Turkish republic.

In addition to using an outdated U.S.-based scientific manual to declare homosexuality a psychosexual illness, the military decides what constitutes homosexuality according to Turkish folk constructions of queerness. It limits the definition of homosexuality to so-called "traditional" gender-inversive and role-dependent models, accepting only non-gender-normative men and those who play the "passive" role in relationships as ineligible for service. All male Turkish citizens are required to serve in the Turkish military. Thus, in order to discourage malingerers, the army subjects men to humiliating psychological and physical exams and requests photos of the applicant being voluntarily sodomized as proof of homosexuality.[75] (Gey men darkly joke that the Turkish army owns the greatest collection of gay porn in Turkey.) Thus, a part of the state apparatus through which every Turkish man must pass upholds the non-Western model of homosexuality, accepting, if not forcing, men who claim the "active" position into the army, even if they exclusively sleep with men. According to a middle-aged informant, sodomy within the ranks can be punished according to the same model, with a focus on the various roles played by each soldier. As a private in the army, Mehmet witnessed firsthand how two men's sexual actions were punished: the insertee's parents were called and told to come and take their "girl" home; the inserter, on the other hand, was told he would be kept in the army indefinitely as punishment.[76]

This policy posits undifferentiated "active" penetrative sexuality as the norm for all Turkish men; "passive" men and other non-gender-normative people who were assigned male at birth must be excluded lest they subvert the whole system by seducing all the "normal" soldiers. The power of the military in defining the terms of normative male sexuality cannot be underestimated. As mentioned in chapters 1 and 2, the military is the primary masculinizing force in Turkish culture: it sets the terms of manliness as well as male citizenship. Being drafted into the military is often a rural young man's most extensive and influential encounter with the state apparatus, comparable only to state-run primary education. Successfully completing one's military service is often a requirement for gainful employment, housing, and marriage. No matter how enthusiastically the popular media and activists disseminate egalitarian gey identity, private industries remain limited in their audience and authority in a country that is celebrated as a "military nation" and built upon the foundations of Kemalist statism.[77]

The Turkish state, however, has also shown itself more than ready and willing to bolster the Western egalitarian model of homosexuality at strategic movements, especially in conversations with Western representatives. Halil Yılmaz, former deputy head of the Istanbul police, for example, responded to a presentation by a Canadian activist on homophobic murders by saying the Turkish murders were not like those in the West, because they were committed by "homosexuals" themselves: "Our colleague has discussed crimes against homosexuals in Canada. . . . However, in our country, homosexual homicides do not result from discrimination. The violence is not against homosexuals, but between homosexuals."[78] The same state, however, would refuse a place in the military only to the victim of such crimes, classifying the insertive "homosexual" as a red-blooded, ordinary young man ready to serve the country.

In contemporary Turkey, individuals and organizations utilize the good/bad dialectic of westernization in figuring gender and sexual identities. Identifying as gey in Turkey comes with complications and dangers, as gey-identified men (and women) regularly become the target of discourses of westoxication. However, this subject position also comes with a symbolic association with modernity, the West, and upper-class sophistication aligned with "a mass-mediated consumer lifestyle."[79] Since the late twentieth century, these symbolic associations have facilitated tentative alliances with various governments implementing selective westernization measures, including the Islamically oriented AKP, as I will explore later in this chapter. State and private regimes of selective westernization also treat non-gey-identified "active" men strategically, depending on the circumstances. Associated with backwardness and criminality in courts, LGBT activists' accounts, and the mainstream liberal media, they are nevertheless seen as indispensable assets for the Turkish military. Travesti, on the other hand, have become dispensable for both the state and activists. Travesti risk being harassed and murdered by their "active" clients. They are often a central target of violent urban renewal projects. In addition, scholars, authors, and activists regularly submit the category of "travesti" to epistemological attack. The next section explores and connects these two modes of social engineering through the underlining ideology of selective westernization.

ERASING TRAVESTI: SELECTIVE WESTERNIZATION AND SOCIAL ENGINEERING

Since the late nineteenth century, Turkey's ruling elite has seen the social sciences as an important tool for selective westernization. The CUP government's ethnic engineering projects, sociologist Ziya Gökalp's writings on Turkish folklore, and Kemalist educational reforms have all been influenced by the Western social sciences and their promise of "order" and "progress."[80] As Susan Pearce puts it, "Turkish sociology has, in part, given the nation-state its structural and ideational base, as well as some of its more controversial critics."[81] Regardless of alignment with the state, the Turkish school of sociology remains deeply committed to diagnosing and curing social ills. Current scholarly and activist treatment of travesti identities must be placed within this discursive context, recognizing the explicit or implicit push of all sociologically oriented texts (including this chapter) toward social change, whether progressive or conservative.

A dialogue between Selin Berghan, a feminist sociologist, and Güneş, a travesti sex worker, epitomizes the category confusion wreaked by travesti when inserted into Western-style social science projects. In this interview, the scholar reminds the interviewee of her official sexual identity. The informant replies by saying she simply made the shift from homosexuality to trans identity, and excuses her past by noting her ignorance of these taxonomies:

—But didn't you feel like you didn't fit among homosexuals? After all, you are not homosexual, you are a transsexual.

—But, at that time, when I was living with my family, I was a homosexual. We didn't know anything about all that anyway. I thought I was the only one in the world.[82]

A few pages later, Berghan reinforces the lesson by asking, "Do you know the difference between a transvestite, transsexual, and homosexual?" Güneş admits that she had not "before [Berghan] explained it scientifically."[83]

Berghan, of course, needs to insist on the distinction between trans identity and homosexuality instead of glorifying the anticategory "queer" or the classed folk category travesti: hers is a particularly modernist project, a social science study, specifically examining trans women and, by design, aiming to exclude other non-heteronormative positionalities. It is also more than an academic investigation: this is sociologist as social activist. She lectures the sex workers on "feminism" and identity politics throughout the book and champions the country's nascent LGBT rights movement in every single interview. For Güneş, however, the difference between trans-womanhood and homosexuality is one of degree, not of type. Her transition from homosexual to trans woman is a plausible movement along a gradient of femininity and masculinity, not a giant leap between unrelated categories of being. She asserts that 85 percent of travesti's customers come to them "with the identity of men" but ask to be "fucked" and call the sex workers "my husband" in bed. Continuing to conflate gender identity, partner preference, and sex role, she continues, "What else can I say, they are even more homosexual than we are!"[84]

Berghan's insistence on keeping figures clear is not only directed toward her informants. The introduction to the book also informs the reader of the "scientific" difference between different identity categories: "Medicine aligns homosexuality with sexual preference, transvestitism with fetishism, and differentiates them both from transsexualism. . . . Despite the prevalent opinion, gays do not have to be 'like women' and lesbians do not have to be 'like men.'"[85] After this direct homage to modern medical truth, Berghan reprints a several-pages-long didactic monologue by an MD PhD from Ankara's prestigious Hacettepe University, one of the longest uninterrupted interview pieces in the book—the others being with the trans subjects themselves. Professor Ayşe Uluşahin, in turn, establishes her own authority by strategically citing the United States at the beginning of her explanation. She then delineates the proper categories:

> We use the criteria established by the American Psychiatric Association. . . . The definition of transsexualism is [for an individual] to feel like the opposite sex, to live as the opposite sex and to wear the clothing of the opposite sex.[86] Transvestitism is a totally different thing. Transvestitism is wearing the clothing of the opposite sex for sexual satisfaction. It is not the same thing as transsexualism. . . . Homosexuality and transsexualism are also very different. . . . Therefore, these aren't grades [of something]; they are totally different statuses that can co-exist.[87]

The repeated disavowals ("transvestitism is a totally different thing"; "it is not the same thing as transsexualism") here demonstrate the perceived stakes in this insistence on clear-cut categories. In fact, the paragraph mobilizes APA criteria like a culturally aseptic cure to a homegrown mistake, which itself remains largely unnamed. The local figure of the travesti, evoked in repeated references to people who "wear the clothing of the opposite sex," haunts both Berghan's feminist sociology project and Uluşahin's scientific definitions.

Travesti, a category that includes cross-dressed male sex workers as well as trans female sex workers, form the most visible symbols of non-heteronormativity in Turkey. Unlike Turkish gay and lesbian identities, which often imply the ability and willingness to "pass," travesti identity is built on conspicuousness: it is an essential part of the definition of a travesti that you know one when you see one. Their customers, who are looking not for cisgender women but specifically for travesti, do—as do the Turkish police who are out to enforce the vaguely worded prohibitions of the criminal code on "public exhibitionism" and "offenses against public morality." As KAOS GL, an Ankara-based LGBT rights organization, explain in their online dictionary, "[I]t is possible to spot a travesti from outward appearance."[88] A travesti called Beste explains the close alignment of travesti identity with a kind of violently marginalizing public gaze: "Sometimes I want to dress up as a man and wander around comfortably. I really miss walking and feeling no one is looking at me. It is so much easier to live as a *gey*."[89]

As Deniz Kandiyoti notes, "[A] whole continuum of identities may co-exist under the broad label of *travesti*."[90] Some Turkish travesti think of themselves as male cross-dressers, others as transgender women, and still others profess an identity distinct from men or women. To modify their primary and secondary sexual characteristics, many may take hormones and some pursue gender confirmation surgery. All publicly wear feminine clothing, particularly while doing sex work. Travesti have historically lived and worked together; many call themselves *lubunya*, and speak Turkish with a coded vocabulary based on a Roma dialect.[91] Others may use the acronym "CD," which stands for "cross-dresser." Some have a distinct sense of identity that is different from both men and women. When Berghan asks how thirty-year-old Ceylan learned he was actually a woman, Ceylan forcefully resists the sociologist's politically correct move: "I'm not a woman, I'm a travesti. I have never presented myself as a woman. Even if I become a transsexual this will not change. I have not shed this cover, and I will not. I do not want to lose my essence, and I will not."[92] Those who are active in the LGBT movement often prefer "trans," which de-emphasizes surgery and obscures denotations of sex work.[93] This newly imported term, though limited in use outside of activist circles, thus allows individuals to figure themselves as belonging to a more "modern" identity category.

As Catherine Lutz reminds us, even in progressive social movements, "the margins have their own margins"; in the world of Turkish non-heteronormativity, travesti inhabit a margin that moved further away from the increasingly "homonormative" middle class in the early twenty-first century.[94] An unwritten *don't ask, don't tell* policy allows gender-normative queers and a small minority of trans individuals, who can pass and have obtained the appropriate "sex-change" papers, to secure legal jobs. The government's refusal to include a clause against gender identity–based discrimination in the constitution, however, pushes individuals who cannot afford or do not want to have gender confirmation surgery into sex work. The government's refusal to allow brothels to employ any-one other than cisgender women pushes travesti into illegal sex work.[95] The association of travesti with illicitness is so complete that police can simply pick them off the street and jail them without having to accuse them of anything specific. Condoms in their houses are used as incriminating evidence of prostitution. A section of the guidelines for police on whom they can arrest for bonuses simply reads, "travesti."[96] Trans activists, therefore, list the right to legal employment among their top demands.[97] Many travesti protests simply involve groups of activists entering government unemployment offices and filling out applications.[98]

Yet travesti have had to battle with nonstate forces as well, including some LGBT activists. A great deal of early Turkish gay activism aimed to undo the active/passive distinction, divorce gender identity from sexual object choice, and thus "dehyperfeminize the homosexual in society."[99] The public visibility of travesti and their complex practices of identification and disidentification complicated these efforts. Gey men have historically blamed local role-dependent and gender-inversive categories for the dismal state of LG rights in Turkey.[100] Politically active travesti often complain of the "transphobia" of gay men and lesbians in the movement. This is indeed a familiar narrative: cisgender gay men and women, in search of respectability, have tried to distance themselves from gender-inversive identities associated with working-class cultures in many social milieus in the United States as well.[101] In Turkey, this marginalizing move takes on an additional twist because of the semiotics of westernization. Many travesti are exiles or immigrants from inner or eastern Anatolia; their abjectification combines the discourse of inadequate westernization with markers of easternness/Kurdishness and criminality.

In a particularly telling essay, published in 1995 in the journal *KAOS GL*, a gay man called Esat blamed the public effeminacy of travesti for perpetuating the association of homosexuality with sex (as opposed to love) and with passivity:

> In Lubunya identity, being passive is true not only sexually but also socially. On the other hand, in gayness, there is a stance for more equality, more braveness, as someone who cannot stand being socially insulted, as someone who lives his "passiveness" only in sexual role, but does not accept passivity in social directions.[102]

The assumption that travesti are passive in sexual and social relations is simply false. The unmistakably public nature of their identity forces travesti to take risks gey men rarely encounter, showing them to be just as "brave," if not more. Many travesti are specifically expected to perform as penetrators during paid sex, and those who have undergone gender confirmation surgery admit to having lost quite a few customers because of this decision.[103] More importantly, travesti were the first queer group to become politically active in Turkey, organizing hunger strikes against police harassment in 1987 and joining radical left parties almost a decade before Western-influenced LGBT organizations came into being.[104] Demet Demir, a trans woman who worked as travesti, was the first openly queer Turkish person to run in local elections.

Despite connotations of backwardness, travesti is no less a transculturated category than gey, and equally the result of historical processes of "overlay and accretion."[105] In Turkey, the word *travesti* came into use in the late 1950s in relation to cross-gender performances on stage and in nightclubs.[106] The word is clearly of Latin roots, and has not even become "neutralized" or Turkified through the introduction of vowel harmony. Despite roots in traditional gender-inversive identities, the postwar availability of hormones, silicone injections, and surgeries has meant that this wild-westernized, hybrid identity is "a uniquely modern possibility"—the result of negotiations between the state, psychiatrists, surgeons, travesti, and their clients.[107]

Esat's argument, therefore, makes sense only figuratively: while gey identity is associated with Western modernity and progressivism, travesti are seen as premodern relics of a traditional and oppressive gender regime, holding gey men back and denying them their active masculinity. As Çintay's descriptions also show, the stereotypical travesti, with her/his makeup "falling off of her/his face," garish, cheap, nightclub-style clothing, and urban criminalization, appears to be inadequately westernized in a deeply abject way. Thus this figure compares negatively to both "Eastern" "active" males and "Western" gey men. The travesti category is so firmly situated at the intersection of gender, sexuality, and class that one trans woman, threatening to kill herself because potential employers consistently mistake her for a travesti, differentiated herself from this category by citing her (westernized) class status: "I know three foreign languages and I have two university degrees, yet people think I am one of *them* and refuse to give me a job."[108]

Toward the end of the first decade of the twenty-first century, Turkey's LGBT organizations had made great strides in addressing the "transphobia" they identified in the early gay rights movement. They had also become weary of serving as study subjects for social scientists whose aims clashed with theirs. Instead, they began to seize the power/knowledge dynamic, publishing and disseminating data about queer subjects in Turkey and organizing academic conferences around Pride Week. While this next generation of LGBT intellectuals' and activists' rhetorical treatment of trans identities differed greatly from the simplistic polemics of the 1990s, even the most radical "queer" writings still tended to depict travesti identity as more or less a mistake caused by the country's inadequate development. According to KAOS GL, for example, "transgender" would be the right term for travesti had it not been for the category confusion characteristic of the backwardness of Turkey:

> The concept of TRANSGENDER, which refers to those who modify their biological sex and their appearance in some way with or without an operation, is used in foreign countries but has not been practically adopted in our country where everything is confused with everything else.[109]

This statement cites a category imported from the English-speaking United States (disguised here under the euphemism "foreign countries") as the point of comparison. The disapproval of "everything being confused with everything else" contrasts with the celebrations of "queer" politics that can also be found elsewhere on the website. Instead, this description echoes early selective westernizers' concern with "anomie," disseminating figures of inadequate westernization to fuel sociocultural and political progress.[110]

Attempts to theorize travesti identity as the Third World route to Western-style trans womanhood, a local mistake to be replaced by the politically correct category "transgender," or as a traditional form of being gay, however, have failed because travesti is not merely a sexual identity but a professional one. The two constants include a public performance of femininity and sex work. Cross-dressed men and trans women, including those who have had gender confirmation surgery, can all "work as *travestis*."[111] The classed dimensions of this identity/profession are best made clear in the jarring work of photographer Halil Koyutürk, who has studied children of the street (*sokak çocukları*) as well as travesti, and identified working as travesti as one of the few financial opportunities open to the former.[112] The socioeconomic necessity of working as travesti hampers the wishful thinking of many advocates that, with enough consciousness-raising and education, all travesti will one day turn into gay men, trans women, or genderqueer people, and everyone will live happily ever after.

As Rosemary Hennessy made painfully clear in *Profit and Pleasure*, we do not have the luxury of theorizing sexual identities as if they exist outside the economy.[113] As the "gay or travesti bridge" discussions opening this chapter show, gey identity is symbolically connected to Western refinement and modernity in Turkey, whereas the category travesti continues to be associated with Eastern backwardness, inauthenticity, and lower-class aesthetics. While the Turkish government intervenes in "gey" and "traditional" homosexualities strategically, supporting one model over the other depending on the context, the state has adopted a much more consistent policy against travesti: erasure. Trans activist Seyhan put it poignantly: "they are trying to make us not exist."[114]

In addition to their primary persecution regarding employment opportunities, the oppression of travesti regularly takes place in terms of space and mobility: the government restricts their movements and attacks their visibility in "European" Istanbul. Thus, the state's treatment of travesti shows how discourses conflating transgressive sexualities and mobility, explored in chapter 2 in the context of upper class women, may turn deadly in the case of low-income queer subjects. The harassment of travesti began in earnest during the early 1980s under the rule of the military junta. Their homes were raided and wrecked; they were beaten and tortured in accordance with a general "clean-up" campaign. After the transition to civilian rule under the Özal government, projects of urban renewal—and the police enforcing them—replaced soldiers as "the rod of the state."[115] The oppression of travesti intensified during the month of Ramadan in 1987, when police suddenly arrested seventy travesti, tortured them for days, shaved their heads, maimed their breasts and bodies, and exiled them from the European side of Istanbul. No matter how much the timing seemed to imply that this was a religious and moral campaign, it was also a part of a larger project of selective westernization. The year 1987 was a proud one for European Istanbul; under the new mayor Bedrettin Dalan, the city had begun a "feverish urban renewal campaign" a year before.[116] Travesti, along with many other "unwanted" residents of the slums by Beyoğlu were kicked out and their houses were razed to make space for the new Tarlabaşı Boulevard, separating the cosmopolitan touristy sections of the municipality from ethnically mixed, working-class neighborhoods.[117]

The "urban renewal" of 1986–1988 foreshadowed 1996 chillingly. In 1995, Turkey took a huge step in strategic westernization by joining the European Customs Union, erasing domestic duties and tariffs and facilitating international mergers, under the leadership of its first female prime minister, Tansu Çiller—a neoliberal economist educated at the American College for Girls and the University of Connecticut. The rising popularity of the Islamist Welfare Party and the European Union's continuing resistance to political integration with Turkey, however, exacerbated concerns about the country's place within the symbolic East/West binary.[118] In the summer of 1996, the Turkish government, worrying about the kind of impression that would be made on Westerners visiting the city for the 1996 United Nations Human Settlements Program (Habitat II) conference, began another "purification" campaign in Beyoğlu. Travesti living there were driven from their homes into exile in Anatolia. Many were arrested and subjected to violence and torture. The fights that broke out between the travesti defending their homes and groups of ultranationalist ruffians precipitated the chaos trans activist Demet Demir calls "Turkey's Stonewall."[119]

Recep Tayyip Erdoğan, who had been the mayor of Istanbul during Habitat II, broke with the Welfare Party to lead the newly founded AKP in 2001. Welfare had been clear about its policies regarding LGBT individuals and economic liberalism, and used the rhetoric of overwesternization to oppose both. In 1995, Necmettin Erbakan, the leader of the party, opposed the country's application for membership in the European Union, warning his constituents that union with Europe "will bring homosexuality" to Turkey.[120] Using the Turkish transliteration "homoseksüellik," which sounds jarringly foreign because it lacks vowel harmony and echoes a slur ("homo"), instead of the Turkish translation (eşcinsellik), Erbakan utilized a common conservative strategy, doubling down on connotations of homosexuality as an unwelcome Western export. He also called the proposed membership a "European mandate," referencing the gendered/sexualized histories of the American mandate.[121] Yet where Necmettin Erbakan's rhetoric was fervently anti-European, Erdoğan pursued membership in the European Union and, as prime minister (2002–2014), presided over the greatest neoliberal restructuring of the economy and civil society since the 1980s. Where Erbakan had spewed hate over any nonmarital relationship, Erdoğan and his then minister of foreign affairs Abdullah Gül at least pretended to consider the recommendations laid out in the KAOS GL report "The Turkey of Homosexuals" [Eşcinsellerin Türkiyesi] in 2008.[122]

The position of LGBT rights under the AKP has been a mixed bag, directly tied to the incumbents' use of selective westernization in their foreign correspondences and their sporadic use of the populist rhetoric of over-westernization locally.[123] Despite countless incidents of backpedaling from the government, attempts to close LGBT institutions, and the ever-present specter of censorship and punishment, the first era of the AKP's majority rule (2002–2007) coincided with the improved status of mainstream LGBT organizations in Turkey. These organizations gained some grudging legitimacy and greater visibility during this period. Lambdaistanbul and KAOS GL were both able to secure grants from several international organizations, publish brochures on LGBT rights, and organize and attend international conferences. Governments of all political backgrounds had consistently banned LGBT pride marches during the 1990s; in 1993, the ban had led to the founding of Lambdaistanbul. In 2003, under the first AKP government, Lambdaistanbul led a peaceful march of about fifty activists. In 2005, KAOS GL became the first Turkish LGBT organization to gain legal status from the Ministry of the Interior. In 2006, Rainbow Solidarity and Cultural Association for Transgenders, Gays, and Lesbians in Bursa became the second legally registered LGBT organization in the country, and in February 2007, Lambdaistanbul also gained legal recognition. In 2004, Istanbul held its first international gay and lesbian film festival, "OutIstanbul." Between 2006 and 2007, Istanbul pride parade participation increased tenfold, from 150 to 1,500. In 2008, the nation's capital Ankara hosted its first LGBT pride march.[124]

In 2007, Uğur Yüksel, the editor of *KAOS GL* magazine, argued that this newfound visibility and respectability were due to a shift in strategy by LGBT organizations, which "stopped fighting with institutions such as the media and the state they had previously rejected, and began learning their codes and working to transform them from within."[125] Selective westernization is one of those codes. While members of Lambdaistanbul and KAOS GL regularly advocate anticapitalist queer politics, in the first decade of the new century, these gay- and lesbian-dominated organizations found middle-class decorum and "civilized" self-presentation to be useful political tools. They adopted the tactics of selective westernization, both to court Western funds for their projects and to impress upon fellow citizens that they are a part of the country's progress on the road to modernity and belonging within Western civilization. In stark contrast to travesti, middle-class activists were even able to hitch their activism to the government's authoritarian westernization projects. Habitat II, which led to the clean-up campaigns against travesti, also housed a "homosexual stand," offering *KAOS GL* magazine to visitors. Again during Habitat II, major media outlets publicized the movement and its fight for "G-L rights" for the first time.[126]

In the early twenty-first century, the AKP's membership talks with the European Union similarly provided possibilities for organizations including KAOS GL and Lambdaistanbul to petition the government and to argue in the mainstream press that attention to LGBT civil rights would be essential for entry into the Western club.[127] For a while, the AKP's "moderate" Muslims played along. On June 5, 2008, Zafer Üskül, an AKP minister and leader of the parliament's human rights commission, made mainstream news by becoming the first government official to attend an LGBT meeting. When asked how his conservative party viewed homosexuals, Üskül said the party was against discrimination based on "sexual object choice."[128] No other party sent a representative to the meeting, which hosted International Lesbian, Gay, Bisexual, Trans and Intersex Association (ILGA) representatives as well as an openly gay member of the European Parliament, Michael Cashman. Conservative members of the AKP and the religious press soon attacked Üskül for attending a meeting of "perverts." However, KAOS GL sued the newspapers involved, and the high court found them guilty of insulting "gays and lesbians," marking another public victory for these identity categories in Turkey.[129]

After the 2007 election solidifying its majority, the AKP decelerated its reforms, "shedding liberal ballast" in an effort to please right-wing voters who had become impatient with the party's selective westerniza-tion policies.[130] Turkish enthusiasm for entry into the European Union also faded in response to discriminatory roadblocks, and the relations between LGBT activists and the AKP cooled off considerably between 2008 and 2010.[131] In 2012, the AKP made it clear that it would not sup-port the insertion of an amendment banning discrimination based on "sexual orientation and gender identity" into the new constitution, show-ing their previous liberal rhetoric to be a mere utilization of the language of selective westernization without any real commitment. By 2012, the banner for LGBT constitutional rights had been taken over by left-leaning opposition parties.

Even during the early AKP rule, many Turkish LGBT activists seri-ously doubted the government's motives and insisted that any gains made under the administration had been the result of unrelenting grassroots pressure.[132] However, the AKP's grudging role in opening up the politi-cal possibilities for LGBT rights in Turkey is undeniable. Doing fieldwork with Lambdaistanbul in the summer of 2008, Evren Savcı found many of the group's members sympathized with the AKP at the time.[133] Okay, a leftist member of Lambdaistanbul, acknowledges that in the first half decade of its rule, the AKP oversaw progressive changes that self-declared Kemalist and left-wing governments had not been able or willing to achieve.[134] According to an article in *The Independent*, moreover, these strategic concessions might have had an effect in tempering some crit-ics of the government, at least early on: "[M]any gay activists are reluc-tant to draw a connection with the ruling Justice and Development Party (AKP) [and murders of gay men], noting it was the first party in Turkey's history to send a deputy to attend a conference on gay rights."[135] Among gey men expressing support for AKP then was Cemil İpekçi, a popular fashion designer and one of the most famous gey men in Turkey. İpekçi identifies as a "conservative homosexual," and, during the first era of AKP rule, he argued that the AKP was friendlier to gey men than any other mainstream party. In 2008, the designer told the *Wall Street Journal* that he socialized with AKP leaders and that he had taken his boyfriend to state dinners organized by party officials.[136]

Under its brand of "authoritarian neoliberalism," the AKP has been zealous in its pursuit of privatization and deregulation, fueling an unpre-cedented flow of foreign capital into the country.[137] Neoliberal politics conflates American-style consumerism with identity-based lifestyles and social movements in Turkey as well as in the West. In the early twenty-first century, the AKP's leaders realized that they had to reach some sort of accommodation with LG activists if they wanted their bid for entry into the European Union to be taken seriously, and more importantly, if they wanted the steady stream of foreign investment to continue. The *Wall Street Journal*, after all, interviewed the openly gay İpekçi in an article, not on sexual identities or fashion, but on the economic prospects of Turkey under the AKP. After women's rights, gay rights constitute the new trump card of moral superiority in the hands of the neoliberal West, and the AKP has proven willing to fold on both under the right circumstances.[138]

Travesti, however, are seen as inadequately modern relics at best; even supportive queer activists seem to expect the demise of this category. Thus, travesti sex workers hold a precarious position within liberal LGBT activism and remain dispensable to governments willing to strategically accommodate sexual identities recognized by the West. Even with a selective list, it is difficult to name improvements to the situation of travesti under the AKP. A walk down the street in feminine attire can be read as illegal solicitation or simply as an affront to public serenity under the Law of Offences (*Kabahatler Kanunu*), promulgated in 2005. Travesti continue to live marginalized lives marred by substandard health care, police harassment, and violence, often committed by their "active" clients.[139] While ethnographic research suggests that many clients are primarily interested in travesti's penises, murderers often cite "homosexual panic" in ways that resemble the active/passive narratives that dominate the murders of gey men. In veiled allusions to the country's "Kurdish problem," defendants also utilize the classed and ethnically tinged belief that travesti are violent, uncivilized creatures who "terrorize" law-abiding citizens.[140] The newly imported term "trans," despite all its advantages, erases how travesti identity is situated along a classed and racialized East/West spectrum and collapses male-to-female and female-to-male identities, making it harder to theorize the intersectional nature of travesti oppression.[141] The symbolic associations with inadequate modernization, therefore, hurt travesti both rhetorically and literally.

AGAINST "PROJECTS": LGBT ACTIVISM AND
THE LIMITS OF WESTERNIZATION

In the 1990s and early 2000s, the state's selective westernization projects affected queer identities differently based on cultural capital and racialized class lines. Travesti were banished from public view and pushed outside the city in association with urban renewal projects, even as gey men and lesbians were accommodated under the same projects. Çintay's criticism of one such project—the lighted bridge—as more travesti than gay, therefore, is an ironically fitting metaphor, expressing what she saw as the AKP's inadequate modernity through classed figures of sexuality. A further rift among Turkey's queer subjects hinges on LGBT organizations' ability (and willingness) to engage in civic selective westernization projects and utilize Western funds. In the early twenty-first century, these two fault lines were marked, first by the departure of two veteran trans activists from Turkey's first LGBT organization, Lambdaistanbul, in 2007, and second by the founding of Sosyalist EBT (Socialist Homosexuals, Bisexuals, and Trans People) as a vocal opposition to liberal organizations in 2012. Tellingly, Sosyalist EBT members use the term *projecilik* (project orientation) to criticize both the NGO-ization of the Turkish LGBT movement and its associations with the government's authoritarian westernization projects. Thus ideas about westernization influence not only how figures of sexual identity are mobilized politically, but also how sexual politics are figured in the country.

The year 2007 saw a tenfold increase in participation in the pride march in Istanbul, but also marked the departure of two veteran trans activists from Lambdaistanbul: Demet Demir and Ebru. At the time, Demir was one of the most well-known LGBT activists in Turkey, and she had been involved in left-wing political movements since the late 1970s. Demir worked with Lambdaistanbul for twelve years, marching in the front lines of protests, reading statements for the group, participating in commissions, and keeping the center open once a week. Demir lived through the Habitat II violence of 1996 and was one of the few travesti who refused to give up their homes on Ülker Street. Demir and Ebru, another trans woman listed as one of the founders of Lambdaistanbul, left the organization due to what they perceived to be a secret hierarchy and a lack of transparency.[142] Both activists insisted that they were not informed of the ways in which grant money from European organizations was spent, and their questions were met with a curt answer: "We are not obliged to report to you." In a 2008 email interview, Ebru insisted that cisgender members were deeply patronizing and condescending; in response to her suggestions, they had simply shrugged, "Your problems are not the same as ours. It would be better if you founded your own organization." Of course, it is perfectly normal for rights organizations to specialize based on member profiles. "Yet," notes Ebru, "the letters LGBTT were and are all in the title of the organization," the final Ts standing for "travesti" and "transseksüel."[143] Soon after Demir and Ebru's departure, the category "travesti" was also erased. By mid-2011, Lambdaistanbul's official name still contained two Ts, but a silent consensus developed to use only one T, standing for trans, in public and intergroup correspondence.[144] By 2015, the organization had dropped the second T and adopted LGBTİ for its web presence, the last two letters standing for trans and another recently imported category, "intersex."

According to Demir, the 2007 pride parade was much less peaceful and egalitarian than it seemed.[145] The new gay and lesbian committee, she argued, did not ask for a speaker from travesti sex workers. When Demir managed to convince them to allow one, she was asked to not mention police brutality against the travesti community. This outraged Demir, who later exclaimed, "This is not a festival!" In October 2008, travesti activists united with Demir and Ebru to form their own group, LGBTT Istanbul, and began running a photocopy-reproduced travesti zine called *Gacı/Laço*. (A similar process had already occurred in Ankara with the founding of Pembe Hayat, a trans organization, in 2006 despite the existence of the highly visible KAOS GL.) Since 2010, travesti and trans activists have also held a separate pride parade.

Such "secondary marginalization" within disadvantaged groups and LGBT rights organizations is common outside of Turkey as well.[146] However, it is exceedingly difficult to separate political narratives from personal gripes in the field.[147] Indeed, spokespersons from Lambdaistanbul categorically denied these claims, particularly accusations regarding financial transparency. Lambdaistanbul activists I spoke with insisted their finances are open for examination by all members and suggested that the marginalization Demir and Ebru felt is merely a result of the education gap between travesti and the other members. According to

Sinan, a trans man and activist, members had also been aware of the possibility of the "co-optation" of their political agenda by European gay and lesbian organizations, and tried to resist this as much as possible when seeking grants.[148] Lambdaistanbul did not have any projects supported by Western grants between 2007 and 2012, and internal discussions about the possibilities and pitfalls of seeking Western funding continue.[149] However, Mija Sanders, an activist and LGBT scholar who volunteered with the organization during the summer and fall of 2007, reports that the departure of Demir and Ebru did lead to a change in the member profile and political agenda, and that a gey- and lesbian-dominated atmosphere preceded their resignation.[150] She argues that, by 2008, most of the volunteers were young gay- and lesbian-identified individuals, mainly college students.

In many ways, Lambdaistanbul follows an impressive politics of intersectional queer solidarity: its website continues to protest violence against travesti, and marks collaborations with several trans-majority organizations as well as participation in workers' rights marches.[151] However, the marginalization of trans individuals and travesti sex workers has come up several times since Demir and Ebru's departure, in particular with regard to how salaried positions are tallied based mainly on (westernized) cultural capital, particularly knowledge of English and computer skills. Savcı has provocatively pointed out how belonging also increasingly requires familiarity with the epistemological vocabulary and political attitudes promulgated by queer theory, still largely produced in the ivory towers of the United States and northwestern Europe.[152] Because travesti sex workers do not have the linguistic and cultural training that middle-class gey men and lesbians are more likely to have, they find it difficult to apply for and win grants. Grants secured, on the other hand, have accentuated in-group rifts. Thus travesti disempowerment appears both intersectional and "cumulative."[153]

The 2012 Pride Week, themed "Memory," celebrated how far the movement had come, but none of the panels included any travesti or any trans women, as was protested by several attendees.[154] The week also occasioned moments of disagreement between Kurdish and Turkish activists and the protest of "liberal" LGBT strategies by Sosyalist EBT. Sosyalist EBT was founded in the spring of 2012 in response to Istanbul LGBTT accepting European funds to launch a project called Trans X

Turkey, marking a disagreement between the two trans women who had left Lambdaistanbul in 2007.[155] As Ebru stayed, Demir moved on with several colleagues to create an organization that, based on its mission statement, would refuse funds from Western organizations. Birol İskra, another high-ranking member, and Demet utilize the discourse of excessive westernization to draw attention to the imposition of new identity categories on Turkish queers and to protest the liberal consumerist "multiculturalist" ideology, which they believe underlies the use of the rainbow flag. Adopting a social constructivist outlook, İskra comments on the figurative drive of the imperialist West in determining the rules of modernity: "The same West that once told us, 'you are homosexuals; you are sick; you need to be treated' now tells us 'you are gays; you need to become free.'"[156] Unlike Faces, Mert, and many others, he is reluctant to identify as gey, because he is against "the gay life style," as produced by the capitalist political economy and fed by commercial sectors, such as the fashion and tourism industries "perfected in the United States."

Sosyalist EBT uses strong language about various NGOs' rapprochement with the state, courting of Western donors, and articulation of a liberal multiculturalist ideology. They accuse other organizations of projecilik, project orientation, using a word that left-wing activists often use to attack the AKP government's selective westernization projects, particularly those that seek to "rehabilitate" the urban environment. They have also been critical of the "festival-like" atmosphere of the Istanbul Pride Parade, insisting that the AKP will use the colorful images of Turkish queers dancing and waving rainbow flags as "proof" of their liberalism in their dealings with the West.[157] They argue that there are only two LGBT organizations in contemporary Turkey: those that work within the liberal system as projeci NGOs (i.e., "them") and those that refuse to get their funds, identities, and strategies from "the capitalist West" (i.e., "us").[158]

In retaliation, some members of other LGBT organizations have utilized social media to mock Sosyalist EBT and their archaic-sounding leftist rhetoric. More substantial critiques exist as well. According to a prominent member of Social Policies, Gender Identity and Sexual Orientation Studies Association (SPoD), founded in 2011, Sosyalist EBT critiques Turkey's LGBT rights activism without attention to the local context. Based on this formulation, it is Sosyalist EBT that appears, upon closer examination, to be too influenced by Western discourses:

> It is okay to criticize the LGBT rights movement [in Turkey]. However, one must expect such criticism to address, first and foremost, existing [local] problems. Instead, it appears as if Sosyalist EBT is voicing its concerns from a Western European country, as if it is criticizing the Pride Parade in Cologne and not in Istanbul. Turkish LGBT organizations have always been aligned with the Left. The movement has never become mainstream; no large company has ever sponsored any LGBT organization financially. The number of [paid] workers in all Turkish LGBT organizations is not more than 10 and organizations struggle even to pay rent. Either [members of Sosyalist EBT] do not know all this, or they do and are still shooting themselves in the foot.[159]

Members of Sosyalist EBT insist that soon, given the project orientation of "liberal" organizations and the state's investment in attracting Western goodwill, the Istanbul Pride Parade will not be all that different from the commercialized parades of Europe and the United States. The interviewee from SPoD suggests, however, that even the rise of an organization like Sosyalist EBT can be read as a success of the Turkish LGBT rights movement and its veteran organizations, Lambdaistanbul and KAOS GL. Okay from Lambdaistanbul agrees and notes that Lambdaistanbul regularly collaborates with other organizations, including the trans-dominated Istanbul LGBTT. He believes productive discussions with Sosyalist EBT must be possible as well.[160] It is telling that all of these organizations were active on the ground during the large-scale Gezi Park protests against the AKP's latest urban renewal project during the summer of 2013. Taken together, alliances and contentions between Turkish LGBT organizations reflect the rising self-reflexiveness of a complex movement that intersects with multiple transnational variables and retains a comparative outlook.

In the late twentieth century, having a visible and vibrant gay community began to serve as a potent symbol for a country's civilizational status and openness to foreign investment. The attending neoimperialist agitation for gay rights has certainly inflamed nationalist diatribes against foreign intervention and "over-westernization" in Turkey. However, the Western chimera Massad depicts under the catchy name "Gay International" is not the main culprit in the oppression of travesti or the homophobic violence attributed to non-gey-identified men who have sex with men.[161] Nor is a monolithic Islam to blame, though theological polemics got a boost when the AKP government banned Istanbul's pride parade for the first time in 2015.[162] In fact, blanket denouncements of Western imperialism or Islamic fundamentalism constitute two sides of the same coin, and obscure how complexly figures of "the West" and "the East" saturate debates over sexual identities and politics. The AKP played this new game strategically between 2002 and 2008, leaving the closet door ajar, and announcing it to the world, to reap the benefits of economic globalization.[163] However, because travesti form a class-based category that is largely illegible to the West, and because even self-declared leftists have historically oscillated between disdain and frustration toward this category, individuals classified as travesti experienced further victimization, not benefits, under selective westernization.

International relations and local politics are connected through figures of gender and sexuality, and they mutually influence each other. This may explain why the increasing visibility of LGBT groups in the early twenty-first century did not lead to increasing acceptance in Turkey. According to the 2007 Pew Global Attitudes survey, the percentage of Turks who believe homosexuality should be accepted as a way of life actually decreased to 14 percent in 2007, down from 22 percent in 2002. This preceded the AKP's rightward turn but, tellingly, occurred in the context of increasing anger about America's military ventures in the Middle East and a general turn against neoliberal economics. In the same survey, the percentage of those who completely agree that "most people are better off in a free market economy" also dropped to 18 percent from 36 percent.[164] The same year, Turkey gave the United States its lowest approval rating among all surveyed countries. Communist and socialist queers' currently unpopular criticism of U.S.-flavored "liberal" approaches, therefore, might contain a grain of truth, especially when read critically with an eye toward the rhetorical alignment of "gay" identities, neoliberalism, and the United States in the country. Such an alignment is, of course, in need of both theorization and problematization.

Nevertheless, the persistence of symbolic associations with "the West," even specifically "America," should make us question whether we can truly divorce consumer capitalism from "cultural Westernization" (or backlash against local perceptions of it) while examining so-called Third World sexual identities and politics.[165]

The turn of the twenty-first century saw increasing "visibility" and even limited political recognition for Turkey's "LGBT" "community." This chapter, however, has problematized all of the terms in quotation marks. The impact of vernacular transculturation, oppressive tendencies of selective westernization projects, and the association of gey identity with the West/the United States continue to matter to Turkish queer liberation as the movement evolves. Turkish queer identities have not been imported wholesale from the West, nor are they the results of the country's "inadequate" modernization. However, attempts to set the gendered/sexualized limits of westernization operate daily in the lives of all Turkish subjects. These discursive formations, which code power relations through gender and sexuality, connect culture to politics. They also link domestic and foreign policy. Debates around the limits of westernization deploy figures of gender and sexuality; gendered and sexualized figures, in turn, are read through the dialectics of westernization. Future transnational feminist and queer scholarship, therefore, will have to take into account not just transculturated local figures, but also the conflation of social and economic liberalisms, their symbolic connections to "America," and the current climate of international relations with "the West."

Refiguring Culture in
U.S.–Middle East Relations

The end of the Cold War renewed interest in the connections between culture and foreign affairs, especially with regard to U.S.–Middle East relations. The "Clash of Civilizations" thesis might be the most notorious paradigm to emerge out of the search for new theoretical approaches. In his 1993 *Foreign Affairs* article "The Clash of Civilizations?" and his 1996 book, political scientist Samuel Huntington argued that the world can be divided into seven or eight major civilizations based on shared cultural and religious beliefs. The post–Cold War world, according to Huntington, is ripe for a clash between these civilizations, most significantly between "the West" and "Islam." The Clash of Civilizations thesis, however, was not just a prediction of the future, but also a rewriting of the past. In the essay, and more extensively in the book that followed, Huntington examined historical conflicts through civilizational lenses and declared, "differences among civilizations have generated the most prolonged and the most violent conflicts" across the centuries.[1]

Since then, multiple scholars have persuasively critiqued Huntington's thesis, showing how it minimizes both intracivilizational conflicts and cross-cultural influences, depicting civilizations as timeless, static entities clashing through time.[2] In addition, the idea that "culture" can be a central explanatory factor for international conflicts has come under scrutiny. Mahmood Mamdani, for example, calls theories that advance primarily religious and cultural explanations for crises between the United States and Muslim-majority countries "Culture Talk," demonstrating how they erase political and economic histories.[3] Indeed, historically, American observers have overemphasized the role that "Islamic culture"—however defined—might play in Turkish policies and in U.S.–Middle East conflicts in general. Yet, even before the critics weighed in, Turkey itself seems to have troubled Huntington. In his essay, he calls it "the most obvious and prototypical torn country," a fickle nation unable to decide whether it belongs with the West or with Islamic civilization. His book turns prescriptive in order to make Turkey conform to the Clash of Civilizations model: the country would do well to just shelve its attempts to join "Western civilization" and "resume its much more impressive and elevated historical role as the principal Islamic interlocutor and antagonist of the West."[4] In other words, a bit more Islam and more clashing, please.

Huntington over-reifies both the West and so-called Islamic civilization. Therefore, Turkey, with its Muslim-majority population and its history filled with impactful westernization projects, becomes an annoyance. Huntington's critics, on the other hand, minimize how the idea of "the West" operates as a discursive resource for populations excluded from this moral geography. Across the world, local debates around modernity and national identity continue to be connected to the figure of the West as a model to accept, modify, or counter. The sharp divide between the West and the rest distorts reality, but rhetorical attempts to locate such a divide are real enough.[5] Culture Talk influences politics.

The "obvious" dilemmas of Turkish westernization, which have led Huntington to call the country "torn," cannot be excised. Instead, they make U.S–Turkish relations an exceptionally rich case for reconsidering the connections between cultural life and foreign affairs. Exploring the West, not as a distinct civilization, but as a contested figure in modern Turkish history, *The Limits of Westernization* demonstrates how cultural change and debates around its proper limits have intersected with internal and external power struggles, including between Turkey and the United States. Huntington is heir to the American intellectual tradition of seeing the Middle East primarily through religious lenses. In contrast, I have argued that gender and sexuality, intersecting with ideas about class, region, ethnicity, and religion, have provided the primary tropes for debate on the Turkish side. The book delineates people collectively, discursively negotiating a cross-national dilemma: needing to incorporate "the master's tools" to survive and become legibly "modern" while trying to stay "authentic." Turkey was never formally colonized, which initially appeared to give the nationalist state considerable leeway in selecting the terms of development. The Turkish rhetorical field, therefore, provides a powerful case study for a global phenomenon: the unexpected trajectories, horizons, and thresholds of state-led modernization.

In the early twentieth century, Turkey's political elite institutionalized westernization as a mode of governmentality: a governing apparatus for implementing reforms as well as an ideological doctrine that seeks to create a certain type of citizen-subject. Turkey's opinion leaders, including politicians and intellectuals, generated a double-edged discourse around the proper limits of westernization. Disseminating figures of excessive and inadequate westernization, they sought to police the boundaries of social change. Authoritarian westernization, however, inevitably clashed with unofficial and "wild" aspects of transculturation with the West, particularly the United States, which became a cultural and political hegemon as the twentieth century progressed. Throughout the century, Turks responded to American attempts to figure Turkey in line with U.S. policy goals with various local projections of modernity. "America" thus operated as a complex resource for the construction of modern Turkish identities and politics—at times representing a key reserve for selective westernization, at others the primary fount of westoxication—sometimes even in the absence of the U.S. government's intervention.

Transculturated figures and civilizational rubrics helped shape, and were in turn shaped by, foreign relations in the twentieth century. As this book explains, the "terrible Turk" operated as a figure of extreme otherness in the United States in the late nineteenth and early twentieth centuries. The Turkish elite sought to erase this figure through selective westernization and cultural revolution; they attempted to create a Western-style nation-state out of the ashes of an Old World empire and promote properly "modern" citizens: hat-wearing men, unveiled women, even (eventually) "gay" Turks. In moments when European and American policy goals seemed to overlap with those of the Turkish state—from the false promise of Wilsonianism, to the rise of modernization theory during the early Cold War, to the siren call of the European Union—it seemed possible that Turks would be able to transcend Western figures of race and religion and become accepted to the civilization club. Yet Turkish policy makers were not able to erase local knowledges and affects that became transculturated with Western cultural exports to launch challenges to this project. Moreover, as theorists like Said, Mignolo, and Rodney have demonstrated, the Western concept of civilization (and its later manifestations, including "modernization") was formed through the experience of colonialism, and thus remains deeply dependent on raced foil figures for its existence.[6] Stock figures like the terrible Turk evinced sedimentation and transformation, not erasure, in the twentieth century. Thus by the end of the Cold War, the terrible Turk had become "the Islamic terrorist" (with "the moderate Muslim" as foil), justifying new exclusions and military ventures.

The traces of this political history are apparent in the very development of the Clash of Civilizations thesis, which was closely informed by American figurations of Turkey. It is well known that Huntington adopted this phrase from a 1990 *Atlantic Monthly* essay titled the "Roots of Muslim Rage" by Bernard Lewis, a highly influential and controversial scholar of the Middle East, whom I quote (in somewhat of a trickster spirit) in the introduction. Mamdani considers Lewis and Huntington as big proponents of Culture Talk, with the exception that the former makes a distinction between "good" and "bad" Muslims, whereas the latter delegates all Muslims to the largely unchanging sandheap of "Islamic civilization." It is perhaps less well known, yet no coincidence, that Lewis's theorizations of good and bad Muslims developed in relation to his early work on Turkey. In the highly acclaimed 1961 monograph *The Emergence of Modern Turkey*, Lewis depicted late Ottoman and Turkish history as the story of good Muslims overpowering bad Muslims. In this narrative, various forward-thinking Ottoman leaders attempt (and Atatürk finally manages) to undermine the regressive forces of "Islam," replacing a decentralized Oriental empire with a Western-style nation-state marked by self-responsibility and positivism.[7] Here, Lewis, who was in close contact with Kemalist intellectuals, including Halide Edib Adıvar's husband Dr. Adnan Adıvar, whom he thanks in the acknowledgments, replicates Turkish nationalist history writing with arguments that emphasize the inadequate modernization of the Ottoman Empire and the necessity of authoritarian westernization. He echoes U.S.-based scholarship popularized after World War II, which postulated a division between "traditionalists" and "modernists" in the Middle East.[8] He also models the early Cold War amalgamation of modernization theory, containment, and Orientalism, which depicted Turkey as a good model for her Arab neighbors and found broad acceptance in the State Department.

Whereas Lewis celebrated Turkey's westernization as exemplary in 1961, Huntington in 1993 saw it as more or less a mistake, despite borrowing generously from Lewis. Pure "facts" of Turkish political history do not justify these opposing interpretations of selective westernization. After all, both the late 1950s and the early 1990s, the two eras preceding the publication of these books, saw religiously inflected challenges to Kemalism, which were suppressed by a coup (1960) and a military memorandum (1997). The disagreement between Huntington and Lewis about how to figure Turkey may partially stem from a disciplinary divide between the political scientist Huntington and the old school Orientalist Lewis. *The Emergence of Modern Turkey* has significant strengths in its grounding in Turkish sources and its foregrounding of internal dissent, neither of which can be said about *The Clash of Civilizations*. At times, one does catch glimpses of a latent content underlying Lewis's erudite narrative about the subjugation of retrograde Oriental forces by a modernizing dictatorship. Does not this approving history of strategic westernization at the Turkish level recommend a parallel vision for U.S. policy in the broader Middle East? Couldn't Uncle Sam be a new and improved Atatürk for the entire region? However, the sweeping pontifications about Islam and the West and the attendant policy recommendations for boosting U.S. hegemony that structure much of Lewis's later work are minimized here due to his focus on a single state undergoing transformation—or, less generously, they have been contained in his casting of Turkey itself as the microcosm for a larger clash between Islam and the West.[9] Clearly oriented toward serving empire, unmoored from primary documents, *The Clash of Civilizations* misses out on these scholarly advantages.

Perhaps more important than disciplinary divides and linguistic competencies, however, is the shift that has taken place within the ideological contours of U.S. foreign policy from the Cold War to the War on Terror, from a modernization theory that accommodated Orientalism toward a purer, culturally essentialist Orientalism that suspects the ability of Muslims to modernize (or be "good") beyond the superficial. Clash of civilizations rhetoric has partially displaced modernization theory and its promise of uplift to all who play by America's rules. State Department attempts to boost "moderate" Islam across the world offer an interesting hybrid: an astonishingly robust Orientalism that accommodates a tempered version of modernization theory. No wonder the early twenty-first century saw Kemalists develop a new type of anti-Americanism at the intersection of over- and under-westernization, figuring the United States as a bizarrely regressive force Islamicizing Turkey (see chapter 3).

Racial orderings of the world, which never fully disappeared, have resurfaced under the guise of "culture" and "civilization" in the early twenty-first century. For all the talk about culture, the War on Terror is built on a certain will to ignorance (as opposed to Foucauldian "will to knowledge") regarding the linguistic and cultural complexities of the other.[10] The 2010 *World Affairs* article by Claire Berlinski, "Smile and Smile: Turkey's Feel-Good Foreign Policy," exemplifies how this combination of willful ignorance and Culture Talk operates in relation to Turkey and "Turkish culture." Adopting a snarky pop-psychological approach, "Smile and Smile," explains contemporary Turkish foreign policy toward Israel, Iran, and the United States through the "Turkish national character." That character, according to the author, simply involves being "insane and deceitful." Turks are driven by what feels good: "Long-term, rational economic and geostrategic interests? To hell with those. The patient, subtle advancement of an Islamist agenda? To hell with that, too. This is a logic-free zone."[11] In this logic-free zone, Turks lie both to themselves and to others because of their current "feelings" about this country, or that. It is impossible to examine or understand Turkish culture and, therefore, Turkish politics. In this variety of Orientalism, pundits conveniently do not even need to study—let alone read closely, intertextually, and contextually—local cultural production. Culture becomes the great mystery that is nevertheless conveniently mobilized as explanation for every single political event.

In *The Emergence of Modern Turkey*, Lewis credits "Western Civilization" with inventing the concept of "process": "the tendency to view a sequence of events not as a simple series but as a process in time, or, in organic terms, as a development." He then praises "modern Turkey" for adopting this concept, once again setting the country "apart from her Muslim neighbors."[12] This is Orientalist gobbledygook with a dash of modernization theory, of course, but it works well to describe the (d)evolution of Orientalist scholarship from Lewis's 1961 monograph to the 1993 Huntington and 2010 Berlinski, both of whom largely dismiss process, as if they themselves were stereotypical "bad" Muslims from a Bernard Lewis text. Their texts close avenues of inquiry by "locking individuals and groups a priori into a genealogy."[13] They reify culture to such an extent that it operates as race did in the era of the terrible Turk.

As mentioned, a key merit of Lewis's book on Turkey was its focus on conflict and change over time, demonstrating different stakeholders around the "emergence" of "modern Turkey." Its largest weakness, as has become increasingly clear, is its author's resistance to acknowledging how hegemonic Western discourses like Orientalism and modernization theory color historical scholarship and structure policy recommendations. The book self-assuredly reproduces what Said has called Orientalism's "radical realism": "anyone employing Orientalism, which is the habit of dealing with questions, objects, qualities, and regions deemed Oriental, will designate, name, point to, fix what he is talking or thinking about with a word or phrase, which then is considered either to have acquired, or more simply to be, reality."[14] This insistence on drawing a line between interpretive frameworks and power relations holds an important place in Said's well-known criticism of Lewis, as well as in Lewis's counterattack on Said for "polluting" the field with "political polemic."[15]

Of course, every historically oriented text participates in the politics of refiguring and fixing its subjects, including the book you have just read. By starting with a chapter on historiography, allowing the chapters to overlap chronologically, and following a strategy of interdisciplinary layering throughout, *The Limits of Westernization* signals the multiple ways cultural history can be written. A question interweaves through the narrative: how different disciplinary formations and modes of meaning-making (history, literature, folklore, sociology) have served imperialism and/or authoritarian governmentality and how they might exceed and subvert both. In other words, this book has been my attempt to combine Lewis's strength in depicting how internal debates about the figure of the West may influence a country's political culture with Said's indispensible criticism of scholarly figure-making.

As Dipesh Chakrabarty argues in *Provincializing Europe*, our intellectual categories carry traces of Western Europe's own histories, and often prove inadequate to understanding other lifeworlds and cultural formations. Yet, since these local modernities are historically influenced by European and American imperialism and popularly imagined through transnational moral geographies, no pure, intellectual counter-space exists from whence to discard "the West" either. Careful consideration of local ways of knowing and local understandings of the West, however, offers us the opportunity to reevaluate our conceptual tools and their imperial histories. Examining site-specific transculturated concepts, such as westernization (or, more precisely, batılılaşma), operating in uneasy dialectic with Orientalisms and trying them out as critical tools can help us retheorize culture in U.S.–Middle East relations without reifying our own cultural production.

The Limits of Westernization foregrounds figurative language and stock figures as keys to reconsidering the connections between culture and international relations for three reasons. First, such language engages emotions.[16] Political discourse is essentially discourse about power, and intersectional figures of gender and sexuality are key ways in which power has been represented, naturalized, and contested cross-culturally.[17] The hyperphallic figure of the terrible Turk colored Wilson's approach to the post–World War I Middle East. If the task of Kemalism was to construct representatives of proper modernity out of the new republic's citizens to counter the image of the terrible Turk, the task of Kemalist history was to tidy up complicated political histories through gendered stock figures like the westoxicated woman. Political resistance movements, like the early twenty-first-century secularist pushback against the AKP's "moderate" Muslims, have also employed gendered and classed figures to recruit followers and close ranks. Operating at the junction of conscious policymaking and implicit bias, both deeply local and transculturated, such tropes underscore the transnational formation of the national and highlight the continuing need for intersectional feminist critique.

However essentialized, figures of the other do not emerge from ancient civilizational divides, but from historically and politically specific processes of overlay and adjustment as the ruling elite attempt to manage populations through various modes of governmentality and cultural diplomacy. Lila Abu-Lughod noted the tendency to "plaster neat cultural icons like the Muslim woman over messy historical and political dynamics" in the build-up to the 2001 U.S. invasion of Afghanistan.[18] Although Abu-Lughod underlines the convergence between this contemporary figure and the native Muslim woman from colonial narratives in her foundational essay, she skips over the intermediary figure of the "Third World woman" from Cold War–era development discourse.[19] Linking the age of high imperialism to the War on Terror via the Cold War, however, helps demonstrate how gendered racialized/religious figures may oscillate as they become mobilized for new policies. This is exactly the type of sedimentation that helped the terrible Turk become the good pupil in the transition from World War I to the Cold War. The resurgence of the terrible Turk in the form of the Islamic terrorist, therefore, is a transnational tale about a specific racial "bricolage" emerging at the end of the so-called American century.[20]

Yet another lesson in the adaptability of figures comes from contemporary Turkish politics: in the second decade of the twenty-first century, the AKP government became expert at manipulating the trope of the "American mandate," which was once used against it, to consolidate support for its authoritarian measures. As noted in chapter 1, in January 2016, President Erdoğan attacked academics who had signed a peace petition protesting the AKP's counterinsurgency campaign in the southeast, calling them "mandacı" traitors who were inviting Westerners in to judge and rule Turkey as the Wilsonian Principles League had once done. Following these events at the time, I noticed how Erdoğan's most powerful political adversaries, i.e., the left-leaning Kemalists of the Republican People's Party (CHP) and the right-wing Kemalists of the Nationalist Movement Party (MHP), seemed outmaneuvered by his use of Kemalist rhetoric about national unity and imperialist penetration. Clearly, Erdoğan learned a similar lesson from this gambit. In July 2016, he blamed a violent failed coup attempt on an erstwhile ally, U.S.-based "moderate Muslim" cleric Fethullah Gülen and his followers.[21] Since Gülen resides in the United States and has connections with the CIA, Erdoğan was able once again to successfully mobilize Kemalist popular history about foreign and domestic conspiracies against the nation, in line with the so-called "Sèvres Syndrome" and popular memories of the American mandate. This rhetorical ploy collapsed the deeply polarizing AKP rule with the will of the people, constructing a post-secular *Nutuk* 2.0. Thus came the justification for eliminating opponents (many of them former allies) through a vast ideological purge of the military, judiciary, and academia.

This lability relates to the second reason I chose to focus on stock figures and rhetorical tropes in this book: they travel, albeit with significant modifications, between official and informal domains. Across the world, the vernacular is the level at which ideas about the other gain traction, alternately supporting or destabilizing official policy measures. Indeed, as the book argues, tropes of excessive and inadequate westernization find widespread utilization in everyday, colloquial communications, including within jokes and narratives about sexual identities. Thus we encounter the westoxicated intellectual not just in Kemal's *Nutuk*, but also in the nationalist paperback novel. We find figures of hypermasculine backwardness in folk humor as well as in rules governing military conscription. Stock figures embodying the Islamic terrorist and the moderate Muslim currently abound in American art exhibits, popular culture, and online folk humor, as well as in policy documents.[22] However, the vernacular is both exceptionally difficult to police and prone to transculturation. At this level, we may also find hidden transcripts and reworked figures, expressing and building up resistance to hegemonic projects. Analyzing them will require a transnational American studies more conversant with folkloristics; in fact, "provincializing" the field should require an epistemological commitment to considering the local vernacular as not just a topic for analysis, but also as a possible resource for theory.[23]

Third and finally, I believe a closer engagement with local, transculturated figures can provide glimpses into political lifeworlds that may not be immediately legible from the outside, challenging the "determined incomprehension" U.S. pundits often employ in explaining popular anti-Americanisms in the Middle East.[24] McAlister uses this phrase to describe the corporate media's unwillingness to engage histories of U.S. imperialism as explanatory factors. The attitude can also encompass attempts to analyze political conflicts through "culture," depicted as the inexplicable qualities of a foreign people. Close attention to figurative language and stock figures, on the other hand, allows us to redefine culture as a process as opposed to a product, and as a space of contention as well as consensus. It lets us historicize popular affects, studying intersections between discourse and power, between local cultures and international relations, and between official statements and vernacular sentiments, while keeping both transculturation and internal heterogeneities in mind. Interdisciplinary and multilingual scholarship at the intersection of American studies, area studies, and transnational feminist theory must be a key part of taking "more seriously 'the world' part of 'the U.S. in the world.'"[25] Foregrounding local figures without romanticizing them may even help destabilize the hegemonic stock figures—the "good" and "bad" Muslims—that bolster imperial regimes of racialized surveillance, deportation, and occupation in the era of the War on Terror.

Notes

INTRODUCTION

1. *Yahşi Batı* [The mild west], dir. Ömer Faruk Sorak (Fida Film, 2010). This and all other translations from Turkish are mine, unless noted otherwise.

2. Timothy Marr, *The Cultural Roots of American Islamicism* (New York: Cambridge University Press, 2006), 9.

3. Cengiz Çandar, "The Post-September 11 United States Through Turkish Lenses," in *The United States and Turkey: Allies in Need*, ed. Morton Abramowitz (New York: Century Foundation, 2003), 145–172, 153–154.

4. Brian J. Grim, "Turkey and Its (Many) Discontents," Pew Research Center, http://www.pewglobal.org/2007/10/25/turkey-and-its-many-discontents/, accessed July 11, 2015. See also Joshua W. Walker, "Truly Democratic—and Anti-American," *Jerusalem Post*, July 14, 2007, http://www.jpost.com/servlet/Satellite?cid=1184168563444&pagename=JPost%2FJPArticle%2FShowFull, accessed May 14, 2008.

5. "The American century" itself is a contested temporal metaphor for the rise of American power and interventionism in the mid-twentieth century. As the period immediately after World War I constitutes the first extensive inclusion of the United States within Turkish debates about westernization, I join scholars who emphasize the early roots of U.S. hegemony. See Henry Luce, "The American Century," *Life Magazine*, February 17, 1941; David Harvey, *The New Imperialism* (New York: Oxford University Press, 2003), 50; Michael J. Hogan, *The Ambiguous Legacy: U.S. Foreign Relations in the "American Century"* (New

York: Cambridge University Press, 1999); Neil Smith, *American Empire: Roosevelt's Geographer and the Prelude to Globalization* (Berkeley: University of California Press, 2003), especially 1–31.

6. For "governmentality," as a term signifying the strategic praxes of government and the production of citizen-subjects, see Michel Foucault, "Governmentality," trans. Rosi Braidotti and revised by Colin Gordon, in *The Foucault Effect: Studies in Governmentality*, ed. Graham Burchell, Colin Gordon, and Peter Miller (Chicago: University of Chicago Press, 1991), 87–104.

7. Meltem Ahıska, "Occidentalism: The Historical Fantasy of the Modern," *South Atlantic Quarterly* 102, no. 2/3 (2003): 351–379, 359. Studying Japan, David Strang calls similar practices "defensive westernization." See David Strang, "Contested Sovereignty: The Social Construction of Colonial Imperialism," in *State Sovereignty as Social Construct*, ed. Thomas J. Biersteker and Cynthia Weber (Cambridge: Cambridge University Press, 1996), 22–50. Of course, from a broader perspective, there is no "modernization without colonization," as Europe "modernized" by colonizing Asia, Africa, and the Americas. See Walter D. Mignolo, *Darker Side of the Renaissance: Literacy, Territoriality and Colonization* (Ann Arbor: University of Michigan Press, 1995), and Ann Stoler, *Race and the Education of Desire: Foucault's "History of Sexuality" and the Colonial Order of Things* (Durham, N.C.: Duke University Press, 1995).

8. Nilüfer Göle, *The Forbidden Modern: Civilization and Veiling* (Ann Arbor: University of Michigan Press, 1997), 66–67.

9. Raymond L. M. Lee, "Bauman, Liquid Modernity and Dilemmas of Development," *Thesis Eleven* 83 (November 2005): 61–77. For İlber Ortaylı, as early as the 1839 Tanzimat reforms, which constitute the first wide-scale selective westernization attempt in the Ottoman Empire, rulers sought to combine "conservativism" with "pragmatic reformism." İlber Ortaylı, *İmparatorluğun En Uzun Yüzyılı* [The longest century of the empire] (Istanbul: Alkım, 2005), 226. Cemil Aydın, on the other hand, locates the beginnings of widespread interest in "defining the limits and criteria of Ottoman Westernization" in the late nineteenth century—the apex of European imperialism and scientific racism. Cemil Aydın, *The Politics of Anti-Westernism in Asia: Visions of World Order in Pan-Islamic and Pan-Asian Thought* (New York: Columbia University Press, 2007), 41.

10. Bernard Lewis, *The Emergence of Modern Turkey* (London: Oxford University Press, 1968), 7.

11. Émile Durkheim, who theorized extensively on the dangers of anomie, was a large influence on Ziya Gökalp, the theoretical father of Turkish selective westernization. For more on Durkheim's prescriptive sociology, see Stephen P. Turner, *Emile Durkheim: Sociologist and Moralist* (London: Routledge, 1993).

12. Fernando Ortiz, *Cuban Counterpoint: Tobacco and Sugar*, trans. Harriet de Onís (Durham, N.C.: Duke University Press, 1995), 98. See also Mary Louise Pratt, *Imperial Eyes: Travel Writing and Transculturation* (London: Routledge, 1992).

13. Canclini, referencing Brian Stross. Néstor García Canclini, *Hybrid Cultures: Strategies for Entering and Leaving Modernity*, trans. Christopher L. Chiappari and Silvia L. Lopez (Minneapolis: University of Minnesota Press, 1995), xxv; Brian Stross, "The Hybrid Metaphor: From Biology to Culture," *Journal of American Folklore* 112, no. 445 (Summer 1999): 254–267.

14. For *aşırı batılılaşma*, variously translated as excessive-, over-, or super-westernization, see Şerif Mardin, "Tanzimat'tan Sonra Aşırı Batılılaşma," in *Türk Modernleşmesi* [Turkish modernization] (Istanbul: İletişim, 1971), 21–76. For "westoxication" (*gharbzadegi*), see Valentine M. Moghadam, *Modernizing Women: Gender and Social Change in the Middle East* (London: Lynne Rienner, 2003), 158–159. The operation of selective westernization alongside the gendered discourse of westoxication is reflected in the state's granting increasing rights to women, combined with its suppression of female sexuality. Both Ottoman and republican elites adopted selected reforms regarding women's social status, yet persistently criticized what they saw as over-westernized sexual and social behavior. See Elif Shafak, "Transgender Bolero," *Middle East Report* 34, no. 1 (2004): 26–29; Deniz Kandiyoti, "Gendering the Modern: On Missing Dimensions in the Study of Turkish Modernity," in *Rethinking Modernity and National Identity in Turkey*, ed. Sibel Bozdoğan and Reşat Kasaba (Seattle: University of Washington Press, 1997), 113–132; Ayşe Parla in "The 'Honor' of the State: Virginity Examinations in Turkey," *Feminist Studies* 27, no. 1 (2001): 65–88.

15. Göle, *Forbidden Modern*, 69.

16. Xiaomei Chen, *Occidentalism: A Theory of Counter-Discourse in Post-Mao China* (Lanham, Md.: Rowman & Littlefield, 2002), 8.

17. For the development of shifting ideas of "the West" and "the East," and the role Asia Minor has played in them, see the introduction to Zachary Lockman, *Contending Visions of the Middle East: The History and Politics of Orientalism*, 2nd ed. (New York: Cambridge University Press, 2004).

18. Roland Barthes, *Mythologies* (New York: Noonday, 1972); Henry Nash Smith, *Virgin Land: The American West as Symbol and Myth*, new ed. (Cambridge, Mass.: Harvard University Press, 2007).

19. Reinhold Wagnleitner, *Coca-Colonization and the Cold War: The Cultural Mission of the United States in Austria After the Second World War* (Chapel Hill: University of North Carolina Press, 1994); Emily S. Rosenberg, *Spreading the American Dream: American Economic and Cultural Expansion, 1890–1945*

(New York: Hill and Wang, 1982); Richard Kuisel, *Seducing the French: The Dilemma of Americanization* (Berkeley: University of California Press, 1997); Walter LaFeber, *Michael Jordan and the New Global Capitalism*, exp. ed. (New York: W. W. Norton, 2002); Victoria De Grazia, *Irresistible Empire: America's Advance Through Twentieth-Century Europe* (Cambridge, Mass.: Belknap, 2006).

20. İhsan Yılmaz, "Secular Law and the Emergence of Unofficial Turkish Islamic Law," *Middle East Journal* 56, no. 1 (2002): 113–131, 118. The literature here is extensive, as every history of modern Turkey has had to discuss Europe-oriented westernization reforms. Some influential works include Lewis, *Emergence of Modern Turkey*; Mardin, *Türk Modernleşmesi*; Niyazi Berkes, *Türkiye'de Çağdaşlaşma* [The development of secularism in Turkey] (Istanbul: Yapı Kredi Publishing, 2007); Jacob M. Landau, ed., *Ataturk and the Modernization of Turkey* (Leiden: Brill, 1984); Fatma Müge Göçek, *Rise of the Bourgeoisie, Demise of Empire: Ottoman Westernization and Social Change* (New York: Oxford University Press, 1996); Bozdoğan and Kasaba, eds., *Rethinking Modernity and National Identity*; Erik J. Zürcher, *Turkey: A Modern History* (London: I. B. Tauris, 2004).

21. John M. Vander Lippe, "The 'Terrible Turk': The Formulation and Perpetuation of a Stereotype in American Foreign Policy," *New Perspectives on Turkey* 17 (September 1997): 39–57; John M. Vander Lippe, "Racism and the Making of American Foreign Policy: The 'Terrible Turk' as Icon and Metaphor," *Research in Politics and Society* 6 (1999): 47–63; Justin McCarthy, *The Turk in America: The Creation of an Enduring Prejudice*, Utah Series in Turkish and Islamic Studies (Salt Lake City: University of Utah Press, 2010).

22. Nils Gilman, *Mandarins of the Future: Modernization Theory in Cold War America* (Baltimore: Johns Hopkins University Press, 2007), 30–32; Nathan J. Citino, "The Ottoman Legacy in Cold War Modernization," *International Journal of Middle East Studies* 40 (November 2008): 579–597; Matthew F. Jacobs, *Imagining the Middle East: The Building of an American Foreign Policy, 1918–1967* (Chapel Hill: University of North Carolina Press, 2011). See chapter 2 for more on this subject.

23. Henri J. Barkey, "The Endless Pursuit: Improving U.S.-Turkish Relations," in *United States and Turkey*, 207–249; See also Graham E. Fuller, *The New Turkish Republic: Turkey as a Pivotal State in the Muslim World* (Washington, D.C.: U.S. Institute of Peace, 2007).

24. Edward W. Said, *Orientalism* (New York: Vintage, 1978), 1.

25. John Carlos Rowe, "Edward Said and American Studies," *American Quarterly* 56, no. 1 (2004): 33–47; Jacob S. Dorman, "Ever the Twain Shall Meet: Orientalism and American Studies," *American Quarterly* 67, no. 2 (2015): 491–503.

26. Melani McAlister, *Epic Encounters: Culture, Media, and U.S. Interests in the Middle East Since 1945*, 1st ed., rev. (Berkeley: University of California Press, 2005). Although Said points out the gendering of the East as a "fairly supine, feminine Orient" to be possessed, later feminist readings have emphasized this feature of Orientalist discourse (Said, *Orientalism*, 220). See Reina Lewis, *Gendering Orientalism: Race, Femininity and Representation* (New York: Routledge, 1995); Melda Yeğenoğlu, *Colonial Fantasies: Towards a Feminist Reading of Orientalism* (New York: Cambridge University Press, 1998); Lila Abu-Lughod, "'Orientalism' and Middle East Feminist Studies," *Feminist Studies* 27, no. 1 (2001): 101–113.

27. For example, McAlister, *Epic Encounters*; Douglas Little, *American Orientalism: The United States and the Middle East Since 1945* (Chapel Hill: University of North Carolina Press, 2002); Timothy Marr, *The Cultural Roots of American Islamicism* (Cambridge: Cambridge University Press, 2006); Susan Nance, *How the Arabian Nights Inspired the American Dream, 1790–1935* (Chapel Hill: University of North Carolina Press, 2009); Jacob Rama Berman, *American Arabesque: Arabs, Islam, and the Nineteenth-Century Imaginary* (New York: New York University Press, 2012).

28. For example, Bill V. Mullen, *Afro-Orientalism* (Minneapolis: University of Minnesota Press, 2004); Brian T. Edwards, *Morocco Bound: Disorienting America's Maghreb, from Casablanca to the Marrakech Express* (Durham, N.C.: Duke University Press Books, 2005); Ussama Makdisi, *Artillery of Heaven: American Missionaries and the Failed Conversion of the Middle East* (Ithaca, N.Y.: Cornell University Press, 2008); Waïl S. Hassan, *Immigrant Narratives: Orientalism and Cultural Translation in Arab American and Arab British Literature* (New York: Oxford University Press, 2011); Nadine Naber, *Arab America: Gender, Cultural Politics, and Activism* (New York: New York University Press, 2012); Sohail Daulatzai, *Black Star, Crescent Moon: The Muslim International and Black Freedom Beyond America* (Minneapolis: University of Minnesota Press, 2012); Ella Habiba Shohat and Evelyn Azeeza Alsultany, eds., *Between the Middle East and the Americas: The Cultural Politics of Diaspora* (Ann Arbor: University of Michigan Press, 2013); Alex Lubin, *Geographies of Liberation: The Making of an Afro-Arab Political Imaginary* (Chapel Hill: University of North Carolina Press, 2014); Carol Fadda-Conrey, *Contemporary Arab-American Literature: Transnational Reconfigurations of Citizenship and Belonging* (New York: New York University Press, 2014); Keith P. Feldman, *A Shadow Over Palestine: The Imperial Life of Race in America* (Minneapolis: University of Minnesota Press, 2015); Brian T. Edwards, *After the American Century: The Ends of U.S. Culture in the Middle East* (New York: Columbia University Press, 2016).

29. See, for example, James E. Ketelaar, *Of Heretics and Martyrs in Meiji Japan: Buddhism and Its Persecution* (Princeton, N.J.: Princeton University Press, 1990), 137; James G. Carrier, ed., *Occidentalism: Images of the West* (Oxford: Clarendon, 1995); Chen, *Occidentalism*; and Alastair Bonnett, *The Idea of the West: Culture, Politics and History* (New York: Palgrave Macmillan, 2004); Mohamed Tavakoli-Targhi, *Refashioning Iran: Orientalism, Occidentalism and Historiography* (New York: Palgrave Macmillan, 2001); Afsaneh Najmabadi, *Women with Mustaches and Men Without Beards: Gender and Sexual Anxieties of Iranian Modernity* (Berkeley: University of California Press, 2005). For Turkey, see Meltem Ahıska, "Occidentalism: The Historical Fantasy of the Modern," *South Atlantic Quarterly* 102, no. 2/3 (2003): 351–379, and Aydın, *Politics of Anti-Westernism in Asia*.

30. Brian T. Edwards and Dilip Parameshwar Gaonkar, "Introduction: Globalizing American Studies," in *Globalizing American Studies*, ed. Brian T. Edwards and Dilip Parameshwar Gaonkar (Chicago: University of Chicago Press, 2010).

31. Predominant scholarship on European views on (and uses of) "America" includes Wagnleitner, *Coca-Colonization and the Cold War*; Rob Kroes, *If You've Seen One, You've Seen the Mall: Europeans and American Mass Culture* (Urbana: University of Illinois Press, 1996); Kuisel, *Seducing the French*; Richard Pells, *Not Like Us: How Europeans Have Loved, Hated, and Transformed American Culture Since World War II* (New York: Basic Books, 2008); Uta G. Poiger, *Jazz, Rock, and Rebels: Cold War Politics and American Culture in a Divided Germany* (Berkeley: University of California Press, 2000). A significant body of work focusing on Latin American views of the United States exists as well, boosted by the 1998 publication of Gilbert Michael Joseph and Catherine LeGrand, eds., *Close Encounters of Empire: Writing the Cultural History of U.S.-Latin American Relations* (Durham, N.C.: Duke University Press, 1998).

32. Dipesh Chakrabarty, *Provincializing Europe: Postcolonial Thought and Historical Difference* (Princeton, N.J.: Princeton University Press, 2000).

33. Allow me to cite a few significant precedents associated with my own field of American studies here. Transnational feminist scholars Inderpal Grewal and Caren Kaplan have critiqued "the institutional divide between international area studies and American studies" for foreclosing important areas of inquiry, especially for scholars of sexuality. Inderpal Grewal and Caren Kaplan, "Global Identities: Theorizing Transnational Studies of Sexuality," *Gay and Lesbian Quarterly* 7, no. 4 (2001): 663–679, 668–669. Historian Seth Fein advocates and models bilingual and interdisciplinary scholarship at the intersection of area studies and American studies in his "New Empire Into Old: Making Mexican Newsreels the Cold War Way," *Diplomatic History* 28, no. 5 (2004): 703–748. Edwards and Gaonkar have called for a multilingual, comparative, provincial-

ized American studies in their introduction to the 2010 edited collection *Globalizing American Studies,* which constitutes a significant landmark in the field, as do Amy Kaplan and Donald E. Pease, eds., *Cultures of United States Imperialism* (Durham, N.C.: Duke University Press Books, 1994) and *Re-Framing the Transnational Turn in American Studies,* ed. Winfried Fluck, Donald E. Pease, and John Carlos Rowe (Hanover, N.H.: Dartmouth College Press, 2011). Ella Shohat has argued for a similar approach examining the "co-implicatedness of regions, for example, of America in the Middle East and the Middle East in America." Ella Shohat, "The Sephardic-Moorish Atlantic: Between Orientalism and Occidentalism," in *Between the Middle East and the Americas: The Cultural Politics of Diaspora,* ed. Evelyn Alsultany and Ella Shohat (Ann Arbor: University of Michigan Press, 2013), 42–62, 56. The recent publications of "On Demand and Relevance: Transnational American Studies in the Middle East and North Africa," a special issue of *Comparative American Studies* 13, no. 4 (June 2016), ed. Ebony Coletu and Ira Dworkin; and Alex Lubin and Marwan M. Kraidy, eds., *American Studies Encounters the Middle East* (Chapel Hill: University of North Carolina Press, 2016) demonstrate a new tide of intellectual work committed to bridging this divide.

34. Edwards, *After the American Century,* 37.
35. Ibid., 72.
36. Historians and historically oriented sociologists have written almost all influential accounts of Turkish selective westernization. See note 20.
37. See chapter 2.
38. Examples relevant to my project include Göle, *Forbidden Modern;* Pınar Selek, *Maskeler, Süvariler, Gacılar* [Masks, cavaliers, and the gacıs] (Istanbul: İstiklal Kitabevi, 2007); Alev Çınar, *Modernity, Islam, and Secularism in Turkey: Bodies, Places, and Time* (Minneapolis: University of Minnesota Press, 2005); Öykü Potuoğlu-Cook, "Beyond the Glitter: Belly Dance and Neoliberal Gentrification in Istanbul," *Cultural Anthropology* 21, no. 4 (2006): 633–660; Esra Özyürek, *Nostalgia for the Modern: State Secularism and Everyday Politics in Turkey* (Durham, N.C.: Duke University Press, 2006); Meral Özbek, "Arabesk Culture: A Case for Modernization and Popular Identity," in *Rethinking Modernity and National Identity in Turkey,* 211–232; Ayşe Öncü, "Istanbulites and Others: The Cultural Cosmology of Being Middle Class in the Era of Globalism," in *Istanbul: Between the Global and the Local,* ed. Çağlar Keyder (Lanham, Md.: Rowman & Littlefield, 1999), 95–120; Çağlar Keyder, "Globalization and Social Exclusion in Istanbul," *International Journal of Urban and Regional Research* 29, no. 1 (2005): 124–134.
39. Deniz Kandiyoti and Ayşe Saktanber, eds., *Fragments of Culture: The Everyday of Modern Turkey* (New Brunswick, N.J.: Rutgers University Press, 2002); Yael

Navaro-Yashin, *Faces of the State: Secularism and Public Life in Turkey* (Princeton, N.J.: Princeton University Press, 2002); Nurdan Gürbilek, *Vitrinde Yaşamak: 1980'lerin Kültürel İklimi* [Living in the store windows: The cultural climate of the 1980s] (Istanbul: Metis, 2001); Elif Shafak, *The Flea Palace*, trans. Müge Göçek (London: Marion Boyars, 2004).

40. Shelley Fisher Fishkin, "Crossroads of Cultures: The Transnational Turn in American Studies—Presidential Address to the American Studies Association, November 12, 2004," *American Quarterly* 57, no. 1 (2005): 17–57, 20.

41. Roland Barthes and Richard Howard, *S/Z: An Essay*, trans. Richard Miller (New York: Hill and Wang, 1975).

1. NARRATING THE MANDATE

1. Letter from the founders of the Turkish Wilsonian League to President Wilson, December 5, 1918, Box 207, Folder 2/824, Yale University Manuscripts and Archives.

2. Timothy Marr, *The Cultural Roots of American Islamicism* (New York: Cambridge University Press, 2006), 9.

3. Emily S. Rosenberg, *Spreading the American Dream: American Economic and Cultural Expansion, 1890–1945* (New York: Hill and Wang, 1982), 7–13.

4. Quincy Wright, "The United States and the Mandates," *Michigan Law Review* 23, no. 7 (1925): 717–747, 719.

5. Michael Oren, *Power, Faith, and Fantasy: America in the Middle East, 1776 to the Present* (New York: W. W. Norton, 2007), 377.

6. "The Council of Four: Minutes of Meetings from March 20 to May 24, 1919," in *Papers Relating to the Foreign Relations of the United States* (hereafter cited as *FRUS*), *The Paris Peace Conference, 1919* (Washington, D.C.: U.S. Government Printing Office, 1914–1920), vol. 5, 482.

7. Halide Edib to Mustafa Kemal Atatürk, August 10, 1919, reprinted in Mustafa Kemal Atatürk, *A Speech Delivered by Mustafa Kemal Atatürk, 1927* (Istanbul: Başbakanlık Basımevi, 1981), 76–80. The National Assembly gave Kemal the last name Atatürk in 1934. Since this name and Edib's last name (Adıvar) were not in use during the era on which this chapter focuses, I do not use them.

8. For example, Melani McAlister, *Epic Encounters: Culture, Media, and U.S. Interests in the Middle East Since 1945*, 1st ed., rev. (Berkeley: University of California Press, 2005); Timothy Marr, *The Cultural Roots of American Islamicism* (New York: Cambridge University Press, 2006); Christina Klein, *Cold War Orientalism: Asia in the Middlebrow Imagination, 1945–1961* (Berkeley: University of California Press, 2003).

9. Eric Tyrone Lowery Love, *Race Over Empire: Racism and U.S. Imperialism, 1865–1900* (Chapel Hill: University of North Carolina Press, 2004).

10. Homi K. Bhabha, "Introduction: Narrating the Nation," in *Nation and Narration*, ed. Homi K. Bhabha (New York: Routledge, 1990).

11. For disremembering as a narrative technique, see W. J. T. Mitchell, "Narrative, Memory, and Slavery," in *Picture Theory: Essays on Verbal and Visual Representation* (Chicago: University of Chicago, 1995), 183–208. For overremembering, see Paul Ricoeur, *Memory, History, Forgetting* (Chicago: University of Chicago Press, 2006). Here I use both concepts in reference to collective practices of cultural memory.

12. Mitchell, "Narrative, Memory, and Slavery," 184. Mitchell is referencing Hortense Spillers's depiction of the "knowledge industry," which has turned slavery into "a phenomenon so well known that nothing more is to be known about it." See Hortense J. Spillers, "Changing the Letter: The Yokes, the Jokes of Discourse, or, Mrs. Stowe, Mr. Reed," in *Slavery and the Literary Imagination*, ed. Deborah E. McDowell and Arnold Rampersad (Baltimore: Johns Hopkins University Press, 1989), 25–61. Benedict Richard O'Gorman Anderson, *Imagined Communities: Reflections on the Origin and Spread of Nationalism* (New York: Verso, 1991). For Turkey, see Nergis Canefe, "Turkish Nationalism and Ethno-Symbolic Analysis: The Rules of Exception," *Nations and Nationalism* 8, no. 2 (2002): 133–155.

13. Sabri M. Akural, "Kemalist Views on Social Change," in *Ataturk and the Modernization of Turkey*, ed. Jacob M. Landau (Boulder, Colo.: Westview, 1984), 125–152; Feroz Ahmad, *The Making of Modern Turkey* (London: Routledge, 1993), 80; Ayşe Kadıoğlu, "The Paradox of Turkish Nationalism and the Construction of Official Identity," *Middle Eastern Studies* 32, no. 2 (1996): 177–193; Büşra Ersanlı, "History Textbooks as Reflections of the Political Self: Turkey (1930s and 1990s) and Uzbekistan (1990s)," *International Journal of Middle East Studies* 34, no. 2 (2002): 337–349. Howard Eissenstat, "History and Historiography: Politics and Memory in the Turkish Republic," *Contemporary European History* 12, no. 1 (2003): 93–105; Clive Foss, "Kemal Atatürk: Giving a New Nation a New History," *Middle Eastern Studies* 50, no. 5 (2014): 826–847; Étienne Copeaux, *Tarih Ders Kitaplarında (1931–1993) Türk Tarih Tezinden Türk-İslâm Sentezine* [From the Turkish History Thesis to the Turkish-Islamic Synthesis in History Textbooks], trans. Ali Berktay (Istanbul: İletişim, 2014).

14. Hülya Adak, "National Myths and Self-Na(rra)tions: Mustafa Kemal's *Nutuk* and Halide Edib's *Memoirs* and *The Turkish Ordeal*," *South Atlantic Quarterly* 102, no. 2/3 (2003): 509–529; see also Erik J. Zürcher, *Turkey: A Modern History*, rev. ed. (London: I. B. Tauris, 2004), 175.

15. Fatma Müge Göçek, *The Transformation of Turkey: Redefining State and Society from the Ottoman Empire to the Modern Era* (London: I. B. Tauris, 2011), 23; Büşra Ersanlı, "The Ottoman Empire in the Historiography of the Kemalist Era: A Theory of Fatal Decline," in *The Ottomans and the Balkans: A Discussion of Historiography*, ed. Fikret Adanır and Suraiya Faroqhi (Boston: E. J. Brill, 2002), 115–154.

16. Michel-Rolph Trouillot, "Good Day Columbus," in *Silencing the Past: Power and the Production of History* (Boston: Beacon, 1995), 108–140; James W. Loewen, *Lies My Teacher Told Me: Everything Your American History Textbook Got Wrong* (New York: Simon and Schuster, 2007).

17. Amy Kaplan, "'Left Alone with America': The Absence of Empire in the Study of American Culture," in *Cultures of U.S. Imperialism*, ed. Amy Kaplan and Donald Pease (Durham, N.C.: Duke University Press, 1993), 3–21.

18. Loewen, *Lies My Teacher Told Me*, 97.

19. Mitchell, "Narrative, Memory, and Slavery," 187–188.

20. "A practice not only of recollection of a past *by* a subject, but of recollection *for* another subject." Ibid., 193n17.

21. The 1944 biopic *Wilson*, produced by Darryl F. Zanuck and 20th Century Fox, starring Alexander Knox as President Woodrow Wilson, is a great example of the president's redemption in the mid-century.

22. Mustafa Aydın, introduction to *Turkish-American Relations: Past, Present and Future*, ed. Mustafa Aydın and Çağrı Erhan (London: Routledge, 2004), xvii–xxiv.

23. Leland James Gordon, *American Relations with Turkey, 1830–1930: An Economic Interpretation* (Philadelphia: University of Pennsylvania Press, 1932).

24. Şuhnaz Yılmaz, *Turkish-American Relations, 1800–1952: Between the Stars, Stripes and the Crescent* (London: Routledge, 2015), 16–17; Nur Gürani Arslan, *Türk Edebiyatında Amerika ve Amerikalılar* [America and Americans in Turkish literature] (Istanbul: Boğaziçi, 2000), 6–8.

25. Walter LaFeber, *The New Empire: An Interpretation of American Expansion 1860–1898*, 35th anniv. ed. (Ithaca, N.Y.: Cornell University Press, 1998); Amy Kaplan, *The Anarchy of Empire in the Making of U.S. Culture* (Cambridge, Mass.: Harvard University Press, 2002); Matthew Frye Jacobson, *Barbarian Virtues: The United States Encounters Foreign Peoples at Home and Abroad, 1876–1917* (New York: Hill and Wang, 2001).

26. Rosenberg, *Spreading the American Dream*.

27. Joseph L. Grabill, *Protestant Diplomacy in the Near East: Missionary Influence on American Policy, 1810–1927* (Minneapolis: University of Minnesota Press, 1971), 47; Robert L. Daniel, "The Armenian Question and American-Turkish Relations, 1914–1927," *Mississippi Valley Historical Review* 46, no. 2 (1959): 252–275, 254.

28. Oren, *Power, Faith, and Fantasy*, 293.

29. Kaplan, *Anarchy of Empire*, 3. Kaplan uses these terms in reference to the ambiguous position of Puerto Rico at the end of the nineteenth century; I believe they work just as well to describe the United States' relation to missions in the Near East as "ambiguous spaces" in which U.S. military, economic, and cultural power could function "divorced from political annexation" (15).

30. Jeremy Salt, *Imperialism, Evangelism and the Ottoman Armenians, 1878–1896* (London: Frank Cass, 1993), 48; Donald Bloxham, "Rethinking the Armenian Genocide," *History Today* 55, no. 6 (2005): 28–30.

31. Grabill, *Protestant Diplomacy*, 40.

32. Taner Akçam, *A Shameful Act: The Armenian Genocide and the Question of Turkish Responsibility* (New York: Holt, 2006), 44.

33. Robert L. Daniel, "The United States and the Turkish Republic Before World War II: The Cultural Dimension," *Middle East Journal* 21, no. 1 (1967): 52–63; Suzanne E. Moranian, "The Armenian Genocide and American Missionary Relief Efforts," in *America and the Armenian Genocide of 1915*, ed. Jay Winter (New York: Cambridge University Press, 2003), 185–213. For a primary example, see Edwin Munsell Bliss, *Turkey and the Armenian Atrocities* (Edgewood, 1896), 306.

34. Susan C. Pearce, "The 'Turkish Model' of Sociology: East-West Science, State Formation, and the Post-Secular," *The American Sociologist* 43, no. 4 (2012): 406–427, 412.

35. Fuat Dündar, *Modern Türkiye'nin Şifresi: İttihat ve Terakki'nin Etnisite Mühendisliği, 1913–1918* [The password to modern Turkey: Ethnic engineering of the Committee for Union and Progress, 1913–1918] (Istanbul: İletişim, 2008); Canefe, "Turkish Nationalism and Ethno-Symbolic Analysis," 149.

36. Quoted in Oren, *Power, Faith, and Fantasy*, 313.

37. Statement of the Turkish Ambassador (Rustem) as published in the *Washington Evening Star*, September 8, 1914. Reproduced in U.S. Department of State, *FRUS, The Lansing Papers, 1914–1920* (Washington, D.C.: U.S. Government Printing Office, 1914–1920), vol. 1, 68–75.

38. Henry Morgenthau, "Report of Conversation with Talaat Pasha, 8 August 1915," in *United States Diplomacy on the Bosphorus: The Diaries of Ambassador Morgenthau, 1913–1916*, ed. Ara Sarafian (London: Gomidas Institute, 2004), 298.

39. "Tells of Wilson's Armenian Pledge," *New York Times*, May 3, 1920; Nicole Pope and Hugh Pope, *Turkey Unveiled: A History of Modern Turkey* (New York: Overlook, 2000), 60.

40. Sally Howell, *Old Islam in Detroit: Rediscovering the Muslim American Past* (New York: Oxford University Press, 2014), 67. While outside the scope of this chapter, this perception also affected the Turkish immigrants in the United States, as Howell points out.

41. "President Wilson's Fourteen Points," delivered in Joint Session of U.S. Congress, January 8, 1918, *The World War I Document Archive*, http://wwi.lib .byu.edu/index.php/President_Wilson%27s_Fourteen_Points, accessed July 13, 2008.

42. "The Present Situation: The War Aims and Peace Terms It Suggests," Inquiry Memorandum, December 22, 1917, *FRUS, The Paris Peace Conference, 1919*, 1:41–53.

43. Ahmed Emin Yalman, *Turkey in My Time* (Norman: University of Oklahoma Press, 1956), 71–73.

44. For more on the centrality of Point 12 to the discussions preceding the Turkish Independence War, see Vahdet Keleşyılmaz and Mehmet Şahingöz, "Millî Mücadele Dönemi Türk Basınında Wilson Prensipleri" [Wilsonian principles in the Turkish press in the era of the nationalist resistance], *Atatürk Araştırma Merkezi Dergisi* 12, no. 35 (1996): 357–378.

45. "The Council of Four: Minutes of Meetings from March 20 to May 24, 1919," *FRUS, The Paris Peace Conference, 1919*, 5:13.

46. Halide Edib, *The Turkish Ordeal: Being the Further Memoirs of Halidé Edib* (London: Century, 1928), 15.

47. By all accounts, except her own, Halide Edib was the driving force behind the Wilsonian Principles League. See Gotthard Jäschke, "Ein amerikanisches Mandat für die Türkei?" [An American mandate for Turkey?], *Die Welt des Islams* n.s. 8, no. 4 (1963): 219–234, 220–221.

48. Edib, *Turkish Ordeal*.

49. Erez Manela, *The Wilsonian Moment: Self-Determination and the International Origins of Anticolonial Nationalism* (New York: Oxford University Press, 2007).

50. Ibid., 91–92.

51. Yalman, *Turkey in My Time*, 71–73.

52. Edib to Kemal, 77.

53. Ibid.

54. Theodore Roosevelt to William Wingate Sewall, May 4, 1898, in *The Letters of Theodore Roosevelt*, ed. Elting E. Morison (Cambridge, Mass.: Harvard University Press, 1951–1954), vol. 2, 822.

55. Malcolm D. Magee, *What the World Should Be: Woodrow Wilson and the Crafting of a Faith-Based Foreign Policy* (Waco, Tex.: Baylor University Press, 2008).

56. David Fromkin, *A Peace to End All Peace: The Fall of the Ottoman Empire and the Creation of the Modern Middle East* (New York: Macmillan, 2001), 258.

57. Lawrence Evans, *United States Policy and the Partition of Turkey, 1914–1924* (Baltimore: Johns Hopkins Press, 1965), 102.

58. "The Council of Four: Minutes of Meetings from March 20 to May 24, 1919," *FRUS, The Paris Peace Conference, 1919*, 5:10.

59. Ibid., 757.

60. "Wilson Warns U. S. May Refuse to Rule Turks," *New York Times*, May 25, 1919.

61. Meltem Ahıska, "Occidentalism: The Historical Fantasy of the Modern," *South Atlantic Quarterly* 102, no. 2/3 (2003): 351–379, 360.

62. Anne Classen Knutson, "The Enemy Imaged: Visual Configurations of Race and Ethnicity in World War I Propaganda Posters," in *Race and the Production of Modern American Nationalism*, ed. Reynolds J. Scott-Childress (New York: Routledge, 1999), 195–220; Jacobson, *Barbarian Virtues*, 162.

63. Interestingly, a woman wrote the only American article I could find that mentions Edib's role in setting up "Wilson Societies" at the time. The sensational novelist Marguerite Cunliffe-Owen, using a pen name, called Edib "thoroughly unscrupulous" in this article and claimed (falsely) that she was educated at a women's college in the United States. La Marquise de Fontenoy, "Woman Educated in America Fights Allies in Turkey," *Washington Post*, June 27, 1919.

64. Stanford Shaw, "Halide Edib (Adıvar)'s Appeal to the American Public for Justice for the Turks," *Belleten* 67, no. 249 (2003): 531–539.

65. Paul C. Helmreich, *From Paris to Sèvres: The Partition of the Ottoman Empire at the Peace Conference of 1919–1920* (Columbus: Ohio State University Press, 1974), 28.

66. "Wilson Urges We Take Armenia Mandate," *New York Times*, May 25, 1920.

67. Mark Malkasian, "The Disintegration of the Armenian Cause in the United States, 1918–1927," *International Journal of Middle East Studies* 16, no. 3 (1984): 349–365.

68. Thomas Bryson, *American Diplomatic Relations with the Middle East, 1784–1975: A Survey* (Metuchen, N.J.: Scarecrow, 1977), 73.

69. Thomas Bailey, *Wilson and the Great Betrayal* (New York: Times Books, 1963), 296.

70. Robert L. Daniel, "The United States and the Turkish Republic Before World War II: The Cultural Dimension," *Middle East Journal* 21, no. 1 (1967): 52–63.

71. "The Secretary of State to the High Commissioner in Turkey (Bristol)," *FRUS, 1927*, document number 711.672/540, 3:770.

72. Louis L. Thurstone, "An Experimental Study of Nationality Preferences," *Journal of General Psychology* 1 (1928): 405–423.

73. Adak, "National Myths and Self-Na(rra)tions."

74. Jale Parla, *Babalar ve Oğullar: Tanzimat Romanının Epistemolojik Temelleri* [Fathers and sons: The epistemological foundations of the Tanzimat novel] (Istanbul: İletişim, 1990). I am grateful for this formulation to Naoko Shibusawa, whose work cogently underlines how maturity might work alongside gender in political representations. See Naoko Shibusawa, *America's Geisha*

Ally: Reimagining the Japanese Enemy (Cambridge, Mass.: Harvard University Press, 2010).

75. Dündar, *Modern Türkiye'nin Şifresi*, 71.
76. Yakup Kadri Karaosmanoğlu, *Sodom ve Gomore* [Sodom and Gomorrah] (1928; repr. Istanbul: İletişim, 2004).
77. Kemal, *Speech*, 5.
78. Zürcher, *Turkey*, 148.
79. These words (*Ya İstiklal Ya Ölüm!*) are memorized by Turkish school kids. Kemal, *Speech*, 10.
80. Halide Edib (Adıvar), *Turkey Faces West: A Turkish View of Recent Changes and Their Origin* (New Haven, Conn.: Yale University Press, 1930).
81. "Turk Nationalists Organize to Resist," *New York Times*, March 20, 1920.
82. Quoted in Orhan Koloğlu, "Halide Edib'in Gönüllü Sürgün Yılları" [Halide Edib's years in voluntary exile], *Tarih ve Toplum* 174 (1998): 12–16, 13.
83. Avni Özgürel, "Benzersiz Bir Aydınlık" [An unmatched radiance], *Radikal*, June 17, 2001, 9.
84. Mark Bristol to the Secretary of State, "A Realistic Interpretation of Modern Turkey," RG59, Records of the Department of State Relating to Internal Affairs of Turkey, document dated May 22, 1925, no. 867.401/8, National Archives and Records Administration, College Park, Md.
85. Nilüfer Göle, *The Forbidden Modern: Civilization and Veiling* (Ann Arbor: University of Michigan Press, 1996), 64–66; Deniz Kandiyoti, "Gendering the Modern: On Missing Dimensions in the Study of Turkish Modernity," in *Rethinking Modernity and National Identity in Turkey*, ed. Sibel Bozdoğan and Reşat Kasaba (Seattle: University of Washington Press, 1997), 113–132; Ferhunde Özbay, "Gendered Space: A New Look at Turkish Modernisation," *Gender & History* 11, no. 3 (1999): 555–568.
86. Halide Edib (Adıvar), "Dictatorship and Reform in Turkey" (1929), reprinted in *The Middle East and Islamic World Reader*, ed. Marvin E. Gettleman and Stuart Schaar (New York: Grove, 2004), 129.
87. Ibid.
88. Italics added. "Turks Drop Arabic for Our Alphabet," *New York Times*, April 30, 1928.
89. For example, "Says Turks Resent Kemal's Methods: Mme. Halide Edib Finds Dictator Too Eager to Set Up European Standards and Culture," *New York Times*, February 2, 1931, Business & Opportunity section.
90. G. Howland Shaw, "An Intellectualistic Interpretation of Modern Turkey," RG59, Records of the Department of State Relating to Internal Affairs of Turkey, 1910–1929, document dated September 12, 1924, no. 867.401/8, National Archives and Records Administration, College Park, Md.

91. Ibid.

92. After working as a visiting professor at Columbia University during the 1931–1932 academic year, Edib continued her lectures in British-controlled India, where she compared the Turkish and Indian anticolonial struggles. Alparslan Nas, "Inside India, Outside of Kemalism: Analysis of Halide Edib's Writings on Anti-Colonialism," *International Journal of Humanities and Social Science* 3, no. 7 (2013): 187–193.

93. Halide Edib, "Turkey and America: The Ghazi's Speech," *The Times*, October 21, 1927, 12.

94. "Kemal Is Disputed by Turkish Woman: Halide Edib, Novelist, Denies That She Favored an American 'Protectorate,'" *New York Times*, November 13, 1927, Editorial section.

95. Charles E. Allen, consul in charge, Review of the Turkish Press (October 23–November 5, 1927), November 9, 1927, American Embassy, Constantinople (1927), Diplomatic Posts, Turkey, vol. 17, class 891, National Archives and Records Administration, College Park, Md.

96. Kadir Kasalak, "Sivas Kongresi Öncesinde Manda ve Himayenin Türk Basınında Tartışılması ve Komutanlar Arasında Yazışmalar" [The discussions on the mandate and protectorate before the Sivas Congress and the correspondence between officers], *Atatürk Yolu Dergisi* 10, no. 3 (November 1992): 187–211, 207.

97. Evans, *United States Policy*, 177.

98. Mazhar Müfit Kansu, *Erzurum'dan Ölümüne Kadar Atatürk'le Beraber* [With Atatürk from the Congress of Erzurum until his death], vol. 1 (Ankara: TTK, 1986).

99. Hayri Mutluçag, ed., "Sivas Kongresinin Tutanak ve Kararları" [The records and decisions of the Sivas Congress], *Belgelerle Türk Tarihi Dergisi* 65 (February 1973): 4–10.

100. Kemal, *Speech*, 93.

101. James G. Harbord, *Conditions in the Near East: Report of the American Military Mission to Armenia* (Washington, D.C.: Government Printing Office, 1920), 40.

102. Kasalak, "Sivas Kongresi Öncesinde," 207. See also Deniz Bilgen, *ABD'li Gözüyle Sivas Kongresi: Amerikan Mandası ve Gazeteci L. E. Browne'in Faaliyetleri* [The Sivas Congress in American eyes: The American mandate and the activities of journalist L. E. Browne] (Istanbul: Kaynak, 2004), 182.

103. Kemal, *Speech*, 84.

104. Kansu, *Erzurum'dan Ölümüne Kadar*, 192.

105. Harbord, *Conditions in the Near East*, 16–17.

106. "Big Cities Join Turkish Revolt," *New York Times*, October 14, 1919.

107. Michael J. Shapiro, "Moral Geographies and the Ethics of Post-Sovereignty," *Public Culture* 6, no. 3 (March 20, 1994): 479–502.

108. Roderic H. Davison, "Turkish Diplomacy from Mudros to Lausanne," in *The Diplomats, 1919–1939*, ed. Gordon A. Craig and Felix Gilbert (Princeton, N.J.: Princeton University Press, 1953), 172–209, 178.

109. Cemil Aydın, *The Politics of Anti-Westernism in Asia: Visions of World Order in Pan-Islamic and Pan-Asian Thought* (New York: Columbia University Press, 2013), 133–136. Of course, at the time, the representatives could not have known that Kemal would abolish both the sultanate and the caliphate in 1924.

110. "Meeting Held at President Wilson's House in Place des Etats-Unis, Paris, Saturday, May 17, 1919, at 4:30 p.m.," *FRUS, The Paris Peace Conference 1919*, 5:694.

111. Ibid., 693.

112. "The Council of Four: Minutes of Meetings from March 20 to May 24, 1919," *FRUS, Paris Peace Conference 1919*, 5:708.

113. Anderson, *Imagined Communities*, 204.

114. "The Council of Four: Minutes of Meetings from March 20 to May 24, 1919," *FRUS, Paris Peace Conference 1919*, 5:13.

115. Marr, *Cultural Roots*, 94.

116. Charles Seymour, ed., *The Intimate Papers of Colonel House* (Boston: Houghton Mifflin, 1926–1928), vol. 1, 96.

117. Ibid., 3:323.

118. Aydın, *Politics of Anti-Westernism*, 130.

119. Evans, *United States Policy*, 183.

120. "The Council of Heads of Delegations: Minutes of Meetings, July 1 to August 28, 1919," *FRUS, Paris Peace Conference, 1919*, 7:839.

121. Margaret MacMillan, *Paris 1919: Six Months That Changed the World* (New York: Random House, 2003), 33.

122. James G. Harbord, "Investigating Turkey and Trans-Caucasia," *World's Work* 40, no. 1 (1920): 43; Peter D'Epiro and Mary Desmond Pinkowish, *What Are the Seven Wonders of the World: And One Hundred Other Great Cultural Lists, Fully Explicated* (New York: Random House, 1998), 433; Thomas Paterson, J. Garry Clifford, Shane J. Maddock, Deborah Kisatsky, and Kenneth Hagan, *American Foreign Relations: A History*, vol. 1: *To 1920* (Boston: Cengage Learning, 2009), 290.

123. McAlister, *Epic Encounters*, 200.

124. "Milli Mücadeleye İnanmayanlar" [Those who didn't believe in the national resistance], *Dün ve Bugün* 1 (1955): 24–25.

125. For example, Ziya Somar, "Manda ve Meşhur Mandacılar" [The mandate and famous pro-mandate individuals], *Tarih Konuşuyor* 3, no. 14 (1965): 1144–1147;

Fahrettin Kırzıoğlu, "Amerikan Mandasını Kimler İstiyor ve Nasıl Öneriyorlardı?" [Who wanted the American mandate and how did they propose it], *Belgelerle Türk Tarihi Dergisi* 67–68 (April–May 1973): 30–37.

126. For example, Mine Erol, *Türkiye'de Amerikan Mandası Meselesi* [The issue of the American mandate in Turkey] (Giresun: İleri, 1972); Bilgen, *ABD'li Gözüyle Sivas Kongresi*; İpek Çalışlar, *Halide Edib: Biyografisine Sığmayan Kadın* [Halide Edib: The woman who does not fit inside her biography] (Istanbul: Everest, 2010).

127. Mustafa Barut, *Türkiye Cumhuriyeti Tarihi I* [History of the Turkish Republic I] (Ankara: Alkım, 1997), 86.

128. Compare: Wikipedia katılımcıları, "Manda (diplomasi)," Wikipedia, Özgür Ansiklopedi, http://tr.wikipedia.org/w/index.php?title=Manda_(diplomasi)&oldid =6744869, accessed July 21, 2015, and Wikipedia contributors, "League of Nations Mandate," Wikipedia, The Free Encyclopedia, http://en.wikipedia.org /w/index.php?title=League_of_Nations_mandate&oldid=328029291, accessed July 21, 2015.

129. *The Ottoman Republic*, directed by Gani Müjde (Avşar Film, 2008).

130. John DeNovo, *American Interests and Policies in the Middle East: 1900–1939* (Minneapolis: University of Minnesota Press, 1963), 118.

131. David Arnett, "Problems of Perception and Vision: Turkey and the U.S.," *Turkish Policy Quarterly* 7, no. 1 (March 2008): 13–23.

132. "Cumhurbaşkanı Erdoğan: 'Karanlık Mandacı Aydın Müsveddeleri'" [President Erdoğan: "Dark, pro-mandate fake intellectuals"], *Hürriyet*, January 12, 2016, http://www.hurriyet.com.tr/cumhurbaskani-erdogan-karanlik-mandaci -aydin-musveddeleri-40039665, accessed July 18, 2016; "Erdoğan: Bu Mandacı Zihniyeti Çok İyi Tanıyoruz" [Erdoğan: We know this pro-mandate ideology very well], *Sabah*, January 14, 2016, http://www.sabah.com.tr/gundem/2016 /01/14/erdogan-bu-mandaci-zihniyeti-cok-iyi-taniyoruz, accessed February 9, 2016.

133. Ayça Çubukçu, "It's the Will of the Turkish People, Erdogan Says. But Which People?" *The Guardian*, July 26, 2016, https://www.theguardian.com /commentisfree/2016/jul/26/turkish-people-erdogan-democracy, accessed October 13, 2016.

134. Matthew Weaver, "Turkey Rounds Up Academics Who Signed Petition Denouncing Attacks on Kurds," *The Guardian*, January 15, 2016, World News section, https://www.theguardian.com/world/2016/jan/15/turkey-rounds-up -academics-who-signed-petition-denouncing-attacks-on-kurds, accessed July 19, 2016; Ceylan Yeğinsu, "Turkey Releases Detained Academics Who Signed Petition Defending Kurds," *New York Times*, January 15, 2016, http://www.nytimes .com/2016/01/16/world/europe/turkey-kurds.html, accessed July 19, 2016.

135. Ironically, Erdoğan himself has not escaped being accused of mandacılık. As I explore in chapter 3, his pro-privatization policies, the AKP's collaboration with the United States over Middle East policy, and his ties with U.S.-based cleric Fethullah Gülen earlier in the twenty-first century, in particular, made him a target of this local epithet. See Alev Coşkun, *Yeni Mandacılar* [The new pro-mandate individuals] (Istanbul: Cumhuriyet, 2008). After the falling out with Gülen around 2013, Erdoğan began to use the language of the American mandate to attack his opponent. I plan to examine this in depth in another book project on transnational conspiracy theories and humor around political Islam.

136. "Milli Mücadeleye İnanmayanlar"; Nadir Nadi, "Onbaşı'nın Anıları" [Memoirs of the corporal], *Cumhuriyet*, March 6, 1960, newspaper clipping, Kadın Eserleri Kütüphanesi ve Bilgi Merkezi Vakfı Archives; Özgürel, "Benzersiz Bir Aydınlık."

137. Edib, *Turkish Ordeal*, 285.

138. Quoted in Çalışlar, *Halide Edib*, 359.

139. Quoted in Ibid., 347.

140. Ibid. For more on the exclusion of religious minorities from the racial/cultural category of "Turkishness" despite their citizenship status, see Tanıl Bora, "Nationalism in Textbooks," in *Human Rights Issues in Textbooks: The Turkish Case*, ed. Deniz Tarba Ceylan and Gürol Irzık (Istanbul: The History Foundation of Turkey, 2004), 49–75, and Murat Ergin, "'Is the Turk a White Man?': Towards a Theoretical Framework for Race in the Making of Turkishness," *Middle Eastern Studies* 44, no. 6 (2008): 827–850.

141. Hikmet Bil, "Halide Edib ve Atabey" [Halide Edib and Atabey], n.p., March 12, 1970, newspaper clipping, Kadın Eserleri Kütüphanesi ve Bilgi Merkezi Vakfı Archives, Istanbul. "Adıvar'in Büstü Açıldı" [Adıvar's bust unveiled], *Milliyet*, March 10, 1970, 1.

142. Mümtaz Arıkan, "Tarihte Bugün: Halide Edip'in Büstü Dinamitlendi" [Today in history: Halide Edib's bust attacked with dynamite], *Cumhuriyet*, March 13, 1990, newspaper clipping, Kadın Eserleri Kütüphanesi ve Bilgi Merkezi Vakfı Archives.

143. Fethi Tevetoğlu, *Milli Mücadele Yıllarındaki Kuruluşlar* [Organizations active during the years of the national resistance] (Ankara: Türk Tarih Basımevi, 1988), 148, 190.

144. A recent book in the latter category is İpek Çalışlar's 2010 biography. For a recent example of the former, see Hayri Yıldırım, *1919'da Yabancı Himaye Tartışmaları ve Amerikan Mandacıları* [Debates over foreign protectorate in 1919 and those in favor of an American mandate] (Istanbul: Togan, 2012).

145. Müfide Ferid Tek, *Pervaneler* [The moths] (Istanbul: Kaktus, 2002), 58. See also Çalışlar, *Halide Edib*, 316.

146. Tek, *Pervaneler,* 50.

147. Ibid., 61, 104.

148. Orkun Uçar and Burak Turna, *Metal Fırtına* [Metal storm] (Istanbul: Timaş, 2005), 227.

149. Adak, "National Myths," 511.

150. Ellipses in original. Çetin Yetkin, *Türk Edebiyatında Batılılaşma ve Kimlik Sorunu* [Westernization and the problem of identity in Turkish literature] (Istanbul: Salyangoz, 2008), 127–128.

151. Ibid., 137.

152. Derya İner, "Discovering the Richness of Halide Edib's Memoirs," unpublished conference paper, presented November 18, 2006, at the Second Annual Graduate Student Pre-Conference, American Association of Teachers of Turkic Languages, Boston University.

2. ALLEGORIZING AMERICA

1. Yakup Kadri Karaosmanoğlu, *Sodom ve Gomore* [Sodom and Gomorrah] (1928; repr. Istanbul: İletişim, 2004), 257–259.

2. Peyami Safa, *Fatih-Harbiye* (1931; repr. Istanbul: Ötüken, 1999), 9.

3. Jale Parla, "Car Narratives: A Subgenre in Turkish Novel Writing," *South Atlantic Quarterly* 102, no. 2/3 (2003): 535–550, 535.

4. A third central metaphor is "time/temporality." See Meltem Ahıska, "Occidentalism: The Historical Fantasy of the Modern," *South Atlantic Quarterly* 102, no. 2/3 (2003): 351–379. Ahmet Hamdi Tanpınar's *Saatleri Ayarlama Enstitüsü* [The Time Regulation Institute], serialized in 1954 and published in 1961, epitomizes the use of this metaphor to satirize westernization. See also Perin Gürel, "Sing O, Djinn! Memory, History, and Folklore in *The Bastard of Istanbul,*" *Journal of Turkish Literature* 6 (2009): 59–80.

5. Ian Watt, *The Rise of the Novel* (1957; repr. Berkeley: University of California Press, 2001).

6. M. H. Abrams and Geoffrey Galt Harpham, *A Glossary of Literary Terms*, 9th ed. (Boston: Wadsworth, 2008), 7.

7. Watt, *Rise of the Novel.*

8. Abrams and Harpham, *Glossary,* 8.

9. Jorge Luis Borges, "From Allegories to Novels," in *Other Inquisitions, 1937–1952,* trans. Ruth L. C. Simms (Austin: University of Texas Press, 1964), 154–158, 156.

10. Deidre Lynch and William B. Warner, "The Transport of the Novel," in *Cultural Institutions of the Novel* (Durham, N.C.: Duke University Press, 1996), 1–10, 5.

11. Northrop Frye, *Anatomy of Criticism: Four Essays* (Princeton, N.J.: Princeton University Press, 1957).
12. Fredric Jameson, "Third World Literature in the Era of Multinational Capitalism," *Social Text* 15 (1986): 65–88.
13. Imre Szeman, "Who's Afraid of Allegory? Jameson, Literary Criticism, Globalization," *South Atlantic Quarterly* 100, no. 3 (2001): 803–827.
14. Jameson, "Third World Literature," 73.
15. Parla, "Car Narratives," 548.
16. Meral Özbek, "Arabesk Culture: A Case of Modernization and Popular Identity," in *Rethinking Modernity and National Identity in Turkey*, ed. S. Bozdoğan and R. Kasaba (Seattle: University of Washington Press, 1997), 213.
17. Huri İslamoğlu-İnan, *The Ottoman Empire and the World-Economy* (Cambridge: Cambridge University Press, 2004), 289.
18. Nevin Coşar and Sevtap Demirci, "Incorporation Into the World Economy: From Railways to Highways (1850–1950)," *Middle Eastern Studies* 45, no. 1 (2009): 19–31, 24.
19. Donald Quataert, "The Age of Reforms, 1812–1914," in *An Economic and Social History of the Ottoman Empire, 1300–1914*, ed. Halil İnalcık and Donald Quataert (Cambridge: Cambridge University Press, 1994), 749–743, 840.
20. Halide Edib, *Ateşten Gömlek* [Shirt of flame] (1922; repr. Istanbul: Özgür Yayınları, 2003), 39.
21. Halide Edib, *The Turkish Ordeal: Being the Further Memoirs of Halidé Edib* (London: Century, 1928), 5.
22. Nilüfer Göle, *The Forbidden Modern: Civilization and Veiling* (Ann Arbor: University of Michigan Press, 1997), 64. For a recent best-selling example, see Turgut Özakman, *Şu Çılgın Türkler* [Those crazy Turks] (Istanbul: Bilgi, 2005).
23. Jameson, "Third World Literature," 73.
24. Ibid., 55–56.
25. Ibid., 65.
26. Aijaz Ahmad, "Jameson's Rhetoric of Otherness and the National Allegory" (1987), reprinted in *In Theory: Nations, Classes, Literatures* (New York: Verso, 1994), 95–122.
27. For general reconsiderations, see Christopher Wise, "The Case for Jameson: Or Towards a Marxian Pedagogy of World Literature," *College Literature* 21 (1994): 173–189; Imre Szeman, "Who's Afraid of National Allegory? Jameson, Literary Criticism, Globalization," *South Atlantic Quarterly* 100, no. 3 (2001): 803–827. For specific applications, see Doris Sommer, "Love and Country in Latin America: An Allegorical Speculation," *Cultural Critique* 16 (1990): 109–128, and Margaret Hillenbrand, "The National Allegory Revisited: Writing Private and Public in Contemporary Taiwan," *Positions* 14, no. 3 (2006): 633–662.

28. Murat Belge, "Üçüncü Dünya Ülkeleri Edebiyatı Açısından Türk Romanına Bir Bakış" [A look at the Turkish novel in the context of Third World literature], in *Berna Moran'a Armağan: Türk Edebiyatina Eleştirel Bir Bakış* [Festshrift for Berna Moran: A critical look at Turkish literature], ed. Nazan Aksoy and Bülent Aksoy (İstanbul: İletişim Yayınları: 1997), 51–63.

29. Ibid., 57–58.

30. As novelist Elif Shafak has commented, "in a country like Turkey, a novel is first and foremost a public statement and a novelist is always more than a novelist." Lewis Gropp, "In Turkey, a Novel Is a Public Statement," interview with Elif Shafak, *Qantara*, July 9, 2008, https://en.qantara.de/content/interview-with-elif -shafak-in-turkey-a-novel-is-a-public-statement, accessed July 22, 2015. See also Suzanne Fowler, "Turkey, A Touchy Critic, Plans to Put a Novel on Trial," *New York Times*, September 15, 2006.

31. Sibel Irzık, "Allegorical Lives: The Public and the Private in the Modern Turkish Novel," *South Atlantic Quarterly* 102, no. 2/3 (2003): 551–556, 555.

32. Kabir Helminski, *The Knowing Heart: A Sufi Path of Transformation* (Boston: Shambhala, 1999), 203.

33. Carl Ernst, *Sufism: An Introduction to the Mystical Tradition of Islam* (Boston: Shambhala, 2011), 29; Annemarie Schimmel, *Mystical Dimensions of Islam* (Chapel Hill: University of North Carolina Press, 1975), 98, 137.

34. Victoria Rowe Holbrook, introduction to Şeyh Galip, *Beauty and Love*, trans. Victoria Rowe Holbrook (New York: Modern Language Association of America, 2005), ix–xxix, xi.

35. Azade Seyhan, *Tales of Crossed Destinies: The Modern Turkish Novel in a Comparative Context* (New York: Modern Language Association of America, 2008), 19.

36. Şerif Mardin, *Religion, Society, and Modernity in Turkey* (Syracuse, N.Y.: Syracuse University Press, 2006), 125. Palmira Brummett, *Image and Imperialism in the Ottoman Revolutionary Press, 1908–1911* (New York: State University of New York Press, 2000).

37. Şerif Mardin, *The Genesis of Young Ottoman Thought* (Princeton, N.J.: Princeton University Press, 1962); Selim Deringil, *The Well-Protected Domains: Ideology and the Legitimation of Power in the Ottoman Empire, 1876–1909* (London: I. B. Tauris, 1998); Deniz Kandiyoti, "End of Empire: Islam, Nationalism, and Women in Turkey," in *Women, Islam and the State*, ed. Deniz Kandiyoti (Basingstoke: Macmillan, 1991), 25; İlber Ortaylı, *İmparatorluğun En Uzun Yüzyılı* [The longest century of the empire] (Istanbul: Alkım, 2005).

38. Ahmet O. Evin, *Origins and the Development of the Turkish Novel* (Minneapolis: Bibliotheca Islamica, 1983), 10.

39. Berna Moran, *Türk Romanına Eleştirel Bir Bakış: Ahmet Mithat'tan Ahmet Hamdi Tanpınar'a* [A critical look at the Turkish novel: from Ahmet Mithat to Ahmet Hamdi Tanpınar] (1983; repr. Istanbul: İletişim, 2007), 11.

40. Ibid., 20.

41. Evin, *Origins*, 17. The criticism of these homosexual elements remained largely implicit until the 1968 publication of *Divan Şiirinde Sapık Sevgi* [Perverted love in court poetry] by the well-known journalist İsmet Zeki Eyüboğlu (Istanbul: Broy, 1991). See also Walter G. Andrews and Mehmet Kalpaklı, *The Age of Beloveds: Love and the Beloved in Early-Modern Ottoman and European Culture and Society* (Durham, N.C.: Duke University Press, 2005).

42. Evin, *Origins*, 47.

43. Ibid., 81.

44. Elif Bilgin, "An Analysis of Turkish Modernity Through Discourses of Masculinities," PhD dissertation, Middle East Technical University, 2004, 87.

45. Ahmet Mithat, *Felatun Bey ve Rakım Efendi* [Mr. Felatun and Master Rakım] (1876; repr. Istanbul: Özgür Yayınları, 2003). See also Moran, *Türk Romanı*, 48–49.

46. John Kucich and Jenny Bourne Taylor, *The Oxford History of the Novel in English*, vol. 3: *The Nineteenth-Century Novel 1820–1880* (Oxford: Oxford University Press, 2012), 95–115.

47. Nurdan Gürbilek, "Dandies and Originals: Authenticity, Belatedness, and the Turkish Novel," *South Atlantic Quarterly* 2003 102, no. 2/3 (2003): 599–628, 609. Also see chapter 1 in this book.

48. Recaizade Mahmut Ekrem, *Araba Sevdası* [The carriage affair] (1896; repr. Istanbul: Bordo Siyah, 2004).

49. Gürbilek identifies a connection between being overly influenced by literature and effeminacy in Ottoman novels. See her "Erkek Yazar, Kadın Okur: Etkilenen Okur, Etkilenmeyen Yazar" [The man writes, the woman reads: The influenced reader, the non-influenced author], in *Kör Ayna, Kayıp Şark: Edebiyat ve Endişe* [Blind mirror, lost East: Literature and anxiety] (Istanbul: Metis, 2004), 19–50.

50. Ekrem, *Araba Sevdası*, 42.

51. Ibid., 305–306. "Sorry" in French.

52. Doris Summer, "Love and Country in Latin America: An Allegorical Speculation," *Cultural Critique* 16 (Autumn 1990): 109–128.

53. Moran, *Türk Romanı*, 84. For a detailed analysis of Ekrem's complex use of language in this novel, see Nergis Ertürk, *Grammatology and Literary Modernity in Turkey* (New York: Oxford University Press, 2011), chap. 1.

54. Moran, *Türk Romanı*, 83. Ekrem, *Araba Sevdası*, 242–243.

55. Jale Parla, *Babalar ve Oğullar: Tanzimat Romanının Epistemolojik Temelleri* [Fathers and sons: The epistemological foundations of the Tanzimat novel] (Istanbul: İletişim, 1990), 15; Gürbilek, *Kör Ayna*, 78.

56. Cemil Aydın, *The Politics of Anti-Westernism in Asia: Visions of World Order in Pan-Islamic and Pan-Asian Thought* (New York: Columbia University Press, 2007), 39–69.

57. Gürbilek, *Kör Ayna*, 89.

58. Moran, *Türk Romanı*, 259–269. See also Deniz Kandiyoti, "Slave Girls, Temptresses and Comrades: Images of Women in the Turkish Novel," in *Women and Sexuality in Muslim Societies*, ed. Pınar İlkkaracan (Istanbul: Women for Women's Human Rights, 2000), 91–106.

59. Serpil Çakır, "Osmanlı Kadın Dernekleri" [Ottoman women's associations], *Toplum ve Bilim* 53 (1991): 139–159; Serpil Çakır, *Osmanlı Kadın Hareketi* [Ottoman women's movement] (Istanbul: Metis, 1994); Elif Gözdaşoğlu Küçükalioğlu, "Imagi-Nation of Gendered Nationalism: The Representations of Women as Gendered National Subjects in Ottoman-Turkish Novels (1908–1938)," PhD dissertation, Bilkent University, 2015.

60. Ahmet Mithat, *Jön Türk* [The Young Turk] (1908; repr. Istanbul: Balina, 2005).

61. Diary entry transliterated and printed in Tahir Alangu, "Ömer Seyfettin," introduction to Ömer Seyfettin, *Perili Köşk* (Istanbul: Dünya, 2003), 33.

62. Nur Gürani Arslan, *Türk Edebiyatında Amerika ve Amerikalılar* [America and Americans in Turkish literature] (Istanbul: Boğaziçi Üniversitesi Yayınları, 2002), 139.

63. Nükhet Sırman, "Writing the Usual Love Story: The Fashioning of Conjugal and National Subjects in Turkey," in *Gender, Agency, and Change: Anthropological Perspectives*, ed. Victoria Ana Goddard (London: Routledge, 2000), 250–273, 254.

64. Halide Edib Adıvar, *Vurun Kahpeye* [Thrash the whore] (1923; repr. Istanbul: Özgür, 2002).

65. Sırman, "Writing the Usual Love Story," 255.

66. Ayşe Parla, "The 'Honor' of the State: Virginity Examinations in Turkey," *Feminist Studies* 27, no. 1 (2001): 65–88, 66; see also Deniz Kandiyoti, "Slave Girls, Temptresses, and Comrades: Images of Women in the Turkish Novel," *Feminist Issues* 8 (1988): 35–49; Ayşe Durakbaşa, "Cumhuriyet Döneminde Kadın Kimliğinin Oluşumu" [The formation of women's identity during the Republican period], *Tarih Toplum* 51 (March 1988): 39–43; Nükhet Sırman, "Feminism in Turkey: A Short History," *New Perspectives on Turkey* 3, no. 1 (1989): 1–34; Ayşe Durakbaşa, "Kemalism as Identity Politics in Turkey," in *Deconstructing Images of the Turkish Woman*, ed. Zehra Arat (New York: St. Martins, 1998), 139–155; Jenny White, "State Feminism, Modernization, and the Turkish Republican Woman," *NWSA Journal* 15, no. 3 (2003): 145–159.

67. Müfide Ferid Tek, *Pervaneler* [The moths] (Istanbul: Kaktüs, 2002), 61.

68. Arslan, *Türk Edebiyatında*, 59.

69. Ahmet Haşim, "Kediler Mezbahasında" [In the slaughterhouse of cats] (1928), in *Bütün Eserleri III: Gürabahane-i Laklakan* (Istanbul: Dergah, 2004), 61–63.

70. Arslan, *Türk Edebiyatında*, 375–376.

71. Karaosmanoğlu, *Sodom ve Gomore*, 70.

72. Ibid., 88.

73. Ibid., 87.

74. Ibid., 133.

75. Schimmel, *Mystical Dimensions of Islam*, 72.

76. Karaosmanoğlu, *Sodom ve Gomore*, 183.

77. Ibid., 15.

78. Ali Asghar Seyed-Gohrab, *Layli and Majnun: Love, Madness, and Mystic Longing in Nizami's Epic Romance* (Leiden: Brill, 2003).

79. Karaosmanoğlu, *Sodom ve Gomore*, 86.

80. Melani McAlister, *Epic Encounters: Culture, Media, and U.S. Interests in the Middle East Since 1945*, 1st ed., rev. (Berkeley: University of California Press, 2005), 80–83.

81. Eugen M. Hinkle, "Cevat—The Portrait of a Turkish Petty Official," enclosed in September 6, 1932, dispatch from G. Howland Shaw to the U.S. secretary of state, National Archives and Records Administration, College Park, Md., RG59, Records of the Department of State Relating to Internal Affairs of Turkey, 1930–1944, document dated September 6, 1932, no. 867.00/2077. Reprinted in Rıfat Balı, *The First Ten Years of the Turkish Republic Thru the Reports of American Diplomats* (Istanbul: Isis, 2009), 45–57, 56.

82. Roger R. Trask, *The United States Response to Turkish Nationalism and Reform, 1914–1939* (Minneapolis: University of Minnesota Press, 1971), 65–93.

83. "The Greatest Turk Since Suleiman Disdains Paradise," *Life*, October 31, 1938, 23–24. Atatürk's reforms, especially those focused on women's voting rights, helped differentiate him from the regressive policies of other interwar dictators. Şirin Tekeli, "Women in Turkish Politics," in *Women in Turkish Society*, ed. Nermin Abadan-Unat (Leiden: Brill, 1981), 293–310. They made possible a *Washington Times* article that noted, "Alone of all the bloody opportunists who have climbed to power in Europe over the past 18 years, Ataturk has done his country great good. He has completely westernized Turkey." Quoted in Rıfat Balı, *New Documents on Atatürk: Atatürk as Viewed Through the Eyes of American Diplomats* (Istanbul: Isis, 2007).

84. Şuhnaz Yılmaz, *Turkish-American Relations, 1800–1952: Between the Stars, Stripes and the Crescent* (New York: Routledge, 2015), 65.

85. Hakan Yılmaz, "The Formation of the American-Turkish Alliance and Its Impact on Domestic Political Developments in Turkey from 1940 to 1960," in *American Turkish Encounters: A Contested Legacy, 1833–1989*, ed. Nur Bilge

Criss, Selçuk Esenbel, Tony Greenwood, and Louis Mazzari (Cambridge: Cambridge Scholars Publishing, 2011), 236–260, 241.

86. Italics in original. Nils Gilman, *Mandarins of the Future: Modernization Theory in Cold War America* (Baltimore: Johns Hopkins University Press, 2007), 31.

87. Gilman, *Mandarins of the Future*, 30–32; Nathan J. Citino, "The Ottoman Legacy in Cold War Modernization," *International Journal of Middle East Studies* 40 (November 2008): 579–597; Matthew F. Jacobs, *Imagining the Middle East: The Building of an American Foreign Policy, 1918–1967* (Chapel Hill: University of North Carolina Press, 2011). Key texts advocating this formation include Walter Livingston Wright Jr., "Truths About Turkey," *Foreign Affairs* 26, no. 2 (January 1948): 349–359; Richard Robinson, "The Lesson of Turkey," *Middle East Journal* 5, no. 4 (1951): 424–438; Lewis V. Thomas and Richard N. Frye, *The United States and Turkey and Iran* (Cambridge, Mass.: Harvard University Press, 1951); Richard N. Frye, ed., *Islam and the West: Proceedings of the Harvard Summer School Conference on the Middle East, July 25–27, 1955* (The Hague: Mouton, 1957); Daniel Lerner, *The Passing of Traditional Society: Modernizing the Middle East* (New York: Free Press, 1958); Bernard Lewis, *The Emergence of Modern Turkey* (London: Oxford University Press, 1968); Robert Ward and Dankwart Rustow, eds., *Political Modernization in Japan and Turkey* (Princeton, N.J.: Princeton University Press, 1964); Niyazi Berkes, *The Development of Secularism in Turkey* (Montreal: McGill University Press, 1964).

88. Walter R. Rostow, *The Stages of Economic Growth: A Non-Communist Manifesto* (Cambridge: Cambridge University Press, 1960); for an overview, see Nick Cullather, "Modernization Theory," in *Explaining the History of American Foreign Relations*, ed. Michael J. Hogan and Thomas G. Paterson (New York: Cambridge University Press, 2004), 212–220.

89. Citino, "Ottoman Legacy in Cold War Modernization," 589; Jacobs, *Imagining the Middle East*, 63; Gilman, *Mandarins of the Future*, 185.

90. Alastair Bonnett, *The Idea of the West: Culture, Politics and History* (New York: Palgrave Macmillan, 2004), 3; Mahmood Mamdani, *Good Muslim, Bad Muslim: America, the Cold War, and the Roots of Terror* (New York: Doubleday, 2005), 120–122; Jacobs, *Imagining the Middle East*, 77–94.

91. Begüm Adalet, "Mirrors of Modernization: The American Reflection in Turkey," PhD dissertation, University of Pennsylvania, 2014, 22–25.

92. "The Impatient Builder," *Time*, February 3, 1958, 20.

93. Altemur Kılıç, *Turkey and the World* (Washington, D.C.: Public Affairs, 1959), 159.

94. Thomas and Frye, *United States and Turkey and Iran*, 77. Also cited in Jacobs, *Imagining the Middle East*, 68–69.

95. Sezgi Durgun, "Cultural Cold War at the İzmir International Fair: 1950s–60s," in *Turkey in the Cold War: Ideology and Culture*, ed. Cangül Örnek and Çağdaş Üngör (New York: Palgrave Macmillan, 2013), 67–86, 73.

96. "İstanbul Heyecanlı Mitinglere Sahne Oldu" [Istanbul became stage to exciting rallies], *Milliyet*, October 21, 1957, 5.

97. Feroz Ahmad, *The Making of Modern Turkey* (London: Routledge, 1993), 90–91.

98. Coşar and Demirci, "Incorporation Into the World Economy," 24.

99. Adalet, *Mirrors of Modernization*.

100. Dwight J. Simpson, "Development as a Process: The Menderes Phase in Turkey," *Middle East Journal* 19, no. 2 (1965): 141–152.

101. Nur Gürani Arslan, "Bir Zamanlar Türk Edebiyatında Amerika" [America in the Turkish literature of past eras], *Doğu Batı* 32 (2005): 241–258, 252.

102. Arslan, *Türk Edebiyatında*, 293.

103. Nazım Hikmet, "Bu Vatana Nasıl Kıydılar" [How they sacrificed this land], 1959, http://siir.gen.tr/siir/n/nazim_hikmet/bu_vatana_nasil_kiydilar.htm, accessed October 12, 2016.

104. For example, Fakir Baykurt, "Nato Yolu" [The road to NATO], in *Anadolu Garajı* (Istanbul: Remzi, 1984), 201–214.

105. Fahri Erdinc, *Diriler Mezarlığı* [Graveyard for the living] (Istanbul: Hür, 1969); Aziz Nesin, "Medeniyetin Yedek Parçası" [The spare part of civilization] (1958), reprinted in Mehmet Kaplan, ed., *Hikaye Tahlilleri* [Story analyses] (Istanbul: Dergah, 1986), 220–229.

106. Report by Kenneth A. Byrns, "Village Trends," April 26, 1963, National Archives and Records Administration, College Park, Md., RG 59, General Records of the Department of State, Central Foreign Policy File 1963, Box 4219 File: SOC TUR. Reprinted in *Turkey in the 1960's and 1970's Through the Reports of American Diplomats*, ed. Rıfat Balı (Istanbul: Libra, 2010), 39–53, 44–45.

107. "A.B.D. Elçisinin Arabası Yakıldı" [USA ambassador's car was burnt], *Milliyet*, January 7, 1969.

108. Fakir Baykurt, *Amerikan Sargısı* [The American bandage] (1967; repr. Istanbul: Adam, 2003), 193. See chapter 1 on earlier American depictions of Turks as Muslim "Apaches."

109. Seyhan, *Tales of Crossed Destinies*, 90.

110. USAID Graphic Standards Manual, January 2005, https://www.usaid.gov/sites/default/files/documents/1869/USAID_Graphic_Standards_Manual.pdf, accessed May 27, 2016.

111. Baykurt, *Amerikan Sargısı*, 65.

112. Ibid., 267.

113. Burçak Keskin-Kozat, "Reinterpreting Turkey's Marshall Plan: Of Machines, Experts and Technical Knowledge," in *American Turkish Encounters: Politics*

and Culture, 1830–1989, ed. Nur Bilge Criss, Selçuk Esenbel, Tony Greenwood, and Louis Mazzari (Cambridge: Cambridge Scholars Publishing, 2011), 182–218, 218n50.

114. Ibid., 185.

115. President Johnson to Prime Minister İnönü, "Correspondence Between President Johnson and Prime Minister Inonu, June 5, 1964, as Released by the White House, January 15, 1966," *Middle East Journal* 20, no. 3 (1966): 386–393.

116. Ambassador Robert S. Dillon, interview by Charles Stuart Kennedy, May 17, 1990, Association for Diplomatic Studies and Training Foreign Affairs Oral History Project, http://www.adst.org/OH%20TOCs/Dillon,%20Robert%20S.toc .pdf, accessed March 8, 2012.

117. Durgun, "Cultural Cold War," 78.

118. See, for example, "Ruslarla Aramızdaki Buzlar Nasıl Çözüldü?" [How the ice between us and the Russians thawed], *Milliyet*, February 4, 1969.

119. Fikret Şenses, "Turkey's Experience with Neoliberal Policies Since 1980 in Retrospect and Prospect," *New Perspectives on Turkey* 47 (2012): 11–31.

120. For an excellent cultural history of the 1980s, a definitive decade in Turkey's late modernity, see Nurdan Gürbilek, *Vitrinde Yaşamak: 1980'lerin Kültürel İklimi* [Living in the store windows: The cultural climate of the 1980s] (Istanbul: Metis, 2001). See also Nilüfer Göle, "80 Sonrası Politik Kültür: Yükselen Değerler" [Post-80s political culture: Ascendant values], in *Melez Desenler: İslam ve Modernlik Üzerine* [Hybrid designs: On Islam and modernity] (İstanbul: Metis, 2000).

121. Erik J. Zürcher, *Turkey: A Modern History*, rev. ed. (London: I. B. Tauris, 2004), 295; Nilüfer Göle, "Toward an Autonomization of Politics and Civil Society in Turkey," in *Politics in the Third Turkish Republic*, ed. Metin Heper and Ahmet Evin (Boulder, Colo.: Westview, 1994), 213–222; Bilge Yeşil, *Media in New Turkey: The Origins of an Authoritarian Neoliberal State* (Urbana: University of Illinois Press, 2016).

122. Hugh Pope and Nicola Pope, *Turkey Unveiled: A History of Modern Turkey* (New York: Overlook, 2011), 162.

123. Cengiz Çandar, "Some Turkish Perspectives on the United States and American Policy Toward Turkey," in *Turkey's Transformation and American Policy*, ed. Morton Abramowitz (New York: Century Foundation, 2000), 120.

124. Cengiz Çandar, "The Post-September 11 U.S. Through Turkish Lenses," in *The United States and Turkey: Allies in Need*, ed. Morton Abramowitz (New York: Century Foundation, 2003), 150.

125. Özbek, "Arabesk Culture."

126. Ufuk Güldemir, *Teksas-Malatya* (Istanbul: Tekin 1992).

127. Quoted in Pope and Pope, *Turkey Unveiled*, 170.

128. Zürcher, *Turkey*, 298.

129. Seyhan, *Tales of Cross Destinies*, 89.

130. Börte Sagaster, "Canon, Extra Canon, Anti-Canon: On Literature as a Medium of Cultural Memory in Turkey," in *Turkish Literature and Cultural Memory: "Multiculturalism" as a Literary Theme after 1980*, ed. Catharina Dufft (Wiesbaden: Harrassowitz, 2009), 63–77.

131. Yıldız Ecevit, *Türk Romanında Postmodernist Açılımlar* [Postmodernist openings in the Turkish novel] (Istanbul: İletişim, 2002).

132. Orhan Pamuk, *The New Life*, trans. Güneli Gün (1994; repr. New York: Vintage, 1998), 39.

133. Ibid., 44.

134. Pamuk is not exaggerating the deadliness of bus travel in Turkey, as McGaha has also observed. See Michael McGaha, *Autobiographies of Orhan Pamuk: The Writer in His Novels* (Salt Lake City: University of Utah Press, 2008), 129.

135. Pamuk, *New Life*, 87.

136. *Bayii*, or seller of general merchandise (historically produced by the state), is the term used in Turkish. The translator has chosen the term "dealer," with all its ominous connotations.

137. Pamuk, *New Life*, 83.

138. María Rosa Menocal, *The Arabic Role in Medieval Literary History: A Forgotten Heritage* (Philadelphia: University of Pennsylvania Press, 1990).

139. Neil Larsen, "Imperialism, Colonialism, Postcolonialism," in *A Companion to Postcolonial Studies*, ed. Henry Schwartz and Sangeeta Ray (Oxford: Blackwell, 2004), as quoted by Irzık in "Allegorical Lives," 564.

140. Pamuk, *New Life*, 243.

141. Marinos Pourgouris, "The Addiction of Our Time: Orhan Pamuk and the Nobel Prize," *Free Associations*, November 3, 2006, http://www.watsonblogs.org /freeassociations/2006/11/the_addiction_of_our_time_orha.html, accessed July 31, 2012. Similar comments, of course, have been made about many other non-Western authors, such as Gabriel García Márquez, coinciding with the rise of multiculturalism in the West.

142. McGaha, *Autobiographies of Orhan Pamuk*, 6–7.

143. Sagaster, "Canon, Extra Canon, Anti-Canon," 67.

144. Ibid. For more on "the Sèvres syndrome" in Turkish political culture, see Dietrich Jung, "The Sèvres Syndrome: Turkish Foreign Policy and Its Historical Legacies," in *Oil and Water: Cooperative Security in the Persian Gulf*, ed. Bjorn Moller (London: I. B. Tauris, 2001), 131–159, and Fatma Müge Göçek, *The Transformation of Turkey: Redefining State and Society from the Ottoman Empire to the Modern Era* (London: I. B. Tauris, 2011), 105–110.

145. Orkun Uçar and Burak Turna, *Metal Fırtına* [Metal storm] (Istanbul: Timaş, 2005), 102.
146. Gustav Sieber's *Quo Vadis, Austria? Ein Roman der Resignation* (Berlin: "Vita" Deutsches Verlagshaus, 1913), imagining the end of the Habsburg Empire, constitutes a precedent from European history. See John Deak, "The Politics of Impending Doom: Military Elites and their Fictional Fantasies of the End of the Habsburg Monarchy," unpublished paper shared at the "Cultural Transformations in Modern Europe" reading group meeting, September 2, 2016, Nanovic Institute for European Studies, Notre Dame, Ind., and Ian Foster, *The Image of the Habsburg Army in Austrian Prose Fiction, 1888 to 1914* (Bern: Lang, 1991), 279–310. A year after the publication of *Metal Fırtına*, an Egyptian comedy called *The Night Bagdat Fell* (2005) similarly depicted a U.S. invasion of Egypt, referencing actual events. See Susan Kollin, *Captivating Westerns: The Middle East in the American West* (Lincoln: University of Nebraska Press, 2015), 200–205. These texts all seem to be autonomous developments arising from similar concerns.
147. Yigal Schleifer, "Sure It's Fiction. But Many Turks See Fact in Anti-US Novel," *Christian Science Monitor*, February 15, 2005, http://csmonitor.com/2005/0215/p01s04-woeu.html, accessed May 16, 2005.

3. HUMORING ENGLISH

1. "Türk Olmak," *Gazete Vatan*, http://www18.gazetevatan.com/fotogaleri/resim.asp?kat=7761&page_number=136, accessed March 12, 2009.
2. Leonard Feinberg, *The Secret of Humor* (Amsterdam: Rodopi, 1978), 2, 184. See also Thomas R. Shultz and Judith Robillard, "The Development of Linguistic Humour in Children: Incongruity Through Rule Violation," in *Children's Humor*, ed. Paul E. McGhee and Anthony J. Chapman (Chichester: Wiley, 1980), 59–90; Christopher Leeds, "Bilingual Anglo-French Humor: An Analysis of the Potential for Humor Based on the Interlocking of the Two Languages," *Humor: International Journal of Humor Research* 5, no. 1 (1992): 129–148, 129.
3. "İlk Türk Otomobili 'Devrim,' Ziyaretçi Bekliyor" [The first Turkish automobile Devrim awaits visitors], *NTVMSNBC*, October 14, 2004, http://arsiv.ntvmsnbc.com/news/291316.asp, accessed March 12, 2009. The Turkish–Italian joint venture company Tofaş retired its Turkish-named cars in the 1990s.
4. Défense de la Langue Française, http://www.langue-francaise.org/Horreurs/Accueil.html, accessed March 18, 2009.
5. Yalçın Pekşen, *The Türkler* (Istanbul: Yay, 2006).
6. Linda Dégh, *American Folklore and the Mass Media* (Indianapolis: Indiana University Press, 1994), 4–5. All in all, I corresponded with twenty Turkish

respondents of varying ages and linguistic backgrounds during the fall of 2006. Needless to say, my random sample does not allow for a full ethnographic study, but I hope it will make a dent in the scarcity of work on bilingual folklore in general and on Turklish humor specifically. Although their English competency and their educational backgrounds differed, I would classify all my subjects as middle class.

7. Anonymous authorship, "multiple existence," and "variation" are three qualities that differentiate folkloric texts from products of mass culture. Alan Dundes and Carl Pagter, *Urban Folklore from the Paperwork Empire* (Austin, Tex.: American Folklore Society, 1975), xviii; Alan Dundes, *Mother Wit from the Laughing Barrel: Readings in the Interpretation of Afro-American Folklore* (Jackson: University Press of Mississippi, 1973), 2; James Scott, *Domination and the Arts of Resistance: Hidden Transcripts* (New Haven, Conn.: Yale University Press, 1992), 251.

8. Roger R. Trask, *The United States Response to Turkish Nationalism and Reform: 1914–1939* (Minneapolis: University of Minnesota Press, 1971), 183.

9. Brian T. Edwards and Dilip Parameshwar Gaonkar, "Introduction: Globalizing American Studies," in *Globalizing American Studies*, ed. Brian T. Edwards and Dilip Parameshwar Gaonkar (Chicago: University of Chicago Press, 2010), 5; Brian T. Edwards, *After the American Century: The Ends of U.S. Culture in the Middle East* (New York: Columbia University Press, 2016). For examples of this attitude regarding Turkey, see Daniel Lerner, *The Passing of Traditional Society: Modernizing the Middle East* (New York: Free Press, 1958); U.S. Information Agency Research Service, *Media Habits Among the USIA Target and General Populations in Ankara and Istanbul, Turkey* (Washington, D.C.: Author, 1970); Sezgi Durgun, "Cultural Cold War at the İzmir International Fair: 1950s–60s," in *Turkey in the Cold War: Ideology and Culture*, ed. Cangül Örnek and Çağdaş Üngör (New York: Palgrave Macmillan, 2013), 67–86.

10. Stith Thompson, *The Folktale* (Berkeley: University of California Press, 1977), 190.

11. Stith Thompson and Jonas Balys, *The Oral Tales of India* (Westport, Conn.: Greenwood, 1976), 294.

12. Hans-Jörg Uther, *The Types of International Folktales: A Classification and Bibliography, Based on the System of Antti Aarne and Stith Thompson*, FF Communications No. 284–286 (Helsinki: Suomalainen Tiedeakatemia, Academia Scientiarum Fennica, 2011).

13. Stith Thompson, *Motif-Index of Folk-Literature: A Classification of Narrative Elements in Folktales, Ballads, Myths, Fables, Mediaeval Romances, Exempla, Fabliaux, Jest-Books and Local Legends* (Bloomington: Indiana University Press, 1960).

14. Pertev Naili Boratav, *Nasreddin Hoca* (Ankara: Edebiyatçılar Derneği, 1996), 101–102.

15. Gary Alan Fine, review of Christie Davies, *The Mirth of Nations* (New Brunswick, N.J.: Transaction, 2002) and Mikita Brottman, *Funny Peculiar: Gershon Legman and the Psychopathology of Humor* (Hillsdale, N.J.: Analytic, 2004), in *Journal of American Folklore* 121, no. 482 (2008): 497–499; Alan Dundes, "Jokes and Covert Language Attitudes: The Curious Case of the Wide-Mouth Frog," *Language in Society* 6 (1977): 141–147.

16. David Viktoroff, *Introduction a la Psycho-Sociologie du Rire* (Paris: Presses Universitaires de France, 1953), 14. Quoted as translated in Victor Raskin, *Semantic Mechanisms of Humor* (Dordrecht: Synthese Language Library, 1985), 17.

17. Geoffrey Lewis, *The Turkish Language Reform: A Catastrophic Success* (Oxford: Oxford University Press, 1999).

18. Ibid., 4.

19. Dror Ze'evi, *Producing Desire: Changing Sexual Discourse in the Ottoman Middle East, 1500–1900* (Berkeley: University of California Press, 2006), 135.

20. Mikhail Mikhaïlovich Bakhtin, *Rabelais and His World*, trans. Helene Iswolsky (Bloomington: Indiana University Press, 2009), 317.

21. Samia Mehrez, "Translating Revolution: An Open Text," in *Translating Egypt's Revolution: The Language of Tahrir*, ed. Samia Mehrez (Cairo: American University in Cairo Press, 2012), 1–23, 7.

22. Donald Quataert, *The Ottoman Empire, 1700–1922* (New York: Cambridge University Press, 2000), 81.

23. Ibid., 82.

24. Osman Ergin, *Türkiye Maarif Tarihi* [History of education in Turkey], vol. 2 (Istanbul: Eser, 1940).

25. For example, "Turks Drop Arabic for Our Alphabet," *New York Times*, April 30, 1928. See also Bilal Şimşir, "American Belgelerinde Türk Yazı Devrimi" [The Turkish language revolution in American documents], *Belleten* 43 (1979): 107–204.

26. Maynard Owen Williams, "Turkey Goes to School," *National Geographic*, January 1929, http://www.turkishculture.org/literature/language/turkey-goes-to-821.htm?type=1, accessed May 15, 2015.

27. Rıfat N. Balı, *New Documents on Atatürk: Atatürk as Viewed Through the Eyes of American Diplomats* (Istanbul: Isis, 2007), cf. 130, 142, 156.

28. Correspondence, American Embassy Angora (Ankara), 1928, Class 840.1-848, vol. 6, Turkey—Languages Dispatch No. 251, September 21, No. 506, National Archives and Records Administration, College Park, Md.

29. Sabri Büyükdüvenci, "John Dewey's Impact on Turkish Education," in *The New Scholarship on Dewey*, ed. James W. Garrison (Dordrecht: Kluwer, 1995), 224–232.

30. Müfide Ferid Tek, *Pervaneler* [The moths] (Istanbul: Kaktüs, 2002), 97.

31. Kezban Acar, "Globalization and Language: English in Turkey," *Sosyal Bilimler* 2, no. 1 (2004): 1–10, 6.

32. İpek Çalışlar, *Halide Edib: Biyografisine Sığmayan Kadın* [Halide Edib: The woman who does not fit inside her biography] (Istanbul: Everest, 2010), 286.

33. Roger R. Trask, *The United States Response to Turkish Nationalism and Reform: 1914–1939* (Minneapolis: University of Minnesota Press, 1971), 152.

34. Ömer Demircan, *Dünden Bugüne Türkiye'de Yabancı Dil* [Foreign language in Turkey, past to present] (Istanbul: Remzi, 1988), 102.

35. Andreas Tietze, "The Influence of English on the Turkish Language," in *English in Contact with Other Languages, Studies in Honour of Broder Carstensen on the Occasion of His 60th Birthday*, ed. Wolfgang Viereck and Wolf Dietrich Bald (Budapest: Akademiai Kiado, 1986), 387–406.

36. Aziz Nesin, *Vatan Sağolsun* [May the homeland prosper] (Istanbul: Düşün Yayınevi, 1968), as translated by Tietze in "Influence of English on the Turkish Language," 390.

37. Ibid. See also Tom McArthur, *The Oxford Guide to World English* (New York: Oxford University, 2002), 306.

38. Demircan, *Dünden Bugüne Türkiye'de Yabancı Dil*, 116.

39. Ibid.

40. Lewis, *Turkish Language Reform*, 133.

41. Acar, "Globalization and Language," 7.

42. İlhan Durusoy, *Temel's 800 Temel Fıkra* [Temel's 800 main jokes] (Istanbul: Altıner, 1995), 174. The title of this collection of Temel jokes is itself in Turklish: note the use of the English possessive "-'s," in "Temel's."

43. Ziya Gökalp, *Turkish Nationalism and Western Civilization* (Westport, Conn.: Greenwood, 1959), 277.

44. Durusoy, *Temel's 800 Temel Fıkra*, 107.

45. Ibid., 41.

46. See Perin Gürel, "Folklore Matters: The Folklore Scholarship of Alan Dundes and the New American Studies," *Columbia Journal of American Studies* 7 (2005): 120–135, and "Bilingual Humor, Authentic Aunties, and the Transnational Vernacular at Gezi Park," *Journal of Transnational American Studies* 6, no. 1 (2015): 1–30. In contrast, consider the continuing centrality of cross-lingual folklore to work on the U.S.–Mexico borderlands, from the scholarship of Américo Paredes to Gloria Anzaldúa's focus on "the wild tongue" in *Borderlands/La Frontera: The New Mestiza* (San Francisco: Aunt Lute, 1987), to, more

recently, Alicia Schmidt Camacho's *Migrant Imaginaries: Latino Cultural Politics in the U.S.–Mexico Borderlands* (New York: New York University Press, 2008).

47. See Hasan M. El-Shamy, *Folk Traditions of the Arab World: A Guide to Motif Classification* (Bloomington: Indiana University Press, 1995), 404; Hasan M. El-Shamy, *Types of the Folktale in the Arab World: A Demographically Oriented Tale Type Index* (Bloomington: Indiana University Press, 2004), 742. Other freestanding examples include Robert Bohdan Klymasz and Bohdan Medwidsky, "Macaronic Poetics in Ukrainian Canadian Folklore," *Canadian Slavonic Papers* 25, no. 1 (1983): 206–215, and Arvo Krikmann, "Jokes in Soviet Estonia," *Folklore: Electronic Journal of Folklore* 43 (2009): 43–66. Leeds's "Bilingual Anglo-French Humor" also contains many folkloric texts.

48. Jan Harold Brunvand, *The Study of American Folklore: An Introduction* (New York: Norton, 1997), 121.

49. İlhan Başgöz and Andreas Tietze, *Bilmece: A Corpus of Turkish Riddles* (Berkeley: University of California Press, 1973), 14. An example Başgöz collected in Sivas is "Doğmadan ölen kimdir?" (Who died before he was born?), with the answer "Adem," Adam (71).

50. Francis Lee Utley and Dudley Flamm, "The Urban and the Rural Jest (With an Excursus on the Shaggy Dog)," *Journal of Popular Culture* 2, no. 4 (1969): 563–577.

51. Daniel Wickberg, *The Senses of Humor: Self and Laughter in Modern America* (Ithaca, N.Y.: Cornell University Press, 1998), 158.

52. Perin Gürel, "Amerikan Jokes: The Folk Politics of Unlaughter in Turkey," paper presented at the Annual Meeting of the American Studies Association, October 11, 2005, Toronto, Ontario.

53. Edwards and Gaonkar, "Introduction: Globalizing American Studies," in *Globalizing American Studies*, 39.

54. Lewis, *Turkish Language Reform*, 40.

55. Pertev Naili Boratav, *100 Soruda Türk Halkedebiyatı* [Turkish folk literature in 100 questions] (Istanbul: Gerçek Yayınevi, 1991), 157–158.

56. Recaizade Mahmut Ekrem, *Araba Sevdası* [The carriage affair] (1896; repr. Istanbul: Bordo Siyah, 2004). See chapter 2 for more on this seminal novel.

57. Ze'evi, *Producing Desire*, 137; Palmira Johnson Brummett, *Image and Imperialism in the Ottoman Revolutionary Press, 1908–1911* (Albany: State University of New York Press, 2000), 194.

58. Willard R. Espy, *The Game of Words* (New York: Bramhall House, 1972), 194.

59. Catherine Soanes and Angus Stevenson, eds., *The Oxford Dictionary of English*, rev. ed. (Oxford: Oxford University Press, 2005), http://www.oxfordreference.com/views/ENTRY.html?subview=Main&entry=t140.e45600, accessed March

19, 2009. See also Diego Zancani, "Macaronic Literature," preface to *Oxford Companion to Italian Literature*, ed. Peter Hainsworth and David Robey (Oxford: Oxford University Press, 2008); Roland Greene et al., *The Princeton Encyclopedia of Poetry and Poetics* (Princeton, N.J.: Princeton University Press, 2012), 837.

60. Mikhail Mikhaïlovich Bakhtin, *The Dialogic Imagination: Four Essays*, trans. Michael Holquist, Caryl Emerson, and Vadim Liapunov (Austin: University of Texas Press, 1981), 81–82.

61. John F. Szwed, "Metaphors of Incommensurability," *Journal of American Folklore* 116, no. 459 (2003): 9–18.

62. "İngilizce Oku, Türkçe Anla" [Read English, understand Turkish], *Hürriyet*, July 16, 2006.

63. Bakhtin, *Rabelais and His World*, 317.

64. *Ekşi Sözlük*, founded in 1999, with over 150,000 users in 2008 and around 400,000 in 2013, constitutes one of the largest online Turkish communities and is a fertile field for online vernacular humor, including Turklish humor. "Ambulance," *Ekşi Sözlük*, http://sozluk.sourtimes.org/show.asp?t=ambulance, accessed March 22, 2009.

65. Espy, *Game of Words*, 15. Also see his *An Almanac of Words at Play* (New York: Clarkson N. Potter, 1975).

66. Alan Dundes, "Pecking Chickens: A Folk Toy as a Source for the Study of Worldview," *Folklore Matters* (Knoxville: University of Tennessee Press, 1989), 83–91, 83.

67. Marjorie D. Kibby, "Email Forwardables: Folklore in the Age of the Internet," *New Media & Society* 7, no. 6 (2005): 770–790; Russell Frank, "The Forward as Folklore: Studying E-Mailed Humor," in *Folklore and the Internet: Vernacular Expression in a Digital World*, ed. Trevor Blank (Logan: Utah State University Press, 2009), 98–122; Trevor J. Blank, ed., *Folk Culture in the Digital Age: The Emergent Dynamics of Human Interaction* (Logan: Utah State University Press, 2012).

68. Anonymous post in Genckolik.net, http://www.genckolik.net/english-forums /173380-only-the-turkish-people-can-understand-the-following-translations .html, accessed October 23, 2006.

69. William Hugh Jansen, "The Esoteric-Exoteric Factor in Folklore," *Fabula* 2 (1959): 205–211.

70. As opposed to proverbs, these texts are notable for their grammatical and rhetorical adaptability. Archer Taylor, "Problems in the Study of Proverbs," *Journal of American Folklore* 47 (1934): 1–21, 18.

71. In October 2006, there were fourteen pages of data; in March 2009, there were eighteen pages. See "Türkçeden ingilizceye direkt çeviri," *Ekşi Sözlük*,

https://eksisozluk.com/turkceden-ingilizceye-direkt-ceviri—379844, accessed December 21, 2015.

72. Perin Gürel, "America, the (Oppressively) Funny: Humor and Anti-Americanisms in Modern Turkish Cinema," in *Humor in Middle Eastern Cinema*, ed. Najat Rahman and Gayatri Devi (Detroit: Wayne State University Press, 2014), 188–213.

73. Savaş Arslan, *Cinema in Turkey: A New Critical History* (Oxford: Oxford University Press, 2011), especially 52–77.

74. Ayşe Öncü, "Turkish Women in the Professions: Why So Many?" in *Women in Turkish Society*, ed. Nermin Abadan-Unat, Deniz Kandiyoti, and Mübeccel Kıray (Leiden: Brill, 1981), 181–193, 186.

75. Review of Turkish press for the period July 3–16, 1927. Correspondence American Embassy Constantinople 1927, Class 891, Turkish Press, Diplomatic Posts TURKEY, vol. 17, National Archives and Records Administration, College Park, Md.

76. Correspondence, American Embassy Angora (Ankara) 1928, Class 840.1-848, vol. 6, Turkey—Languages Dispatch No. 251, September 21, No. 506, National Archives and Records Administration, College Park, Md.

77. Arzu Öztürkmen, "Individuals and Institutions in the Early History of Turkish Folklore, 1840–1950," *Journal of Folklore Research* 29 (1992): 172–198, 180–181.

78. İsmet Çetin, "Ziya Gökalp'in Halk, Halk Kültürü, Halk Edebiyatı, Türk Fıkracılığı ve Nasreddin Hoca Hakkındaki Düşünceleri" [Ziya Gökalp's views on the folk, folk culture, folk literature, Turkish jokes, and Nasreddin Hoca], in *Fikri ve Felsefi Yönüyle Nasreddin Hoca Sempozyumu Bildirileri* (Konya: Sebat Ofset, 1991), 32–43, 40.

79. Ze'evi, *Producing Desire*, 146–147. Also see chapter 4 in this book.

80. Arzu Öztürkmen, *Türkiye'de Folklor ve Milliyetçilik* [Folklore and nationalism in Turkey] (Istanbul: İletişim, 1998), 217.

81. Eighteen-year-old female, response to author's emailed questionnaire, October 26, 2006. The informant learned this item in primary school in Istanbul in the 1990s. There are many variations of this joke circulating in the United States, featuring Native Americans, Irish nuns, or Norwegian immigrants. See James P. Leary, *So Ole Says to Lena: Folk Humor of the Upper Midwest* (Madison: University of Wisconsin Press, 2001), 204n9. The hot dog is in fact a central trope in the American jocular tradition. See Leonard Pines, *Hot Dog Jokes— Told with Relish* (New York: Grosset & Dunlap, 1976), and Rosemary Zumwalt, "Plain and Fancy: A Content Analysis of Children's Jokes Dealing with Adult Sexuality," *Western Folklore* 35, no. 4 (1976): 258–267.

82. Durusoy, *Temel's 800 Temel Fıkra*, 56.

83. Ferhat Aslan has reported multiple jokes that depict Hodja as a hacker, interacting with Bill Gates. However, these are not new jokes but parodies of

well-known Hodja anecdotes, which owe their humor to the juxtaposition of the "traditionalness" of these canonical Hodja jokes with the newness of the Internet. Ferhat Aslan, "Sanal Kültür ortamında Güncellenen Nasreddin Hoca Fıkraları" [Updated Nasreddin Hodja jokes in virtual culture], *Turkish Studies* 6, no. 4 (2011): 39–60.

84. Ulrich Marzolph, "'Focusees' of Jocular Fiction in Classical Arabic Literature," in *Story-Telling in the Framework of Non-Fictional Arabic Literature*, ed. Stefan Leder (Wiesbaden: Harrassowitz, 1998), 118–129, 123.

85. Kathleen Anne Farmer, "The Trickster Genre in the Old Testament," PhD dissertation, Southern Methodist University, 1979, 50.

86. JoAnn Conrad, "The Political Face of Folklore: A Call for Debate," *Journal of American Folklore* 111 (1998): 409–411, 410.

87. Şükrü Elçin, "Bir Nasreddin Hoca Mecmuasi" [A journal of Nasreddin Hodja], *Hacettepe Sosyal ve Beşeri Bilimler Dergisi* 4 (1972): 1–19.

88. Şükrü Kurgan, "Nasrettin Hoca Üzerine" [On Nasreddin Hodja], in *I. Milletlerarası Nasreddin Hoca Sempozyumu Bildirileri* [The Reports of the First International Nasreddin Hodja Symposium] (Ankara: Ankara Universitesi Basımevi, 1990), 225–233, 228.

89. Saim Sakaoğlu, "Nasreddin Hoca'nın Fıkralarında Açık Saçıklık" [Vulgarity in Nasreddin Hodja jokes], in *Nasreddin Hoca'ya Armağan* [Gift to Nasreddin Hodja], ed. Sabri Koz (Istanbul: Oğlak, 1996), 301–311.

90. Boratav, *Nasreddin Hoca*, 91. I know of only one popular Turkish collection which contains obscene Hodja jokes: Günel Altıntaş, *Erotikle Karışık Nasrettin Hoca Fıkraları* [Nasreddin Hodja jokes, mixed in with the erotic] (Istanbul: Seçme, 1997), which contains reprints of selected tales from Boratav's 1996 collection, as well as a very defiant foreword protesting the sanitization of Nasreddin Hodja.

91. Seyfi Karabaş, "The Use of Eroticism in Nasreddin Hoca Anecdotes," *Western Folklore* 49, no. 3 (1990): 299–305, 299.

92. Forty-three-year-old female, response to author's emailed questionnaire, October 20, 2006. In fact, in 1996, Boratav published 594 Hodja tales transcribed from manuscripts across the world, including many that are obscene.

93. Ulrich Marzolph, "Sanitizing Humor: Islamic Mediterranean Jocular Tradition in a Comparative Perspective," in *Europa e Islam tra i secoli XIV e XVI/Europe and Islam Between the 14th and 15th Centuries*, ed. M. Bernardini et al. (Naples: Instituto Universitaro Orientale, 2002), vol. 2, 757–782, 772.

94. Ahmed Emin Yalman, *Yakın Tarihte Gördüklerim ve Geçirdiklerim 1888–1922* [Things I have seen and experienced in recent history], ed. Erol Şadi Erdinç (Istanbul: Pera Yayınları, 1997), vol. 1, 455–456.

95. Erez Manela, *The Wilsonian Moment: Self-Determination and the International Origins of Anticolonial Nationalism* (Oxford: Oxford University Press, 2007), 26.

96. Conrad, "Political Face of Folklore," 410.

97. The association of Hodja jokes with children and innocence is so entrenched that a viral online list making fun of inappropriate children's books included the cover of Günel Altıntaş's 1997 collection of Hodja tales because it contained the word *Erotik* (Erotic) in the title. Of course, this is not a children's book, but a folklore collection containing archived Hodja jokes. See "Çocuk Kitaplarından, Bu Neyin Kafası? Dedirten 16 Fantastik Alıntı" [16 bizarre excerpts from children's books, making us ask what are these people on?], *Liste Kitap*, August 16, 2015, http://listekitap.com/liste/cocuk-kitaplarindan-bu-neyin-kafasi-dedirten-16-fantastik-alinti/, accessed October 19, 2015.

98. Twenty-six-year-old female, response to author's emailed questionnaire, October 29, 2006.

99. Twenty-five-year-old female, response to author's emailed questionnaire, October 30, 2006.

100. Forty-three-year-old female, response to author's emailed questionnaire, October 20, 2006.

101. Theo Meder, "There Were a Turk, a Moroccan and a Dutchman: Narrative Repertoires in the Multi-Ethnic Neighbourhood of Lombok in the Dutch City of Utrecht," in *Erzählen Zwischen den Kulturen*, ed. Sabine Wienker-Piepho, Klaus Roth, and Lutz Röhrich (Münster: Waxmann, 2004), 234–258, 245.

102. Fahrettin Şanal, "TRT ve Kovboy Filmleri!" [TRT and cowboy movies], *Başak Gazetesi*, October 24, 2014, http://www.basakgazetesi.com/makale/trt-ve-kovboy-filmleri-37093.html, accessed December 22, 2015; "Babanın Pazar Günleri Western Film İzleme Tutkusu" [The dad's passion for watching westerns on Sundays], https://eksisozluk.com/babanin-pazar-gunleri-western-film-izleme-tutkusu—1937636, accessed December 22, 2015. While Şanal is critical of what he identifies as cultural imperialism, contributors on *Ekşi Sözlük* reminisce about watching westerns with their fathers later in the century when private TV channels expanded available offerings, even though this meant not being able to watch cartoons.

103. Cengiz Çandar, "Some Turkish Perspectives on the United States and American Policy Toward Turkey," in *Turkey's Transformation and American Policy*, ed. Morton Abramowitz (New York: Century Foundation, 2000), 119. Kollin has noted how the figure of the "cowboy" may function as a symbol of the U.S. military in contemporary Middle Eastern and North African media. Susan Kollin, *Captivating Westerns: The Middle East in the American West* (Lincoln: University of Nebraska Press, 2015), 199.

104. Durusoy, *Temel's 800 Temel Fıkra*, 116.

105. Anthony Giddens, *The Consequences of Modernity* (Stanford, Calif.: Stanford University Press, 1991), 136.

106. Forty-three-year-old female, email forward to author, September 23, 2006. I am reproducing this text here directly from the forwarded email, with all the original typos and misspellings. Note that some Turkish words are rendered properly, whereas others appear to have been typed on an English-language "qwerty" keyboard.

107. İlker Aytürk, "Turkish Linguists Against the West: The Origins of Linguistic Nationalism in Ataturk's Turkey," *Middle Eastern Studies* 40, no. 6 (2004): 1–25.

108. Aziz Nesin, "Otuz Beşinci Yılındayız" [On the 35th anniversary], *Akşam*, September 27, 1967, reprinted in *Dil Yazıları II* (Ankara: Türk Dil Kurumu, 1974), 43–47.

109. Murat Ergin, "'Is the Turk a White Man?': Towards a Theoretical Framework for Race in the Making of Turkishness," *Middle Eastern Studies*, 44, no. 6 (2008): 827–850, 838.

110. Dankwart Rustow, "Politics and Islam in Turkey, 1920–1955," in *Islam and the West*, ed. Richard N. Frye (The Hague: Mouton, 1956), 81.

111. Robert Philipson, *Linguistic Imperialism* (Oxford: Oxford University Press, 1992), 7.

112. Roderic H. Davison, "Westernized Education in Ottoman Turkey," *Middle East Journal* 15, no. 3 (Summer 1961): 289–301, 299.

113. Burçak Keskin-Kozat, *Negotiating Modernization Through U.S. Foreign Assistance: Turkey's Marshall Plan (1948–1952) Re-Interpreted*, PhD dissertation, University of Michigan, 2006, 211.

114. Güray Çağlar König, "The Place of English in Turkey," in *The Birth and Growth of a Department: Department of English Language and Literature, 25th Anniversary*, ed. Deniz Bozer (Ankara: Hacettepe University Press, 1990), 157–167; Oktay Sinanoğlu, "Uluslarası Bilim-Ulusal Eğitim Dili" [Language of international science and national education], in *Bilim Kültür ve Öğretim Dili Olarak Türkçe* (Ankara: Türk Tarih Kurumu, 1978), 1–5, 3.

115. Aydın Köksal, "Yabancı Dille Eğitimden Caymak Zorundayız!" [We must give up education in foreign language], *Bilgicik*, n.d., http://www.bilgicik.com/yazi/yabanci-dille-egitimden-caymak-zorundayiz-prof-dr-aydin-koksal/, accessed August 16, 2010.

116. Poster reproduced on *İlköğretim Türkçe*, a website for teachers of Turkish language and literature in primary and secondary schools, www.ilkogretimturkce.com, accessed March 27, 2009.

117. Rob Kroes, "Americanization and Anti-Americanism," *American Quarterly* 58, no. 2 (2006): 503–515, 503. See also Kroes's *If You've Seen One, You've Seen*

the *Mall: Europeans and American Mass Culture* (Urbana: University of Illinois Press, 1996); Jongsuk Chay, ed. *Culture and International Relations* (New York: Praeger, 1990); Reinhold Wagnleitner, *Coca-Colonization and the Cold War: The Cultural Mission of the United States in Austria After the Second World War* (Chapel Hill: University of North Carolina Press, 1994); Richard Kuisel, *Seducing the French: The Dilemma of Americanization* (Berkeley: University of California Press, 1997); Edwards, *After the American Century*.

118. The nonsense English sentence "leave the door December," building on a pun on the Turkish word *Aralık*, which can mean both "December" and "ajar," became popular in high school classes in late-sixties Istanbul (sixty-two-year-old female, conversation with author, June 26, 2016, Istanbul, Turkey).

119. "Morning morning" is the direct (false) translation of the vernacular expression "*sabah sabah*," which implies a very early hour. "Circle" is the direct (false) translation from the Turkish word *daire*, which denotes both an apartment flat and a geometric circle.

120. Sixty-year-old female, response to author's emailed questionnaire, October 26, 2006. This interviewee attended Middle East Technical University (METU) in Ankara, one of the first Turkish universities to conduct education in English, as well as one that is famous for its students' left-wing leanings.

121. Zeynep Kızıltepe, "Attitudes and Motivation of Turkish EFL Students Towards Second Language Learning," *ITL Journal of Applied Linguistics* 129–130 (2000): 141–168.

122. Twenty-five-year-old-female, response to author's emailed questionnaire, October 30, 2006.

123. Twenty-six-year-old female, response to author's emailed questionnaire, October 28, 2006.

124. Ömer Taşpınar, "The Anatomy of Anti-Americanism in Turkey," Brookings Project on Turkey, November 16, 2005, http://www.brookings.edu/articles/2005 /1116turkey_taspinar.aspx, accessed April 20, 2009; Banu Eligür, *The Mobilization of Political Islam in Turkey* (Cambridge: Cambridge University Press, 2010), 249; Mark L. Haas, *The Clash of Ideologies: Middle Eastern Politics and American Security* (New York: Oxford University Press, 2012), 216–217. For more on America's promotion of "moderate Islam," see Saba Mahmood, "Secularism, Hermeneutics, and Empire: The Politics of Islamic Reformation," *Public Culture* 18, no. 2 (March 20, 2006): 323–347.

125. Perin Gürel, "'Capitalism with Ablutions': Visualizing America's 'Moderate' Islam in Turkey," paper presented at the Annual Meeting of the American Academic of Religion, November 23–26, 2013, Baltimore, Md.; Perin Gürel, "Transnational Conspiracy Theories and Vernacular Visual Cultures: Political Islam in Turkey and America," *In Media Res*, April 11, 2014, http://www

.criticalcommons.org/Members/MCIMR/clips/transnational-conspiracy
-theories-and-vernacular/embed_view, accessed June 24, 2016.

126. Minxin Pei, "The Paradoxes of American Nationalism," *Foreign Policy* (May/ June 2003): 31–37; Kollin, *Captivating Westerns.*

127. Often noted in the context of diasporic and transnational nationalisms as well as vis-à-vis the weakening of the nation-state under globalization. Gerard Delanty, "Nationalism: Between Nation and State," in *Handbook of Social Theory,* ed. George Ritzer and Barry Smart (London: Sage, 2000), 472–484.

128. Doğan Gürpınar, "Türk Milliyetçiliğinin Batılılaşmasının Mutlu Sonu" [The happy end of the westernization of Turkish nationalism], *Birikim* 202 (February 2006): 73–82, 78.

129. Roland Barthes, "Operation Margarine," *Mythologies* (New York: Farrar, Straus and Giroux, 1972), 41–42.

130. Paul Lewis, *Cracking Up: American Humor in a Time of Conflict* (Chicago: University of Chicago Press, 2006), 116, 123.

131. Tunç Taylan, ed., *İşgale Yan Çiziyoruz* [We are (drawing) in opposition to the invasion] (Istanbul: Dünya, 2004), 36.

132. "40,000 Protest Bush in Turkey," *Global Policy Forum,* June 27, 2004, http:// www.globalpolicy.org/ngos/advocacy/protest/iraq/2004/0627turkey.htm, accessed August 15, 2010.

133. Ellen Knickmeyer, "Lifting of Head-Scarf Ban Cleverly Timed, Some Say," *Washington Post,* February 29, 2008, http://seattletimes.nwsource.com/html /iraq/2004249952_iraq29.html, accessed August 15, 2010.

134. Ahmet Kuru, *Secularism and State Policies Toward Religion: The United States, France, and Turkey* (Cambridge: Cambridge University Press, 2008); Ümit Cizre, "Parameters and Strategies of Islam-State Interaction in Republican Turkey," *International Journal of Middle East Studies* 28, no. 2 (1996): 231–251.

135. Esra Özyürek, *Nostalgia for the Modern: State Secularism and Everyday Politics in Turkey* (Durham, N.C.: Duke University Press, 2006).

136. Perin Gürel, "Bilingual Humor, Authentic Aunties, and the Transnational Vernacular at Gezi Park," *Journal of Transnational American Studies* 6, no. 1 (2015), https://escholarship.org/uc/item/2md6f6fr.

137. Scott, *Domination and the Art of Resistance,* 178.

138. Lane Crothers, *Globalization and American Popular Culture,* 3rd ed. (Lanham, Md.: Rowman & Littlefield, 2013), 154.

139. Sigmund Freud, *Jokes and Their Relation to the Unconscious,* trans. James Strachey (New York: W. W. Norton, 1989), 119.

140. George Orwell, "Funny, but Not Vulgar," in *The Collected Letters, Essays, and Journalism of George Orwell,* ed. Sonia Orwell and Ian Angus (London: Secker & Warburg, 1968), 284.

141. William Shakespeare, *The Tempest: Sources and Contexts, Criticism, Rewritings and Appropriations*, ed. Peter Hulme and William H. Sherman (New York: W. W. Norton, 2004), 362–363.

142. The primary data for this chapter was collected in 2006, before the election of Barack Obama as the first black president of the United States.

143. Audre Lorde, *Sister Outsider: Essays and Speeches* (Berkeley, Calif.: Crossing, 2007), 110–114.

144. Julianne Burton-Carvajal, "'Surprise Package': Looking Southward with Disney," in *Disney Discourse: Producing the Magic Kingdom*, ed. Eric Smoodin (New York: Routledge, 1994), 131–147, 144.

145. See, for example, Kalman Applbaum, "'I Feel Coke': Why the Japanese Study English," *Asian Thought and Society* 17 (1992): 18–30.

146. Unlike "extractive" empires, settler colonies involve large-scale immigration, territorial appropriation, and a persistent structure of invasion that is "complex, multifaceted, and enduring." Tom Lynch, "'Nothing but Land': Women's Narratives, Gardens, and the Settler-Colonial Imaginary in the U.S. West and Australian Outback," *Western American Literature* 48, no. 4 (2014): 374–399, 377.

147. Doris Sommer, *Bilingual Aesthetics: A New Sentimental Education* (Durham, N.C.: Duke University Press, 2004), 7; Luis Martínez-Fernández, "Just Like Us? Not Likely," *Chronicle of Higher Education* 53, no. 16 (December 8, 2006): B20.

148. James Poniewozik, "'Homeland,' Graffiti and the Problem of Only Seeing Squibbly," *New York Times*, October 15, 2015, http://artsbeat.blogs.nytimes.com/2015/10/15/homeland-graffiti-racist/, accessed December 13, 2015.

149. Fifty-two-year-old female, response to author's emailed questionnaire, November 3, 2006. Another version depicts a couple with a landlord in England, changing the power dynamic. See Erol Özışık, "Yabancı Kelimeler Türkçe Sanılırsa" [When foreign words are thought to be Turkish], *Milliyet Blog*, June 7, 2010, http://blog.milliyet.com.tr/yabanci-kelimeler-turkce-sanilirsa——/Blog/?BlogNo=247403, accessed June 30, 2016.

150. Taylor, "Problems in the Study of Proverbs," 11.

151. "We Will Bury You," *Wikipedia, The Free Encyclopedia*, December 4, 2006, http://en.wikipedia.org/w/index.php?title=We_will_bury_you&oldid=91896789, accessed December 30, 2006.

152. *Borat: Cultural Learnings of America for Make Benefit Glorious Nation of Kazakhstan*, DVD, dir. Larry Charles (Twentieth Century Fox, 2006).

153. Henry Louis Gates Jr., *The Signifying Monkey: A Theory of Afro-American Literary Criticism* (New York: Oxford University Press, 1988), 217.

154. Inderpal Grewal, *Transnational America: Feminisms, Diasporas, Neoliberalisms* (Durham, N.C.: Duke University Press, 2005), 41.

155. Christian Moraru, *Rewriting: Postmodern Narrative and Cultural Critique in the Age of Cloning* (New York: State University of New York Press, 2001), 87.
156. Bakhtin, *Rabelais and His World*, 20.

4. FIGURING SEXUALITIES

1. Turkish does not mark gender in personal pronouns, using the same word ("o") for he, she, and it. Nur Çintay, "Boğaz Köprüsü Gay mi, Travesti mi?" [Is the Bosphorus Bridge gay or a travesti], *Radikal*, July 11, 2008, http://www.radikal.com.tr/Radikal.aspx?aType=RadikalDetayV3&ArticleID=887810&CategoryID=96, accessed July 23, 2012.
2. See Afsaneh Najmabadi, "Beyond the Americas: Are Gender and Sexuality Useful Categories of Analysis?" *Journal of Women's History* 18, no. 1 (2006): 11–21.
3. On "class racism" in Turkey, see Tanıl Bora, "Nationalist Discourses in Turkey," *The South Atlantic Quarterly* 102, no. 2/3 (2003): 433–451, 442–443.
4. Nur A. Çintay, " 'Boğaz Köprüsü Gay mi?' Meselesi" [The issue of "Is the Bosphorus Bridge gay?"], *Radikal*, July 13, 2008, http://v3.arkitera.com/news.php?action=displayNewsItem&ID=31593, accessed July 23, 2012.
5. Ibid.
6. See, for example, Mehmet Ümit Necef, "Turkey on the Brink of Modernity," in *Sexuality and Eroticism Among Males in Moslem Societies*, ed. Arno Schmitt and Jehoeda Sofer (Binghamton, N.Y.: Hayworth, 1992), 71–76; Jehoeda Sofer, "The Dawn of a Gay Movement in Turkey," in *Sexuality and Eroticism*, 77–82; Hüseyin Tapınç, "Masculinity, Femininity, and Turkish Male Homosexuality," in *Modern Homosexualities: Fragments of Gay and Lesbian Experiences*, ed. Ken Plummer (London: Routledge, 1992), 39–51.
7. Necef, "Turkey on the Brink of Modernity," 72.
8. Introduction to *Occidentalism: Images of the West*, ed. James G. Carrier (Oxford: Clarendon, 1995), 1–31, 22.
9. To quote the *Istanbul Gay Guide*, "Hetero-flexible/bisexual guys are supposedly top (*aktif*= active is the common word in local culture) and do not have sex with each other." "Gay Life in Istanbul," *Istanbul Gay Guide*, http://www.istanbulgay.com/guide.html, accessed May 24, 2015.
10. Joan W. Scott, "The Evidence of Experience," *Critical Inquiry* 17, no. 4 (1991): 773–779.
11. Nilüfer Göle, *The Forbidden Modern: Civilization and Veiling* (Ann Arbor: University of Michigan Press, 1997); Elif Bilgin, "An Analysis of Turkish Modernity Through Discourses of Masculinities," PhD dissertation, Middle East Technical University, 2004; Gökçen Ertuğrul Apaydın, "Modernity as Masquerade: Representations of Modernity and Identity in Turkish Humour Mag-

azines," *Identities: Global Studies in Culture and Power* 12, no. 1 (2005): 107–142, 121. Also see chapter 3 in this book.

12. David M. Halperin, "Is There a History of Sexuality?" *History and Theory* 28, no. 3 (1989): 257–274.

13. Anna Tsing, *Friction: An Ethnography of Global Connections* (Princeton, N.J.: Princeton University Press, 2005).

14. For a theoretical discussion of globalization as a set of flows and scapes, see Arjun Appadurai, *Modernity at Large: Cultural Dimensions of Globalization* (Minneapolis: University of Minnesota Press, 1996).

15. Joseph Massad, *Desiring Arabs* (Chicago: University of Chicago Press, 2007).

16. Lisa Duggan, *The Twilight of Equality? Neoliberalism, Cultural Politics, and the Attack on Democracy* (Boston: Beacon, 2003); Jasbir K. Puar, *Terrorist Assemblages: Homonationalism in Queer Times* (Durham, N.C.: Duke University Press, 2007); David L. Eng, *The Feeling of Kinship: Queer Liberalism and the Racialization of Intimacy* (Durham, N.C.: Duke University Press, 2010). For a phenomenological exploration of the queer contingencies between "the Orient" and "sexual orientation," see chapter 3 in Sara Ahmed, *Queer Phenomenology: Orientations, Objects, Others* (Durham, N.C.: Duke University Press, 2006).

17. Mija A. Sanders, "'Stolen Stories': Kurdish LGBTT Activism in Diyarbakır," M.A. thesis, University of Arizona, 2012.

18. The U.S. government elevated LGBT issues as a part of its foreign policy agenda only in December 2011 under Barack Obama. "Presidential Memorandum—International Initiatives to Advance the Human Rights of Lesbian, Gay, Bisexual, and Transgender Persons," http://www.whitehouse.gov/the-press-office/2011/12/06/presidential-memorandum-international-initiatives-advance-human-rights-l, accessed February 25, 2013.

19. Mert [pseudonym], conversation with author, Istanbul, Turkey, August 12, 2007.

20. See chapter 2 for the association of Beyoğlu with "the West" in Turkish literature.

21. Rob Kroes, "Americanization and Anti-Americanism," *American Quarterly* 58, no. 2 (2006): 504.

22. Kenan [pseudonym], conversation with author, Istanbul, Turkey, August 12, 2007.

23. These categories, invented in 1992 and popularized in the early twenty-first century, demonstrate how class is racialized in Turkey. "White Turks and Black Turks," *Wikipedia, the Free Encyclopedia*, August 7, 2013, http://en.wikipedia.org/w/index.php?title=White_Turks_and_Black_Turks&oldid=553429022. See also, Beyza Sümer, "White vs. Black Turks: The Civilizing Process in Turkey in the 1990s," M.A. thesis, Middle East Technical University, 2003; Emre Arslan,

"Türkiye'de Irkçılık" [Racism in Turkey], in *Modern Türkiye'de Siyasi Düşünce* [Political thought in modern Turkey] (Istanbul: İletişim, 2002), vol. 4, 409–426; Murat Ergin, "'Is the Turk a White Man?': Towards a Theoretical Framework for Race in the Making of Turkishness," *Middle Eastern Studies* 44, no. 6 (2008): 827–850, 842–845.

24. *Istanbul Gay Guide*, n.d., http://www.istanbulgay.com/guide.html, accessed November 7, 2008.

25. See Kenan Çayır, "90'lar Türkiyesi'nde Eşcinsel Hareket: Kimlik, Görünürlük ve Sınırlar" [The homosexual movement in the Turkey of 1990s: Identity, visibility, and boundaries], *Lambdaistanbul*, May 16, 2003, http://www.lambdaistanbul .org/php/main.php?menuID=7&altMenu ID=49&icerikID=357, accessed November 4, 2008; Tarık Bereket and Barry Adam, "Emergence of Gay Identities in Turkey," *Sexualities* 9, no. 2 (2006): 131–151; Tarık Bereket and Barry Adam, "Navigating Islam and Same-Sex Liaisons Among Men in Turkey," *Journal of Homosexuality* 55, no. 2 (2008): 204–222; Gül Özyeğin, "Reading the Closet Through Connectivity," *Social Identities: Journal for the Study of Race, Nation, and Culture* 18, no. 2 (2012): 201–222; Serkan Görkemli, "'Coming Out of the Internet': Lesbian and Gay Activism and the Internet as a 'Digital Closet' in Turkey," *Journal of Middle East Women's Studies* 8, no. 3 (2012): 63–88.

26. "Nefret Cinayetleri Sürüyor" [Hate murders continue], *Birgün*, November 28, 2007, http://www.birgun.net/bolum-56-haber-54065.html#haber_basi, accessed April 20, 2008.

27. Nicolas Cheviron, "Turkey's Gays, Transsexuals Decry Increasing Homophobia," *Agence France-Presse*, April 3, 2010, www.google.com/hostednews/afp /article/ALeqM5i_mI_smXF4WPvvhaQwkZqoC8Ap, accessed August 17, 2010; Volkan Yılmaz, "LGBT Meselesinde Siyasi Tehditler ve Olanaklar" [Political dangers and possibilities in the LGBT issue], *KAOS GL*, July 23, 2012, http://www.kaosgl.com/sayfa.php?id=11930, accessed July 29, 2012.

28. "Kombinezon Cinayetinde Müebbet İstemi" [Life in prison request in the lingerie murder], *En Son Haber*, May 2, 2007, http://www.ensonhaber.com/news _detail.php?id=47525, accessed May 12, 2007.

29. Eve Kosofsky Sedgwick, *Epistemology of the Closet* (Berkeley: University of California Press, 1990), 19.

30. Bahri Karataş, "'Kombinezon Cinayeti' Sanığına 18 Yıl Hapis Cezası" [18 years to the convict in the lingerie murder], *Hurriyet*, March 31, 2008, http://www.hurriyet .com.tr/kombinezon-cinayeti-sanigina-18-yil-8586737, accessed July 25, 2016.

31. Judith Butler, *Bodies That Matter: On the Discursive Limits of "Sex"* (London: Routledge, 1993).

32. Fatih Şendil, "Kocam Gay Olsa Hiç Durmazdım" [Had my husband been gay, I wouldn't have stayed], *SABAH*, April 18, 2007, http://www.sabah.com.tr/2007

/04/18/haber,C2CCF68E93C34A348FD95599C01BD891.html, accessed November 7, 2008.

33. For example, Karataş, "'Kombinezon Cinayeti' Sanığına 18 Yıl Hapis Cezası."

34. Sedgwick, *Epistemology of the Closet*, 47.

35. As Ferguson puts it, culture is "a phenomenon of hierarchical relation and interconnection." James Ferguson, *Global Shadows: Africa in the Neoliberal World Order* (Durham, N.C.: Duke University Press, 2007), 67. For the role of difference and deferral in meaning-making, see Jacques Derrida, *Of Grammatology*, trans. Gayatri Chakravorty Spivak (Baltimore: Johns Hopkins University Press, 1998).

36. Michel Foucault, *The History of Sexuality: An Introduction* (New York: Vintage, 1990), vol. 1, 103.

37. Butler, *Bodies That Matter*, 2.

38. For a quick summary, see Leila J. Rupp, "Toward a Global History of Same-Sex Sexuality," *Journal of the History of Sexuality* 10, no. 2 (2001): 287–302.

39. Stephen Murray and Will Roscoe, introduction to *Islamic Homosexualities: Culture, History, and Literature*, ed. Stephen Murray (New York: New York University Press, 1997), 3–54, 6.

40. Arno Schmitt, "Different Approaches to Male-Male Sexuality/Eroticism from Morocco to Usbekistan," in *Sexuality and Eroticism*, 1–24; Khaled El-Rouayheb, *Before Homosexuality in the Arab-Islamic World, 1500–1800* (Chicago: University of Chicago Press, 2005), 22. Of course, this idea is not limited to the "traditional" Middle East, but saturates contemporary American understandings of "tops" and "bottoms" in gay relationships as well.

41. The first word comes from the Persian word *obnai*, implying an adult male who desires to be penetrated. Both *obnai* and *ibne* are derived from *ma'būn*, an Arabic term for the "habitual bottom" in sex between men. See "Liwāṭ," in *Encyclopaedia of Islam*, 2nd ed., ed. P. Bearman, T. Bianquis, C. E. Bosworth, E. van Donzel, and W. P. Heinrichs, *Brill Online*, 2015, http://referenceworks .brillonline.com/entries/encyclopaedia-of-islam-2/liwat-SIM_4677, accessed October 20, 2016. "Kulampara" entered Ottoman Turkish from the Persian *ghulam-barah*, used for a man inclined to have sex with young males (Schmitt, "Different Approaches," 10).

42. I am grateful to Irvin Cemil Schick for this formulation. See also, Irvin Cemil Schick, "Orta Doğu'nun Geçmişi ve LGBTİ: Günümüz Cinsellik Tasniflerinin Tarihselliği Üzerine" [The Middle Eastern past and LGBTI: On the historicity of contemporary depictions of sexuality], paper presented at the Sosyal Politikalar, Cinsiyet Kimliği ve Cinsel Yönelim Çalışmaları Derneği (SPoD), Akademik Çalışma Grubu Spring Seminars, May 10, 2014, Istanbul, Turkey. As Schick also notes, the language of "same-sex" desire fails us here, since the

"two-sex" system, marking an irreconcilable, categorical binary opposition between males and females, was itself an eighteenth-century European invention. Thomas Walter Laqueur, *Making Sex: Body and Gender from the Greeks
to Freud* (Cambridge, Mass.: Harvard University Press, 1990).

43. El-Rouayheb, *Before Homosexuality*, 13–51. This is not to say active sodomy always escaped religio-judicial or even societal condemnation (23–25). In fact, a
bibliographical note of caution against over-reifying the active/passive power
division is due here: Dror Ze'evi notes that early Ottoman authors generally did
not single out passivity in male-to-male intercourse as exceptionally problematic. Dror Ze'evi, *Producing Desire: Changing Sexual Discourse in the Ottoman
Middle East, 1500–1900* (Berkeley: University of California Press, 2006), 39. Andrews and Kalpaklı suggest that the "fluid shifting of domination and submission" constituted a primary appeal in Ottoman homoeroticism. Walter G.
Andrews and Mehmet Kalpaklı, *The Age of Beloveds: Love and the Beloved in
Early-Modern Ottoman and European Culture and Society* (Durham, N.C.:
Duke University Press, 2005), 20. Joseph Boone has also convincingly argued
that the linkages between age, social status, gender presentation, and sexual
position have never been as fixed as some scholars have assumed. Joseph A.
Boone, *The Homoerotics of Orientalism* (New York: Columbia University Press,
2014), chapter 2. This chapter demonstrates a similar role-flexibility in terms
of travesti and clients.

44. See Dror Ze'evi, "Hiding Sexuality: The Disappearance of Sexual Discourse in
the Late Ottoman Middle East," *Social Analysis* 49, no. 2 (2005): 34–53; Ze'evi,
Producing Desire, especially chapter 6 and conclusion.

45. On Istanbul's central role in Western visions of the perverse Orient, see Boone,
Homoerotics of Orientalism, chapter 3. For formulations of the civilizational
other as sexually deviant, see Irvin Cemil Schick, *The Erotic Margin: Sexuality
and Spaciality in Alteritist Discourse* (London: Verso, 1999), and Rudi C. Bleys,
*The Geography of Perversion: Male-to-Male Sexual Behavior Outside the West
and the Ethnographic Imagination, 1750–1918* (New York: New York University
Press, 1996).

46. Danielle J. van Dobben, "Dancing Modernity: Gender, Sexuality and the State
in the Late Ottoman Empire and Early Turkish Republic," M.A. thesis, University of Arizona, 2008; Evren Savcı, "Queer in Translation: Paradoxes of
Westernization and Sexual Others in the Turkish Nation," PhD dissertation,
University of Southern California, 2011, 70–73, 168–172.

47. Thus we find a quiet transition toward heteronormativity based on understandings of proper, Western-style modernity, which echoes findings of Najmabadi
regarding Iran and Pflugfelder regarding Japan. Afsaneh Najmabadi, *Women
with Mustaches and Men Without Beards: Gender and Sexual Anxieties of*

Iranian Modernity (Berkeley: University of California Press, 2005); Afsaneh Najmabadi, "Types, Acts, or What? Regulation of Sexuality in Nineteenth-Century Iran," in *Islamicate Sexualities: Translations Across Temporal Geographies of Desire*, ed. Kathryn Babayan and Afsaneh Najmabadi (Cambridge, Mass.: Center for Middle Eastern Studies/Harvard University Press, 2008), 282–283; Gregory Pflugfelder, *Cartographies of Desire: Male-Male Sexuality in Japanese Discourse, 1600–1950* (Berkeley: University of California Press, 2007).

48. Compare original reports by the sympathetic American Ambassador Joseph C. Grew and the unsympathetic Consul General Charles E. Allen, reproduced in *New Documents on Atatürk: Atatürk as Viewed Through the Eyes of American Diplomats*, ed. Rıfat Balı (Istanbul: Isis, 2007).

49. See the archives of *Milliyet*, http://gazetearsivi.milliyet.com.tr, and *Cumhuriyet*, http://www.cumhuriyetarsivi.com.

50. Tapınç, "Masculinity, Femininity, and Turkish Male Homosexuality," 46–47.

51. Doğu Perinçek, *Eşcinsellik ve Yabancılaşma* [Homosexuality and alienation] (Istanbul: Kaynak Yayınları, 2000). See also Tunca Özlen, " 'Eşcinsellik ve Yabancılaşma'nın Eleştirisi I" [Critique of "homosexuality and alienation"], *Sol Haber*, August 29, 2011, http://haber.sol.org.tr/serbest-kursu/escinsellik -ve-yabancilasma-nin-elestirisi-i-tunca-ozlen-haberi-45901, accessed July 25, 2016.

52. Arslan Yüzgün, "Homosexuality and Police Terror in Turkey," *Journal of Homosexuality* 24, no. 3/4 (1993): 159–170, 165. Görkemli highlights the role of private television channels of the 1990s in expanding vernacular discourse, however problematically, around sexual identities. Popular newspapers, magazines, and cheap broadsides also played an important, even earlier, role. See Görkemli, " 'Coming Out of the Internet,' " 63–88.

53. Ali Kemal Yılmaz, *Erkek ve Kadında Eşcinsellik* [Homosexuality in men and women] (Istanbul: Özgür Yayınları, 1998), 54; Bereket and Adam, "Emergence of Gay Identities in Turkey," 132; Tapınç, "Masculinity, Femininity, and Turkish Male Homosexuality," 46; Deniz Yıldız, "Türkiye Tarihinde Eşcinselliğin İzinde: Eşcinsellik Hareketinin Tarihinden Satır Başları-1:8o'ler" [Tracking homosexuality through Turkish history: Headlines from the history of the homosexual movement—1: 1980s], *KAOS GL* 92 (January/February 2007): 48–51, http://kaosgldergi.com/dosyasayfa.php?id=2186, accessed June 15, 2015.

54. Özyeğin, "Reading the Closet," 209.

55. David M. Halperin, *How to Do the History of Male Homosexuality* (Chicago: University of Chicago Press, 2002), 109. My research supports the work of multiple scholars who contest the notion of the "global gay," i.e., the spread of a Western gay identity across the globe, as popularized by Dennis Altman's 1997 article "Global Gaze, Global Gays," *GLQ: A Journal of Lesbian and Gay Studies* 3,

no. 4 (1997): 417–437. Instead, I join scholars who depict individuals maneuvering within various transculturated scripts of sexuality, some of which might be symbolically associated with the West/modernity or the East/tradition. See, for example, Barry D. Adam, Jan Willem Duyvendak, and André Krouwel, "Gay and Lesbian Movements Beyond Borders? National Imprints of a Worldwide Movement," in *The Global Emergence of Gay and Lesbian Politics: National Imprints of a Worldwide Movement*, ed. Barry D. Adam, Jan Willem Duyvendak, and André Krouwel (Philadelphia: Temple University Press, 1999), 344–371; Héctor Carillo, *The Night Is Young: Sexuality in Mexico in the Time of AIDS* (Chicago: University of Chicago Press, 2002); Martin F. Manalansan, *Global Divas: Filipino Gay Men in the Diaspora* (Durham, N.C.: Duke University Press, 2003); Megan J. Sinnott, *Toms and Dees: Transgender Identity and Female Same-Sex Relationships in Thailand* (Honolulu: University of Hawaiʻi Press, 2004); Tom Boellstorff, *Gay Archipelago: Sexuality and Nation in Indonesia* (Princeton, N.J.: Princeton University Press, 2005); Gayatri Gopinath, *Impossible Desires: Queer Diasporas and South Asian Public Cultures* (Durham, N.C.: Duke University Press, 2005); Peter A. Jackson, "Capitalism and Global Queering: National Markets, Parallels Among Sexual Cultures, and Multiple Queer Modernities," *GLQ: A Journal of Lesbian and Gay Studies* 15, no. 3 (2009): 357–395.

56. For the United States, see Regina Kunzel, *Criminal Intimacy: Prison and the Uneven History of Modern American Sexuality* (Chicago: University of Chicago Press, 2008); Paula Claire Rust and Rodríguez Rust, eds., *Bisexuality in the United States: A Social Science Reader* (New York: Columbia University Press, 2000), especially part 2; Garcia Moctezuma, "Sexuality in Men of Color: The Impact of Culture," *The Body: The Complete HIV/AIDS Resource*, Winter 2005/2006, http://www.thebody.com/content/art14132.html?ts=pf, accessed November 10, 2008; Jane Ward, *Not Gay: Sex Between Straight White Men* (Durham, N.C.: Duke University Press, 2015).

57. For a sample articulation of Muslim "situational homosexuality," see Stephen O. Murray, "The Will Not to Know: Islamic Accommodations of Male Homosexuality" in *Islamic Homosexualities*, 14–54, 42.

58. Ward, *Not Gay*, 150.

59. Puar, *Terrorist Assemblages*; Melani McAlister, *Epic Encounters: Culture, Media, and U.S. Interests in the Middle East Since 1945*, 1st ed., rev. (Berkeley: University of California Press, 2005), 291.

60. See Massad, *Desiring Arabs*; Lionel Cantú, "De Ambiente: Queer Tourism and the Shifting Boundaries of Mexican Male Sexualities," *GLQ: A Journal of Lesbian and Gay Studies* 8, no. 1/2 (2002): 139–166.

61. Faces [pseudonym], email interview by author, August 20, 2008.

62. Cenk Özbay, "Rent Boy'ların Queer Öznelliği: İstanbul'da Norm Karşıtı Zaman, Mekan, Cinsellik ve Sınıfsallık" [Queer subjectivity of rent boys: Counter-normative time, space, sexuality and class in Istanbul], in *Cinsellik Muamması: Türkiye'de Queer Kültür ve Muhalefet* [Dilemma of sexuality: Queer culture and opposition in Turkey], ed. Cüneyt Çakırlar and Serkan Delice (Istanbul: Metis, 2012), 299.

63. *Istanbul Gay Guide.* See Cantú, "De Ambiente" on the "Latin guys."

64. Kenan [pseudonym], conversation with author.

65. For gey men's classed denigrations of rent boys as "ghetto" and as flashy per-formers of "active" heterosexuality, see Özbay, "Rent Boy'ların Queer Öznelliği," 294.

66. Don Kulick, *Travesti: Sex, Gender and Culture Among Brazilian Transgendered Prostitutes* (Chicago: University of Chicago Press, 1998), 212.

67. Yılmaz, *Erkek ve Kadında Eşcinsellik.*

68. Murat Hocaoğlu, *Eşcinsel Erkekler: Yirmi Beş Tanıklık* [Homosexual men: Twenty-five testimonials] (Istanbul: Siyah Beyaz, 2002), 149.

69. Ibid.

70. See for example, "Gazeteci Baki Koşar'ın Katiline 16 Yıl Hapis" [16 years im-prisonment to the murderer of journalist Baki Kosar], *Gündem Online*, March 1, 2007, http://www.gundemonline.org/haber.asp?haberid=31309, ac-cessed November 7, 2008; "A Gay Murder and Injustice in Turkey," *KAOS GL*, March 5, 2007, http://news.kaosgl.com/item/2007/3/5/a-gay-murder-and-injustice-in-turkey, accessed November 7, 2008; Human Rights Watch, *We Need a Law for Liberation: Gender, Sexuality, and Human Rights in a Changing Turkey*, 2008, http://hrw.org/reports/2008/turkey0508/, accessed August 1, 2012, 22.

71. Note that straight-identified American men also regularly "consolidate their heterosexual masculinity" by engaging in discursive and actual violence around homosexual acts. See Kunzel, *Criminal Intimacy*, 225, and Ward, *Not Gay*, 128.

72. Néstor García Canclini, *Hybrid Cultures: Strategies for Entering and Leaving Modernity*, trans. Christopher L. Chiappari and Silvia L. Lopez (Minneapolis: University of Minnesota Press, 1995), 3. Italics in original.

73. I am grateful to Irvin Cemil Schick for this formulation.

74. Michel Foucault, "Lecture 11, 17 March 1976," in *Society Must Be Defended: Lec-tures at the College de France* (New York: Picador, 2003), 239–264.

75. Human Rights Watch, *We Need a Law for Liberation*, 9. In a 2006 Lambdaist-anbul study, of the twenty-seven queer men who applied for exemption from military service, 67 percent were requested to undergo anal examination to prove their homosexuality, while 29 percent were asked to submit photographs depicting them in the "passive" position. In these photographs, the applicant's face must be visible and they need to be smiling to show that they are willing

participants. Lambdaistanbul, *Ne Yanlış Ne De Yalnızız! Bir Alan Araştırması: Eşcinsel ve Biseksüellerin Sorunları* [We are neither wrong, nor alone! A field research: The problems of homosexuals and bisexuals] (Istanbul: Berdan, 2006). See also Emre Azizlerli, "Proving You're Gay to the Turkish Army," *BBC News*, March 26, 2012, http://www.bbc.com/news/magazine-17474967, accessed June 16, 2016.

76. Mehmet [pseudonym], conversation with author, Istanbul, Turkey, August 12, 2007.

77. Ayşe Gül Altınay, *The Myth of the Military Nation: Militarism, Gender, and Education in Turkey* (New York: Palgrave Macmillan, 2004).

78. Quoted in Douglas Victor Janoff, "Tales from the Turkish Crypt," *Xtra Magazine*, July 1, 2004, http://archives.xtra.ca/Story.aspx?s=3130209, accessed November 7, 2008.

79. David L. Eng, Judith Halberstam, and José Estaban Muñoz, "What Is Queer About Queer Studies Now?" Special Issue, *Social Text* 23, no. 3/4 (2005): 1–17, 1.

80. Niyazi Berkes, "Sociology in Turkey," *American Journal of Sociology* 42, no. 2 (1936): 238–246, 241.

81. Susan C. Pearce, "The 'Turkish Model' of Sociology: East-West Science, State Formation, and the Post-Secular," *American Sociologist* 43, no. 4 (September 28, 2012): 406–427, 407.

82. Selin Berghan, *Lubunya: Transseksüel Kimlik ve Beden* [Lubunya: Transsexual identity and body] (Istanbul: Siyah Beyaz, 2007), 66.

83. Ibid., 77.

84. Ibid., 73.

85. Ibid., 20.

86. Uluşahin uses the standard term *cins*, which literally means "type" or "kind" in Turkish. The word connotes biological sex as well as gender.

87. Berghan, *Lubunya*, 32.

88. KAOS GL, "LGBT Sözlük" [LGBT dictionary], *KAOS GL*, http://www.kaosgl.org/node/274, accessed November 7, 2008.

89. Quoted in Pınar Selek, *Maskeler, Süvariler ve Gacılar* [Masks, cavaliers, and the gacıs] (Istanbul: İstiklal Kitabevi, 2007), 126.

90. Deniz Kandiyoti, "Pink Card Blues: Trouble and Strife at the Crossroads of Gender," in *Fragments of Culture: The Everyday of Modern Turkey*, ed. Deniz Kandiyoti and Ayşe Saktanber (New Brunswick, N.J.: Rutgers University Press, 2002), 277–293, 284.

91. Lubunya call this secret language, which contains around fifty words, *Lubunca*. See Kandiyoti, "Pink Card Blues."

92. Berghan, *Lubunya*, 112.

93. Seyhan, interview by author, Istanbul, Turkey, June 28, 2012.

94. Catherine Lutz, "The Gender of Theory," in *Women Writing Culture*, ed. Ruth Behar and Deborah A. Gordon (Berkeley: University of California Press, 1995), 249–266, 251. Lisa Duggan defines "homonormativity" as "a politics that does not contest dominant heteronormative assumptions and institutions but upholds and sustains them." Duggan, *The Twilight of Equality?*, 50.

95. In addition to travesti who work independently on the streets or via the Internet, Istanbul has several illegal travesti prostitution houses. "Travestilerin Genelevine Gittik" [We went to the prostitution houses of travesti], *Milliyet*, June 25, 2007, http://www.milliyet.com.tr/content/dosya/escinsel/escinsel04.html, accessed July 12, 2012.

96. "Trans Cinsiyet Suç Değildir" [Trans identity is not a crime], *Bianet*, June 24, 2012, http://bianet.org/bianet/lgbtt/139293-trans-cinsiyet-suc-degildir, accessed July 24, 2012.

97. Demet Demir, email interview by author, July 30, 2008. Ebru, email interview by author, July 29, 2008. Both names preferred by interviewees.

98. "Travestiler İş Kurumuna Başvurdu" [Travesti apply for jobs at the state unemployment office], *Haber*, July 17, 2007, http://www.haberler.com/travestiler-is-kurumu-na-basvurdu-haberi/, accessed November 7, 2008.

99. Tapınç, "Masculinity, Femininity, and Turkish Male Homosexuality," 48.

100. Kandiyoti, "Pink Card Blues," 277.

101. See George A. Chauncey, *Gay New York: Gender, Urban Culture, and the Making of the Gay Male World, 1890–1940* (New York: Basic Books, 1994) on the stigmatization of fairies in late nineteenth-century New York. For the masculinization of homosexuality during and immediately after World War II, see Allan Bérubé, *Coming Out Under Fire: The History of Gay Men and Women in World War II* (New York: Free Press, 1990); for the hostile attitude of early homophile activists to genderqueer homosexuals, see John D'Emilio, *Sexual Politics, Sexual Communities: The Making of a Homosexual Minority in the United States, 1940–1970* (Chicago: University of Chicago Press, 1998).

102. Esat, "Gay'liği Yaşa(yama)mak" [(Not) being able to live gayness], *KAOS GL*, October 1995, 5.

103. Kandiyoti, "Pink Card Blues," 283.

104. "Polis Baskısına Karşı 'Açlık Grevi': Eşcinsellerden 'Politik' Eylem" [Hunger strike against police harassment: Political action from homosexuals], *Milliyet*, April 30, 1987, 7. While the headline uses the word "eşcinsel" (homosexual), the photograph shows "gacıvari" lubunya, who later will be classified as travesti. See also "Turkey LGBT History," *KAOS GL*, http://news.kaosgl.com/turkey_lgbt_history.php, accessed October 24, 2008.

105. Halperin, *How to Do the History of Male Homosexuality*, 109.

106. Şehrazad nightclub in Beyoğlu announced "Travesti-Strip Tease (for the first time in Istanbul)" in October 10, 1958, in *Milliyet*. See also Atilla İlhan, *Yanlış Erkekler, Yanlış Kadınlar* [Wrong men, wrong women] (Istanbul: İş Bankası Kültür Yayınları, 1985).

107. Kandiyoti, "Pink Card Blues," 278. Tom Boellstorff similarly critiques ethnographic depictions of "traditional" transgenders and "modern" gays in *A Coincidence of Desires: Anthropology, Queer Studies, Indonesia* (Durham, N.C.: Duke University Press, 2007), 192.

108. My italics. Yusuf Yurdigül, "Türkiye' de Televizyon Haberciliğinde Sıradışı Kimliğin sunumu: Travesti Konulu Haberler" [The presentation of marginal identities in Turkish television news: News depicting travesti], M.A. thesis, Istanbul University, 2002.

109. KAOS GL, "LGBT Sözlük," accessed May 28, 2015. This definition has not changed since at least May 2007.

110. Pearce, "'Turkish Model' of Sociology," 411.

111. Kandiyoti, "Pink Card Blues," 282.

112. Halil Koyutürk, Skype interview by author, July 6, 2012.

113. Rosemary Hennessy, *Profit and Pleasure: Sexual Identities in Late Capitalism* (London: Routledge, 2000). See also John D'Emilio, "Capitalism and Gay Identity," in *Powers of Desire: The Politics of Sexuality*, ed. Ann Snitow, Christine Stansell, and Sharan Thompson (New York: Monthly Review, 1983), 100–113; Donald Morton, ed. *The Material Queer: A LesBiGay Cultural Studies Reader* (Boulder, Colo.: Westview, 1996); Ann Pellegrini, "Consuming Lifestyle: Commodity Capitalism and Transformations in Gay Identity," in *Queer Globalizations: Citizenship and the Afterlife of Colonialism*, ed. Arnaldo Cruz-Malavé and Martin Manalansan (New York: New York University Press, 2002), 134–146; Duggan, *The Twilight of Equality?*; Jackson, "Capitalism and Global Queering."

114. Seyhan, interview by author.

115. For a compelling account of this history, see Veysel Eşsiz, "Devletin Eli, Beli, Sopası: Anlatılmamış Sürgünden 'Kabahatlere' Türkiye'de Trans Bedenin Denetimi" [The state's hand, waist, and rod: The regulation of the trans body from the untold expulsion to "offences"], in *Cinsellik Muamması*, 185–220, 204.

116. Charles P. Wallace, "Gridlock in 'Streets Paved with Gold': Istanbul's Old Charms Fading with Pressure of Fast Growth," *Los Angeles Times*, May 25, 1987, 10.

117. Gökşin Varan, interview by author, Istanbul, Turkey, July 6, 2012. Varan is a photographer whose work has been grounded in Tarlabaşı for over a decade. For the AKP's more recent plans for Tarlabaşı, see Constanze Letsch, "Tarlabaşı Is Renewed," *Near East Quarterly*, June 11, 2011, http://www.neareastquarterly.com/index.php/2011/06/11/tarlabasi-is-renewed/, accessed July 12, 2012.

118. Ümit Cizre Sakallıoğlu, "Rethinking the Connections Between Turkey's 'Western' Identity Versus Islam," *Critique: Critical Middle Eastern Studies* 7, no. 12 (1998): 3–18; Yael Navaro-Yashin, *Faces of the State: Secularism and Public Life in Turkey* (Princeton, N.J.: Princeton University Press, 2002); Alev Çınar, *Modernity, Islam, and Secularism in Turkey: Bodies, Places, and Time* (Minneapolis: University of Minnesota Press, 2005).

119. Demet Demir, interview by author, Istanbul, Turkey, March 12, 2007. In Demir's reference to the Stonewall rebellion we find America as *tertium comparationis* again, operating as a complex resource for imagining local identities and politics.

120. Recounted in Ersan Atar, "Kurtar Beni Avrupa" [Save me, Europe], *Milliyet*, July 24, 2000.

121. Ibid. For more on Welfare's utilization of a binary opposition between West and East, and its focus on countering "the West within," see M. Hakan Yavuz, "Cleansing Islam from the Public Sphere," *Journal of International Affairs* 54, no. 1 (2000): 21–42, 34–35.

122. "Gül ve Erdoğan'ın Masasında 'Eşcinsellerin Türkiye'si' Var" [On the desk of Erdoğan and Gül: "The Turkey of Homosexuals"], *Gazeteport.com*, March 10, 2008, http://www.gazeteport.com.tr/NEWS/GP_169788, accessed August 17, 2010.

123. Kandiyoti makes a similar point in an interview by Serkan Delice, "Bir An Durup Düşünmek: Dayatılan Kimlikler ve Temsil Siyasetinin Bedelleri" [A moment for reflection: The price of imposed identities and the politics of representation], in *Cinsellik Muamması*, 149.

124. This list was culled from the online KAOS GL file "Turkey's LGBT History," http://news.kaosgl.com/turkey_lgbt_history.php, accessed October 24, 2008.

125. Uğur Yüksel, "Kaos GL'den: İyi Temizlikler" [From KAOS GL: Happy cleaning], *KAOS GL* 33 (July–August 2007): 5.

126. "Medya" [Media], *KAOS GL* 22 (June 1996), 1.

127. Hakan Geçim, "LGBT Movement in Turkey and the European Union," *KAOS GL*, September 11, 2006, http://www.kaosgl.org/page.php?id=8719, accessed September 28, 2010; Yıldız, "Türkiye Tarihinde Eşcinselliğin İzinde."

128. Alper Görmüş, "AKP'den Eşcinsellere Herkes Eşittir Mesajı" [AKP gives the message "everyone is equal" to homosexuals], *Akşam*, June 5, 2008, http://www.aksam.com.tr/haber.asp?a=118281,4, accessed November 8, 2008.

129. "Yargıtay Kararı: Gay ve Lezbiyene Sapık Diyemezsiniz" [High Court decision: You cannot call gays and lesbians perverts], *T24*, January 9, 2012, http://T24.com.tr/Haber/Yargitay-Karari-Gay-Ve-Lezbiyene-Sapik-Diyemezsiniz/190734, accessed June 23, 2012.

130. Perry Anderson, "After Kemal," *London Review of Books*, September 25, 2008, https://www.lrb.co.uk/v30/n18/ande01_.html, accessed November 17, 2008.

131. For a thorough analysis of this growing rift, see Savcı, *Queer in Translation*, especially chapter 3.

132. Sinan, interview by author, Istanbul, Turkey, August 10, 2008.

133. Savcı, *Queer in Translation*, 80.

134. Okay, interview by author, Istanbul, Turkey, August 5, 2012.

135. Nicholas Birch, "Was Ahmet Yildiz the Victim of Turkey's First Gay Honour Killing?" *The Independent*, July 18, 2008, http://www.independent.co.uk/news /world/europe/was-ahmet-yildiz-the-victim-of-turkeys-first-gay-honour -killing-871822.html, accessed October 24, 2008.

136. Andrew Higgins and Farnaz Fassihi, "Muslim Land Joins Ranks of Tigers," *Wall Street Journal*, August 6, 2008, http://online.wsj.com/article_email /SB121798369220315407-lMyQjAxMDI4MTA3NjkwODYzWj.html, accessed November 1, 2008.

137. Bilge Yeşil, *Media in New Turkey* (Urbana: University of Illinois Press, 2016), 12.

138. Chandan Reddy, "Asian Diasporas, Neoliberalism, and Family: Reviewing the Case for Homosexual Asylum in the Context of Family Rights," *Social Text* 23, no. 3/4 (2005): 101–119; Massad, *Desiring Arabs*; Puar, *Terrorist Assemblages*.

139. Lambdaistanbul, *İt İti Isırmaz: Bir Alan Araştırması—İstanbul'da Yaşayan Trans Kadınların Sorunları* [A dog won't bite another dog: A field study—the problems of trans women living in Istanbul] (Istanbul: Punto Baskı, 2010); Ceylan Engin, "Gender Discrimination in Turkish Society and Its Effects on Transgender Individuals," M.A. thesis, George Washington University, 2014.

140. For such a defense, see "Öldürülen İrem'in Duruşması Travesti Akınına Uğradı" [Travesti pack the hearing of murdered İrem], *Gazete Bursa*, December 9, 2012. See also Savcı, *Queer in Translation*, particularly chapter 5 for the clients' focus on travesti's penises and the discourse of "travesti terror."

141. For a sophisticated critique of the development of this category, see David Valentine, *Imagining Transgender: Ethnography of a Category* (Durham, N.C.: Duke University Press, 2007).

142. Ebru, email interview by author.

143. Ibid.

144. Okay, interview by author.

145. Demet Demir, interview by author, Istanbul, Turkey, August 17, 2007.

146. Cathy J. Cohen, *The Boundaries of Blackness: AIDS and the Breakdown of Black Politics* (Chicago: University of Chicago Press, 1999), 27; Shane Phelan, *Sexual Strangers: Gays, Lesbians, and Dilemmas of Citizenship* (Philadelphia: Temple University Press, 2010), 84.

147. Evren Savcı, conversation with author, Bodrum, Turkey, July 22, 2012.

148. Sinan, interview by author.

149. Okay, interview by author. See also Evren Savcı, "Who Speaks the Language of Queer Politics? Western Knowledge, Politico-cultural Capital and Belonging Among Urban Queers in Turkey," *Sexualities* 19, no. 3 (March 1, 2016): 369–387.

150. Mija Sanders, email to author, October 28, 2008.

151. For Lambdaistanbul's laudable "intersectionality," see Savcı, "Who Speaks the Language of Queer Politics?" 87–89.

152. See Savcı, *Queer in Translation*, 221–225; Savcı, "Who Speaks the Language of Queer Politics?" For more on the classed politics of the English language in Turkey, see chapter 3.

153. On the "cumulative" nature of resource deficiency for marginalized groups, see Michael Parenti, *Power and the Powerless* (New York: St. Martin's, 1978), 76.

154. The organizing committee noted that one trans woman, Belgin, was invited but could not make it at the last minute. Protestors argued that additional efforts should have been made.

155. Trans X Turkey, http://transxturkey.com/about.php, accessed August 19, 2012.

156. Birol İskra, interview by author, Istanbul, Turkey, June 28, 2012. While this clearly resembles Massad's argument in *Desiring Arabs*, İskra had not read Massad's work at the time of the interview.

157. İskra, interview by author, Istanbul, Turkey, July 2, 2012.

158. Demet Demir, interview by author, Istanbul, Turkey, July 2, 2012.

159. SPoD member, email interview by author, July 26, 2012.

160. Okay, interview by author.

161. Massad, *Desiring Arabs*, chapter 3.

162. See Mustafa Akyol, "What Does Islam Say About Being Gay?" *New York Times*, July 28, 2015, http://nyti.ms/1HYvcFx.

163. For all its inequalities and crises, globalization does have certain benefits, as studies of countries and regions purposefully left out of the circuit of international finance show. See Jennifer Olmsted, "Globalization Denied: Gender and Poverty in Iraq and Palestine," in *The Wages of Empire: Neoliberal Policies, Repression, and Women's Poverty*, ed. Amalia Cabezas, Ellen Reese, and Marguerite Waller (Boulder, Colo.: Paradigm, 2007); Ferguson, *Global Shadows*.

164. Pew Global Attitudes Project, Survey of 47 Publics, Spring 2007, www.pewglobal.org/files/pdf/256topline.pdf, accessed August 12, 2012. For more on this nationalist and statist backlash, see the discussion about Orhan Pamuk and *Metal Fırtına* in chapter 2 and about the AKP's Islamic neoliberalism in chapter 3. Also see Bilge Yeşil, *Media in New Turkey* (Urbana: University of Illinois Press, 2016), 78–87.

165. Jackson, "Capitalism and Global Queering," 362.

POSTSCRIPT

1. Samuel P. Huntington, "The Clash of Civilizations?" *Foreign Affairs* (Summer 1993), http://www.foreignaffairs.com/articles/48950/samuel-p-huntington/the -clash-of-civilizations.

2. For example, Fouad Ajami, "The Summoning: But They Said, We Will Not Hearken," in *The Clash of Civilizations? The Debate* (New York: W. W. Norton, 1996), 26–35; Roy Mottahedeh, "The Clash of Civilizations: An Islamicist's Critique," *Harvard Middle Eastern and Islamic Review* 2, no. 2 (1995): 1–26; Edward Said, "The Myth of 'the Clash of Civilizations'" (Northampton, Mass.: Media Education Foundation, 1998), https://www.mediaed.org/assets/products /404/transcript_404.pdf; Mahmood Mamdani, *Good Muslim, Bad Muslim: America, the Cold War, and the Roots of Terror* (New York: Doubleday, 2005), especially chapter 1.

3. Mamdani, *Good Muslim, Bad Muslim*, 17–62.

4. Samuel P. Huntington, *The Clash of Civilizations and the Remaking of World Order* (New York: Simon & Schuster, 2007), 178.

5. Chiara Bottici and Benoît Challand, *The Myth of the Clash of Civilizations* (Florence, Ky.: Routledge, 2013).

6. Walter Mignolo, *The Darker Side of the Renaissance: Literacy, Territoriality, and Colonization*, 2nd ed. (Ann Arbor: University of Michigan Press, 2003); Edward W. Said, *Orientalism* (New York: Vintage, 1978); Walter Rodney, *How Europe Underdeveloped Africa* (Baltimore: Black Classic, 2011).

7. Bernard Lewis, *The Emergence of Modern Turkey* (London: Oxford University Press, 1968), 484.

8. Matthew F. Jacobs, *Imagining the Middle East: The Building of an American Foreign Policy, 1918–1967* (Chapel Hill: University of North Carolina Press, 2011), 64.

9. This disciplinary divide between Huntington and Lewis threatens to disappear in Lewis's broader policy-oriented texts about Islam and the West, which have been the main focus of Edward Said's criticism (Said, *Orientalism*, 107).

10. Moustafa Bayoumi, *This Muslim American Life: Dispatches from the War on Terror* (New York: New York University Press, 2015), 91–92. See also Zachary Lockman, *Contending Visions of the Middle East: The History and Politics of Orientalism*, 2nd ed. (New York: New York University Press, 2009), x; Jasbir K. Puar, *Terrorist Assemblages: Homonationalism in Queer Times* (Durham, N.C.: Duke University Press, 2007), 84; Ali Behdad and Juliet Williams, "Neo-Orientalism," in *Globalizing American Studies*, ed. Brian T. Edwards and Dilip Parameshwar Gaonkar (Chicago: University of Chicago Press, 2010), 283–299, 285.

11. Claire Berlinski, "Smile and Smile: Turkey's Feel-Good Foreign Policy," *World Affairs* (July/August 2010), http://www.worldaffairsjournal.org/article/smile -and-smile-turkeys-feel-good-foreign-policy.

12. Lewis, *Emergence of Modern Turkey*, 16.

13. Etienne Balibar, "Is There a Neo-Racism?" in *Race, Nation, Class: Ambiguous Identities*, ed. Etienne Balibar and Immanuel Wallerstein (New York: Verso, 1991), 22.

14. Said, *Orientalism*, 72.

15. Bernard Lewis, "The Question of Orientalism," *New York Review of Books* 29, no. 11 (1982): 49–56; Edward Said, Oleg Grabar, and Bernard Lewis, "Orientalism: An Exchange," *New York Review of Books* 29, no. 13 (1982): 44–48.

16. Frank Costigliola, "Reading for Meaning: Theory, Language, and Metaphor," in *Explaining the History of American Foreign Relations*, ed. Michael J. Hogan and Thomas G. Paterson (Cambridge: Cambridge University Press, 2004), 279–303.

17. For an influential theoretical elaboration of the connections between gender and political discourse, see Joan W. Scott, "Gender: A Useful Category of Historical Analysis," *American Historical Review* 91, no. 5 (1986): 1053–1057. Kristin Hoganson's work remains canonical for modeling how gendered constructs influence foreign relations: Kristin Hoganson, *Fighting for American Manhood: How Gender Politics Provoked the Spanish-American and Philippine-American Wars* (New Haven, Conn.: Yale University Press, 2000). See also Emily S. Rosenberg, " 'Foreign Affairs' After World War II: Connecting Sexual and International Politics," *Diplomatic History* 18, no. 1 (1994): 59–70; Elaine Tyler May, "Commentary: Ideology and Foreign Policy: Culture and Gender in Diplomatic History," *Diplomatic History* 18, no. 1 (January 1, 1994): 71–78; Frank Costigliola, "The Nuclear Family: Tropes of Gender and Pathology in the Western Alliance," *Diplomatic History* 21, no. 2 (1997): 163–183; Frank Costigliola, " 'Unceasing Pressure for Penetration': Gender, Pathology, and Emotion in George Kennan's Formation of the Cold War," *Journal of American History* 83, no. 4 (1997): 1309–1339; Cynthia Enloe, *Bananas, Beaches and Bases: Making Feminist Sense of International Politics*, rev. ed. (Berkeley: University of California Press, 2000); Kristin Hoganson, "What's Gender Got to Do with It? Gender History as Foreign Relations History," in *Explaining the History of American Foreign Relations*, 304–322; Naoko Shibusawa, *America's Geisha Ally: Reimagining the Japanese Enemy* (Cambridge, Mass.: Harvard University Press, 2006).

18. Lila Abu-Lughod, "Do Muslim Women Really Need Saving? Anthropological Reflections on Cultural Relativism and Its Others," *American Anthropologist* 104, no. 3 (2002): 783–790, 783.

19. Abu-Lughod cites Spivak, but not Mohanty, for example. Gayatri Chakravorty Spivak, "Can the Subaltern Speak?" in *Marxism and the Interpretation of*

Culture, ed. Cary Nelson and Lawrence Grossberg (Urbana: University of Illinois Press, 1988), 271–313; Chandra Talpade Mohanty, "Under Western Eyes: Feminist Scholarship and Colonial Discourses," *Boundary* 2 12, no. 12.3–13.1 (1984): 333–358.

20. Ann Laura Stoler, *Race and the Education of Desire: Foucault's History of Sexuality and the Colonial Order of Things* (Durham, N.C.: Duke University Press, 1995), 61.

21. Tim Arango and Ben Hubbard, "Turkey Pursues Cleric Living in U.S., Blamed as Coup Mastermind," *New York Times*, July 19, 2016, http://www.nytimes.com /2016/07/20/world/europe/fethullah-gulen-erdogan-extradition.html, accessed July 20, 2016.

22. Jessica Winegar, "The Humanity Game: Art, Islam, and the War on Terror," *Anthropological Quarterly* 81, no. 3 (July 1, 2008): 651; Evelyn Alsultany, *The Arabs and Muslims in the Media: Race and Representation After 9/11* (New York: New York University Press, 2012); Perin Gürel, "Visual Cultures of Internet Islamophobia: Transnational Memes and International Politics," paper presented at the Annual Meeting of the American Historical Association, January 2–5, 2014, Washington, D.C.; Saba Mahmood, "Secularism, Hermeneutics, and Empire: The Politics of Islamic Reformation," *Public Culture* 18, no. 2 (March 20, 2006): 323–347.

23. Walter Mignolo, *Local Histories/Global Designs: Coloniality, Subaltern Knowledges, and Border Thinking* (Princeton, N.J.: Princeton University Press, 2000); Perin Gürel, "Bilingual Humor, Authentic Aunties, and the Transnational Vernacular at Gezi Park," *Journal of Transnational American Studies* 6, no. 1 (January 1, 2015), http://escholarship.org/uc/item/2md6f6fr; Perin Gürel, "Folklore Matters: The Folklore Scholarship of Alan Dundes and the New American Studies," *Columbia Journal of American Studies* 7 (2005): 120–135. Also see chapter 3 in this book.

24. Melani McAlister, *Epic Encounters: Culture, Media, and U.S. Interests in the Middle East Since 1945*, 1st ed., rev. (Berkeley: University of California Press, 2005), 209.

25. Ussama Makdisi, "Author's Response," Roundtable Review of Ussama Makdisi, *Artillery of Heaven: American Missionaries and the Failed Conversion of the Middle East* (Ithaca, N.Y.: Cornell University Press, 2008), *H-Diplo Roundtable Reviews* 10, no. 11 (2009), http://www.h-net.org/~diplo/roundtables/PDF /Roundtable-X-11.pdf, accessed June 17, 2016.

Index

Anatolia (*continued*)
Supreme War Council breaking, 34.
See also Republic of Turkey; Thrash the whore
Anderson, Benedict, 22, 47
Andrews, Walter G., 244n43
Ankara, Turkey, 81, 135, 159, 176
anomie, 4, 173, 200n11
anti-Americanisms, 2–3, 22, 96–99, 103–146, *138*, 196–197
Arab, 7, 49
Araba Sevdası (Ekrem). *See* carriage affair, The
arabesk. *See* hybrid music
Arabic, 106–113, 243n41
armed resistance, 21, 37–38
Armenia, 32, 34–35
Armenians, 20, 25, 26, 27, 32, 96
Asia Minor, nationalism across, 35. *See also* Anatolia
Aslan, Ferhat, 233n83
assassination, 40–41
Association for the Defense of the French Language, 104
Atatürk, Mustafa Kemal, 4, 37–46, 47, 49, 159, 160; caliphate abolished by, 214n29; death of, 50; documentary on, 78; Edib and, 21, 30, 31, 51, 206n7; Islamic rule undermined by, 190–191; modernization used by, 77; name of, 206n7; in novels, 69; reforms of, 110, 222n83; strategic westernization led by, 110; sultanate abolished by, 214n29. *See also* Speech
Ateşten Gömlek (Edib). *See* shirt of flame, The
authoritarian westernization. *See* selective westernization
automobile (*tomofil*), 88, 103–104
Aydın, Cemil, 200n9

bad Muslims, 190–191, 193, 197
bad West, 27, 79, 166
Bailey, Thomas, 34
Bakhtin, Mikhail Mikhaïlovich, 118, 119
bandage, 83, 84
Barthes, Roland, 140
Başgöz, İlhan, 116, 127–128, 231n49
batılılaşma. *See* westernization
Bayar, Celal, 79
bayii. *See* general merchandise dealer
Baykurt, Fakir. *See* American bandage, The
Being Turkish webpage, 103–104, 140
Belge, Murat, 62
belonging, 24–28
benevolent supremacy, 75
Berghan, Selin, 167–169, 170
Berlinski, Claire, 192, 193
Bey, Chekib, 27
Bey, Kara Vasıf, 44–45
Bey, Rustem, 27
Bey, Sami, 73, 74
Beyoğlu, Turkey, 56–57, 154–155, 175
Bhabha, Homi, 22
bilateral friendship associations, 112
bilingual folklore, 120–136, 141, 227n6
bilingual humor, 113–125, 139–46
Bilmece: A Corpus of Turkish Riddles (Başgöz and Tietze), 231n49
bisexuality, 162–163, 240n9
Boone, Joseph A., 244nn43,45
Boratav, Pertev Naili, 234nn90, 92
Borat: Cultural Learnings of America for Make Benefit Glorious Nation of Kazakhstan, 144–145
Borges, Jorge Luis, 58–59
boron reserves, 97–99
Bosphorus Bridge, 147–149

bottoms, 243nn40–41
Bozkurt, Mahmut Esat, 51–52
Brazil, 163, 170
bridge, 147–149, 174, 180
Bristol, Mark Lambert, 40, 43, 45, 48
Britain, 32
British Empire, 48
brothels, 137–139, *138*, 170, 249n95
Browne, L. E., 44, 45
bumper sticker, 103–104
Burdick, Eugene, 81
Bursa, Turkey, 110–111
buses, 89, 90, 93
Bush, George W., 97, 129, 137–139, *138*,
    140, 144–145
Butler, Judith, 156

Çalıkuşu (Güntekin). *See* wren, The
caliphate, 214n29
Canada, 166
"Car Narratives: A Subgenre in Turkish
    Novel Writing" (Parla), 59
carriage affair, The (*Araba Sevdası*)
    (Ekrem), 67–68, 73–74, 117, 130
Carrier, James G., 149
cars, 80–81, 103–104, 115, 227n3
cartoon, 14–15, 32, *33*, 137–139, *138*,
    140
Cashman, Michael, 177
Central Intelligence Agency (CIA),
    195–196
centralization, 26, 38, 64–68
Chakrabarty, Dipesh, 194
Chen, Xiaomei, 5
children, Hodja jokes associated with,
    235n97
children of the street (*sokak çocukları*),
    174
Christendom, in binary opposition to
    Islam, 77

Christianity, girls converting to,
    110–111
Christians, 25–26, 27, 31, 48, 60
Çiller, Tansu, 175
Çintay, Nur, 147–149, 154, 162–163, 172,
    180
citizens, 4, 41
civilizations, 3, 187–197
civil society, 86–87
Clash of Civilizations, The
    (Huntington), 191
"Clash of Civilizations?, The"
    (Huntington), 187–189
Clash of Civilizations thesis, 187–197
class, 38–39, 51–52, 105–106, 114, 172,
    241n23
Clemenceau, Georges, 48
Cohen, Sacha Baron, 144–145
Cold War, 7, 49, 64, 133, 191, 195;
    Khrushchev during, 144; novels,
    76–86, *78*, *85*, 87–88; selective
    westernization in, 76–86, *78*, *85*;
    West in, 77. *See also* modernization
    theory
colleges, American, 110–111
colonies, 25, 239n146. *See also* mandates
colonization, 4, 25, 200n7
comics, 90, 91–92, 105, 129
Committee for Union and Progress
    (CUP), 26, 167
conflicts, culture as explanatory factor
    for, 187–188
Congress, U.S., *78*
Conrad, JoAnn, 126
conspiracies, 50, 93–94. *See also* Metal
    storm; new life, The
coup, 3, 160–161, 195–196. *See also*
    post-coup era
courtesan, 67–68
Crane, Charles Richard, 127

Erbakan, Necmettin, 175–176

Erdinç, Fahri, 80

Erdoğan, Recep Tayyip, 50–51, 195–196, 216n135; AKP led by, 175, 176; in cartoon, 137–139, *138*, 140

Erotikle Karışık Nasrettin Hoca Fıkraları. See Nasreddin Hodja jokes, mixed in with the erotic

"Eşcinsellerin Türkiyesi" (KAOS GL). *See* "Turkey of Homosexuals, The"

Eşcinsellik ve Yabancılaşma. See Homosexuality and alienation

Espy, Willard Richardson, 120

ethnic engineering, 26

ethnicity, 51–52, 114

Europe, 3–4, 6, 8–9, 133, 194, 200n7; economic control ceded to, 73; guardianship over Christian minorities, 25–26, 27; as invader, 69; as over-westernization's source, 45; U.S. differentiated from, 31, 42, 75–76, 153–154

European Customs Union, 175

Europeans, 26, 54, 68, 74, 227n146, 243n42; imperialism, 31, 108–109, 200n9; travelogues, 159

European Union (EU): AKP membership talks, 177, 179; Turkey applying to, 96, 152, 153, 175–176, 177, 178, 179

excessive westernization, 27, 109. *See also* over-westernization

Eyüboğlu, İsmet Zeki, 220n41

Fatih-Harbiye (Safa), 56–57

Felatun Bey ve Rakım Efendi (Mithat). *See* Mr. Felatun and Master Rakım

Ferguson, James, 243n35

fez, 41–42

fifth column, 26, 51

Fifth International Turkish Folklore Congress, 127–128

figurative language, 196–197

First World, 61–62

flapper, 71–76

flatulence, 107, 108, 109, 112–113, 114–115, 119

folk culture, 105, 134–135

folk humor, 104–105, 115–125

folklore, 103–146, *138*, 230n46. *See also* bilingual folklore; Turklish humor

folk traditions, 63–64, 65, 73–74

Fontenoy, La Marquise de. *See* Cunliffe-Owen, Marguerite

foreigners, 51, 54, 106–107

foreign language, 106–113

foreign policy, 31–32, 76–86, *78*, *85*, 191–192, 241n18

forgetting, 23–24, 43–50. *See also* disremembering

Fourteen Points, 31, 47. *See also* Point 12

France, 6, 32

French, 109, 111

friendship, of U.S., 82–84, *85*

"From Allegories to Novels" (Borges), 58–59

Frye, Northrop, 59

"Funny but Not Vulgar" (Orwell), 142

García Márquez, Gabriel, 226n141

Garden of Turkish–American Friendship, 82–83

Gates, Bill, 233n83

Gates, Henry Louis, Jr., 145

"Gay Life in Istanbul" (*Istanbul Gay Guide*), 240n9

gays, *150*, 154, 155–167, 184–185, 243nn40–41, 245n55; bridge, 147–149, 174, 180; transphobia of, 171, 173. *See also* active partner; active position; geys; lesbianism; passive position; tops; travestis

gender, 48–55, *53*, 80, 81–82, 172, 240n1; of East, 203n26; of Edib, 137–139, *138*; of over-westernization, 68–76; in Speech, 38–39, 47; Turkishness forms, 105–106; U.S. and, 68–76. *See also* westoxication

general merchandise dealer (*bayii*), 89–91, 226n136

Georges-Picot, François, 45

German Empire, 20

Germans, 32–34, 46, 110, 111

geys, 150, *150*, 151, 161, 162–167, 171; modernity as connected to, 174; on rent boys, 247n65

Gezi protests, 141, 184

gharbzadegi. *See* westoxication

girls, 56–57, 67–68, 82, 109, 110–111.
   See also *Fatih-Harbiye*; *Sodom ve Gomore*

global gay, 245n55

"Global Gaze, Global Gays" (Altman), 245n55

globalization, 238n127, 253n163

Global Shadows: Africa in the Neoliberal World Order (Ferguson), 243n35

God. *See* Sufism

Gökalp, Ziya, 125–126, 167, 200n11.
   See also Temel jokes

good Muslims, 190–191, 197

good West, 27, 79, 166

Görkemli, Serkan, 245n52

government, 22, 50–51, 86

governmentality, 3–4, 189, 195, 200n6

grants, 181–182

Greece, 24, 76–77; invasion, 29, *29*, 39–40, 46, *53*; Turkey and, *78*, 84, 86

Grew, Joseph C., 245n48

Grewal, Inderpal, 145

Gropp, Lewis, 219n30

Gül, Abdullah, 176

Gülen, Fethullah, 3, 195–196, 216n135

Gulf War, 87

Güntekin, Reşat Nuri, 70

Gürbilek, Nurdan, 9, 220n49

Gürpınar, Doğan, 139

Habitat II, 175, 177

Hagia Irene, 147–149

Halperin, David, 161

Hamidian massacres, 26

"Happy Birthday," 114–115

Harbord, James, 45

Harbord Commission, 29, 34, 44

Haşim, Ahmet, 71

hate crime, 155–167

Hay, John, 27

Hennessy, Rosemary, 174

hetero-flexible guys, 240n9

heterogeneity, 164–165

heteronormativity, 244n47

heterosexuality, 159–160, 247n71

hidden transcripts, 105, 145–146

high school, 237n118

Hikmet, Nazım, 80

histories, *20*, 22–55, *29*, *33*, *36*, *53*; European, 227n146; Kemalist, 194, 195–196; Lewis on, 190–191

homicides, 154–167

homonormativity, 249n94

homophobia, 149, 166

homosexual (*homoseksüel* or *eşcinsel*), 74, *150*, 152, 154–169, 243nn40–41, 247n71; panic, 179; stand, 177. *See also* active partner; active position; gays; lesbianism; passive position; tops

homosexuality, 160–161, 165, 175–176, 220n41, 247n71; models of, 158, 163–164, 166; survey, 185. *See also* gays; lesbianism

Homosexuality and alienation (*Eşcinsellik ve Yabancılaşma*) (Perinçek), 160–161

Hot Spot, 154–155

House, Edward M., 47

Howell, Sally, 209n40

humor, 14–15, 113–125. *See also* bilingual humor; folk humor; Turklish humor

Hun, 32–34

Huntington, Samuel, 187–197, 254n9

hybridization, 5, 134–135. *See also* transculturation

hybrid music (*arabesk*), 87

ibne. See passive position

identity, of travesti, 173–174

imperialism, 38, 69, 133–134, 195; European, 31, 108–109, 200n9; U.S., 6, 21–22, 23, 196. *See also* cultural imperialism

inadequate westernization, 147–186, *150. See also* under-westernization

Incredible Turk, The, 78

Independence Tribunals, 37

Independence War, 39, 41, 52, 93; mobility influencing, 60–61; Treaty of Lausanne and, 35, 37. *See also* Thrash the whore

Indians, 46, 48

Indians (Native Americans), 27–28, 81

indigenization, 5, 94, 105, 134–135

İnönü, İsmet, 40, 86

Inquiry, The, 28–29

intellectuals, 46, 69, 70, 107–108, 126. *See also* Karaosmanoğlu, Yakup Kadri; novelists

intelligentsia, 29, 65–66. *See also* Wilsonian Principles League

International Istanbul Jazz Festival, 147–149

International Lesbian, Gay, Bisexual, Trans and Intersex Association (ILGA), 177

international mandate system, 19–20

Internet, 121–125, 233n83

"In Turkey, a Novel is a Public Statement" (Gropp), 219n30

invasion, 29, 29, 39–40, 46, 52–53, 195; for boron reserves, 97–99; of Cyprus, 86; of Egypt, 227n146; railway system facilitating, 79. *See also* Iraq; *Sodom ve Gomore*

İpekçi, Cemil, 178, 179

Iran, 154, 244n47

Iraq, 3, 96, 136–137

Irzık, Sibel, 62–63, 94

ishq. See love

İskra, Birol, 183, 253n156

Islam, 77, 137–139, 141, 185, 187–197, 254n9. *See also* Sufism

Islamic terrorist, 7, 152, 162, 190, 196

Islamophobia, 7

Istanbul, Turkey, 32, 39, 54, 56–57, 176, 233n81; English in, 111; gays in, 154–155; jazz festival in, 147–149; Pride Parade, 183, 184, 185; prostitution houses in, 249n95; travesti in, 174–175, 249n95; urban renewal campaign of, 175; West viewing, 159

Istanbul Gay Guide, 155, 163, 240n9

Istanbul LGBTT, 181, 182–183

Izmir, Turkey, 29, 39–40, 80, 156–158

LGBTQ (lesbian, gay, bisexual, transgender, queer), 152, 167–168, 170, 171, 176–186, 241n18. *See also* active position; gays; geys; homosexual; homosexuality; lesbianism; passive position; queers; travestis

linguistic imperialism, 133–134

Linguistic Imperialism (Philipson), 133

literature, effeminacy's connection with, 220n49

Lloyd George, David, 20–21, 32, 34, 50

Lorde, Audre, 142

love (*ishq*), 63, 73–74, 76, 94; of U.S., 81–84, *85*; for West, 66, 67–68

lubunya. *See* travestis

Lutz, Catherine, 170

lynchings, 27

macaronic text, 118–121

Mahmut II (sultan), 108

Mamdani, Mahmood, 187–188, 190

mandacı traitors. *See* pro-mandate traitors

mandates, 19–55, *29*, *33*, *53*, 84, 195–196

Marr, Timothy, 47

marriages, 41, 69–70, 137–139, *138*, 157, 159

Marshall Plan, 79, 80, 84

masjid. *See* prayer room

massacres, 20, 26, 27, 32, 96

Massad, Joseph Andoni, 152, 185, 253n156

McAlister, Melani, 8, 196–97

meanings, 158, 160–161

memory, 23–24

men, 73–74, *78*, 116, 247n71. *See also* active position; dandy; geys; passive position; travestis

Merle, Edward Mead, 39

Metal storm (*Metal Fırtına*) (Uçar and Turna), 52, 96–99, 227n146

metrosexual (*metroseksüel*), 157, 158, 161

Middle East, 5, 7, 22, 32, 152; culture and, 187–197; U.S. and, 25, 187–197, 235n103

Middle East Technical University (METU), 81, 237n120

Mild West, The (*Yahşi Batı*), 1–2, 14

military, 86, 152, 164–167, 235n103, 247n75. *See also* junta

Ministry of Culture and Tourism, 126, 127, 147–149

Ministry of Education, 54

Ministry of Interior, 176

minorities, 27, 28–29, 37–38, 87.

missionaries, 25, 32, 47, 75–76

Mitchell, W. J. T., 23, 207n12, 208n20

Mithat, Ahmed, 64, 65–66, 69–70, 73, 98

mobility, 60–61, 83–84, 98

model village, 81–84, *85*

moderate Islam, 137, 141, 192

moderate Muslim, 7, 194, 195–196

modern citizens, 4, 41

modernity, 7, 31, 42, 58–59, 161–162, 174; heteronormativity as an aspect of, 244n47; secularization equated with, 140–141; transculturated figures of, 38–39

modernizations, 42–43, 79, 189. *See also* inadequate westernization; modernization without colonization; Wilsonian Principles League

modernization theory, 7, 77–79, *78*, 84, 137, 191–193

modernization without colonization, 4, 200n7. *See also* selective westernization

Orientalism, 8, 21, 68, 125, 203n26; modernization theory influencing, 77, 191–193; societies' line drawn by, 149

Orientalism (Said), 8

Ortaylı, İlber, 200n9

Oruk, Fikret, 156–158, 161–162

Orwell, George, 142

Osmanlı İmparatorluğu. See Ottoman Empire

Other, 8, 194–195. *See also* Orientalism

Ottoman Empire (*Osmanlı İmparatorluğu*), 7, 14, 60–61, 110–111, 134, 190–191; centralization pursued by, 26, 38, 64–68; death of, 109; elite, 31; extraterritoriality agreement agreed to by, 25; massacres, 20, 26; navy, 24–25; same-sex intercourse in, 158–159; territory, 19, 20; treatment of minorities by, 27; U.S.'s relations with, 24–55, 29, 33, 36, 53. *See also* Edib, Halide; mandates; Point 12; selective westernization; sultan; Tanzimat reforms; Wilsonian Principles League

Ottomanism, 65

Ottoman Public Debt Administration, 60, 73

Ottoman Republic, The, 50

Ottomans, 25–26, 107–108, 109, 117, 159, 243n41

OutIstanbul, 176

over-remembering, 22, 49

over-westernization, 22, 26, 38, 41, 54, 109; of Atatürk, 42; Europe as source of, 45; gender of, 68–76; in novel, 56–99, 78, 85; selective westernization controlling, 111; tram influencing, 59–61; U.S. and,

68–76; of WPL, 43. *See also* excessive westernization; westoxication

Özal, Turgut, 86, 87, 112, 129, 174–175

Özbek, Meral, 60

Özyürek, Esra, 141

Pamuk, Orhan, 57, 98–99. *See also* new life, The

Paris Peace Conference, 19–21, 46–50, 127

Parla, Jale, 57, 59

Paşa, Damat Ferit, 38

Pasha, Talaat, 27

passive position (*ibne*), 158–159, 165–166, 171–172, 243n41, 244n43, 247n75

Pearce, Susan, 167

Perinçek, Doğu, 160–161

Persian, 107–108, 109, 110, 243n41

Pervaneler (Tek). *See* moths, The

Perverted love in court poetry (*Divan Şiirinde Sapık Sevgi*) (Eyüboğlu), 220n41

Pew Global Attitudes survey, 2–3, 185

Pflugfelder, Gregory, 244n47

Philippines, 27, 31

Philipson, Robert, 133

Point 12, 28–30, 29, 34, 46–50

political elite, 3–7, 27–28, 31, 189–190, 195; social sciences viewed by, 167–169; U.S. seen by, 79

polygamy, 41

post-coup era, 86–99, 160–161

postmodernism, 86–99

Powell, Colin, 136–137

prayer room (*masjid*), 74

president, 1–2, 239n142

pride parade, 181, 183, 184, 185

stock figures, 5, 105–106, 196–197. *See also* terrible Turk

Stonewall, 175, 251n119

stoning, 80

Strang, David, 200n7

strategic westernization, 31, 41–42, 79, 110

stream of consciousness, 68

students, 109, 110, 112, 136

Sufism, 63–64, 73, 94, 95

suicides, 70

sultan, 1–2, 21, 38, 46, 108. *See also* Abdulhamid II; Mahmut II

Sultanahmet Square, 52, *53*

sultanate, 214n29

Sun Language Theory, 132

Supreme War Council, 21, 34

survey, 2–3, 185

Syria, 3, 29

Tamerlane, 126

Tanzimat reforms, 64–69, 200n9

Tarlabaşı Boulevard, 175, 250n117

Taylor, Archer, 144

Tek, Müfide Ferid. *See* moths, The

television, 123–124, 235n102, 245n52

Temel jokes, 112–113, 114–115, 125–133, 140, 142, 230n42

terakki. See progress

terrible Turk, 7, 27, 42, 47–48, 50, 109–110; *Incredible Turk, The,* challenging, 78; joke influencing, 127; sedimentation evinced by, 190, 195; selective westernization influencing, 76; Texan as equivalent of, 142; transformation evinced by, 190; in U.S., 26, 76; during WWI, 32–34

terrorism, 7, 50–51, 179. *See also* Islamic terrorist

testing, 113–115, 116

Texan, as terrible Turk's equivalent, 142

Texas, 129, 139, 142

Third World, 61–62, 77, 94, 162, 195

"Third-World Literature in the Era of Multinational Capitalism" (Jameson), 61–62

Thrash the whore (*Vurun Kahpeye*) (Edib), 40, 70

Tietze, Andreas, 231n49

tomofil. See automobile

tops, 240n9, 243n40. *See also* active partner; active position

torture, 162

traitors, 22, 43, 49, 50–52, 54

trams, 56–57, 59–61. See also *Fatih-Harbiye*

transculturation, 38–39, 94, 105, 196–197, 245n55; overview, 4–15; selective westernization clashing with, 189. *See also* vernacular transculturation; Wild West; wild westernization

transgender, 173–174, 253n154

trans identity, 167–168, 170, 179, 182

transnational signifying, wild westernization as, 139–146

transphobia, of gays, 171, 173

transportation, 60–61, 79, 80–81, 91, 92. *See also* buses; motorway; railways; roads; trams

transsexualism, 168–169

transvestitism, 168–169, 170

Trans X Turkey, 182–183

travestis (*lubunya*), 148–151, *150*, 161, 167–179, 185, 249n104; boyfriends of, 163; Brazilian, 163; bridge, 180; homicides of, 156; in Istanbul, 249n95; language called by, 248n91

treason, 110–111
Treaty of Berlin, 25–26
Treaty of Lausanne, 35, 37, 109–110
Treaty of Sèvres, 21, 196
tropes, 196, 233n81
truck, minibus, and taxi driver (şöför), 103–104
Truman Doctrine, 76–77, 84
Türk-Amerikan Dostluk Bahçesi. See Garden of Turkish–American Friendship
Turkey, 7, 20–21, 115, 134; dismemberment of, 46–47; Edib on, 41; EU applied to by, 96, 152, 153, 175–176, 177, 178, 179; Greece and, 76–77, 78, 84, 86; NATO membership of, 22, 49, 79, 84, 135–136, 140; railroads, 79, 92; Roosevelt on, 31; in Speech, 37–39; Stonewall of, 175, 251n119; transportation, 79; Truman Doctrine aiding, 76–77; U.S.'s relations with, 2–3, 22, 24–55, 29, 33, 36, 53, 75–99, 78, 85, 105–106, 109–113, 185–186, 188, 251n119; in War on Terror, 49; Wilson's interest in, 31–32, 43, 50. See also Ankara, Turkey; Beyoğlu, Turkey; Bursa, Turkey; Istanbul, Turkey; Izmir, Turkey; mandates; Republic of Turkey; Sivas, Turkey
Turkey Faces West (Edib), 39
"Turkey of Homosexuals, The" (KAOS GL), 176
"Turkey on the Brink of Modernity" (Necef), 149
Türkilizce humor. See Turklish humor
Turkish, 107–108, 109, 111, 192, 209n40, 240n1; history thesis, 22–23; nationalism, 35. See also Ottomans

Turkish Language Association (TLA), 104, 109
Turkish National Assembly. See Speech
Turkishness, 104–106, 154
Turkish Ordeal, The (Edib), 54, 61
Turkish Republic. See Republic of Turkey
Türkler, The (Pekşen). See Turks, The
Turklish (Türkilizce) humor, 103–146, 138, 227n6, 232n64. See also Temel jokes
Türk Olmak webpage. See Being Turkish webpage
Turks, 25, 28, 32–34, 33, 49, 155; in national preference test, 35, 36; Turkish spoken by, 107–108. See also terrible Turk
Turks, The (Türkler, The) (Pekşen), 104
Turna, Burak. See Metal storm

Uçar, Orkun. See Metal storm
Ugly American, The (Burdick and Lederer), 81
ultra-nationalist novels, 96–99
Uluşahin, Ayşe, 168–169, 248n86
United States, 1–2, 3–4, 6–15; allegorizing, 56–99, 78, 85; Armenians naturalized by, 25; Christians influenced by, 27, 31; conspiracy having to do with, 93–94; culture and, 28, 103–146, 138, 187–197; Edib accused of being in bed with, 39; empire of, 143; Europe differentiated from, 31, 42, 75–76, 153–154; extraterritoriality agreement agreed to by, 25; flapper associated with, 71–76; foreign policy, 76–86, 78, 85, 191–192, 241n18; friendship of, 82–84, 85; garbage, 80; gender and, 68–76;

westernization (*batılılaşma*), 2, 3, 139, 180–186, 189–190, 194; as defensive, 200n7; definition of, 93; limits of, 200n9; novel and, 64–68; pieces using, 149; as U.S. gift, 91–92. *See also* excessive westernization; over-westernization; reforms; selective westernization; strategic westernization; westoxication; wild westernization

Western-language fluency, 110–111

westerns, 128–129, 235n102. *See also* Temel jokes

westoxication (*gharbzadegi*), 5, 14, 38, 43, 69–76, 201n14; Erdoğan on, 51; in fiction, 52; in novels, 97–99; of Pamuk, 96; selective westernization differentiated from, 22. *See also* American bandage, The; dandy

Wickberg, Daniel, 116

Wikipedia, 49–50

Wild West, 6, 80, 86, 128–129, 139. *See also* Temel jokes; Texas

wild westernization, 5–6, 68, 87, 103–146, *138*

Williams, Maynard Owen, 110

Wilson, 208n21

Wilson, Woodrow, 19–22, 23, 24, 27–30, 29; biopic on, 208n21; forgetting of, 46–50; Hodja joke

heard by, 127; Turkey interest of, 31–32, 43, 50. *See also* Fourteen Points; Point 12

Wilsonianism, 7, 75

Wilsonian Principles League (WPL), 19–55, 210n47. *See also* Edib, Halide

Wilson Societies, 211n63

"Woman Educated in America Fights Allies in Turkey" (Fontenoy), 211n63

women, 56–57, 67–76, 80, 195, 201n14, 253n154; death sentence of, 39–40; Kemalists encouraging, 41. *See also* Edib, Halide; *Sodom ve Gomore*

World War I (WWI), 28, 32–34, 56, 60, 195. *See also* Allies; Paris Peace Conference

wren, The (*Çalıkuşu*) (Güntekin), 70

Yahşi Batı. See *Mild West, The*

Yeni Hayat. See *new life, The*

Yetkin, Çetin, 54

Yılmaz, Ali Kemal, 164

Yılmaz, Halil, 166

Young Turks. See Committee for Union and Progress

Yüksel, Uğur, 176–177

Zanuck, Darryl F., 208n21

Ze'evi, Dror, 244n43

züppe. See dandy

CPSIA information can be obtained
at www.ICGtesting.com
Printed in the USA
LVHW040705020720
659270LV00002B/13

9 780231 182034